Institutions and Organizations
Second Edition

FOUNDATIONS FOR ORGANIZATIONAL SCIENCE
A Sage Publications Series

Series Editor
David Whetten, *Brigham Young University*

Editors
Peter J. Frost, *University of British Columbia*
Anne S. Huff, *University of Colorado* and *Cranfield University* (UK)
Benjamin Schneider, *University of Maryland*
M. Susan Taylor, *University of Maryland*
Andrew Van de Ven, *University of Minnesota*

The FOUNDATIONS FOR ORGANIZATIONAL SCIENCE series supports the development of students, faculty, and prospective organizational science professionals through the publication of texts authored by leading organizational scientists. Each volume provides a highly personal, hands-on introduction to a core topic or theory and challenges the reader to explore promising avenues for future theory development and empirical application.

Books in This Series

W. Richard Scott

Institutions and Organizations

Second Edition

Foundations for
Organizational
Science
A Sage Publications Series

Sage Publications
International Educational and Professional Publisher
Thousand Oaks ▪ London ▪ New Delhi

For information:

Sage Publications, Inc.
2455 Teller Road
Thousand Oaks, California 91320
E-mail: order@sagepub.com

Sage Publications Ltd.
6 Bonhill Street
London EC2A 4PU
United Kingdom

Sage Publications India Pvt. Ltd.
M-32 Market
Greater Kailash I
New Delhi 110 048 India

Printed in the United States of America

Library of Congress Cataloging-in-Publication Data

Scott, W. Richard.
    Institutions and organizations / W. Richard Scott. — 2nd ed.
    p.cm. — (Foundations for organizational science)
    Includes bibliographical references and index.
    ISBN 0-7619-2000-5 (cloth: acid-free paper)
    ISBN 0-7619-2001-3 (pbk.: acid-free paper)
    1. Organizational sociology. 2. Social institutions. I. Title. II.
Series.
    HM786 .S3845 2001
    302.3'5—dc21

                        00-011072

    04 05 06 07 7 6 5 4

Acquiring Editor:	Marquita Flemming
Editorial Assistant:	MaryAnn Vail
Production Editor:	Denise Santoyo
Editorial Assistant:	Candice Crosetti
Typesetter:	Denyse Dunn

For Joy—
who constructs and tends institutions
of value to many of us

Contents

Introduction to the Series

The title of this series, **Foundations for Organizational Science** (FOS), denotes a distinctive focus. FOS books are educational aids for mastering the core theories, essential tools, and emerging perspectives that constitute the field of organizational science (broadly conceived to include organizational behavior, organizational theory, human resource management, and business strategy). Our ambitious goal is to assemble the "essential library": for members of our professional community.

The vision for the series emerged from conversations with several colleagues, including Peter Frost, Anne Huff, Rick Mowday, Benjamin Schneider, Susan Taylor, and Andy Van de Ven. A number of common interests emerged from these sympathetic encounters, including: enhancing the quality of doctoral education by providing broader access to the master teachers in our field, "bottling" the experience and insights of some of the founding scholars in our field before they retire, and providing professional development opportunities for colleagues seeking to broaden their understanding of the rapidly expanding subfields within organizational science.

Our unique learning objectives are reflected in an unusual set of instructions to FOS authors. They are encouraged to: (1) "write the way they teach"—framing their book as an extension of their teaching notes, rather than as the expansion of a handbook chapter,(2) pass on their "craft knowledge" to the next generation of scholars—making them wiser, not just smarter, (3) share with their "virtual students and colleagues" the insider tips and best-bets for research that are normally reserved for one-on-one mentoring sessions, and (4) make the complexity of their subject matter comprehensible to nonexperts so that readers can share their puzzlement, fascination, and intrigue.

We are proud of the group of highly qualified authors who have embraced the unique educational perspective of our "Foundations" series. We encourage your suggestions for how these books can better satisfy your learning needs—as a newcomer to the field preparing for prelims or developing a dissertation proposal, or as an established scholar seeking to broaden your knowledge and proficiency.

DAVID A. WHETTEN
SERIES EDITOR

Preface to the First Edition

With the benefit of hindsight, I can now clearly see that, from my earliest days, I have been an institutionalist! My dissertation research, reported in Blau and Scott (1962), addressed the nature of professional work in an organizational setting. The question I pondered then was: If a concern for efficiency and productivity explains the nature of work systems, how is it that the same set of tasks can be differently conceived, and be subject to different normative definitions and different performance criteria? Why is the same work viewed so differently by professional social workers than by bureaucratic administrators? Similar questions were pursued in my later research on authority systems (see Dornbusch and Scott 1975), where we examined differences among workers and between workers and supervisors in their "task conceptions" and explored the effect of these differences on the locus of discretion and the nature of the control systems developed. We discovered that organizational participants not only held different preferences for how work should be organized but also different levels of power, so that preferred authority systems frequently diverged from preferences about such arrangements. And still later in my work on organizational effectiveness (Scott 1977; Scott, Flood, and Forrest 1978),

I asked who—which stakeholders—had the right to set goals and standards and sample work activities and/or outcomes; I noted that the answer to these questions had profound effects on how organizations were structured and on what was regarded as "effective" behavior.

I think that one reason why I came to these questions relatively early was because I tended to concentrate my research on professional organizations—organizations in which professionals share in the determination of goals and standards. Professionals differ from other classes of employees not only in the relative amount of power they exercise, but in what aspects of work they attempt to control. As distinct from unions, professional occupations have sought to exercise control not only over the conditions of work (pay, benefits, safety) but over the definition of the work itself. Professionals attempt to employ their power to shape the institutional frameworks supporting their activities in the broadest possible terms: they seek cultural-cognitive control (insisting that they are uniquely qualified to determine what types of problems fall under their jurisdiction and how these problems are to be categorized and processed); they seek normative control, determining who has the right to exercise authority over what decisions and which actors in what situations; and they seek regulative control, determining what actions are to be prohibited and permitted, and what sanctions are to be used (see Freidson 1986; Flood and Scott 1987; Abbott 1988; Scott & Backman 1990).

The explicit development of an institutional perspective in my own work, however, occurred only in association with my collaboration with John W. Meyer. For more than a decade and in collaboration with various colleagues we pursued studies of teacher behavior as affected by school organization. Gradually, we began to realize that (1) schools were loosely coupled systems, so that apparently "similar" classrooms within the same school might be quite differently organized; (2) schools were open systems (teachers, classrooms, and schools being affected by the organization of their environments); and, in particular, (3) schools reflected in their internal structures the cultural beliefs and rules existing in the wider institutional environment. Meyer and Rowan (1977) produced the first systematic statement of the importance of institutional environments in shaping organizational structures to come out of this work. Later statements were produced by Meyer, Scott, and Deal (1981) and Meyer and Scott (1983b). (For a more detailed discussion of the origin of the institutional perspective in association with our research program in schools, see the preface to Mayer and Scott [1983, pp. 7-17].)

In subsequent years, Meyer has pursued institutional arguments in association with others at the level of the world system (see Meyer and Hannan 1979; Thomas, Meyer, Ramirez, and Boli 1987; Meyer, Kamens, Benavot, Cha, and Wong 1992). And together, Meyer and I with various collaborators have attempted to expand and test institutional theory not only in further studies within educational settings (see Meyer, Scott and Strang 1987; Scott and Meyer 1987; Meyer, Scott, Strang, and Creighton 1988) but also by examining the diffusion of due process and fair employment practices and corporate training programs across diverse types of organizations (see Dobbin, Edelman, Meyer, Scott, and Swidler 1988; Scott and Meyer 1991; Dobbin, Sutton, Meyer, and Scott 1993; Sutton, Dobbin, Meyer, and Scott 1994). Also, with other colleagues, I have pursued the application of institutional theory to health care and mental health settings (see Alexander and Scott 1984; Scott 1985, Scott and Black 1986; Scott and Backman 1990).

My own interests in institutional theory have led me to try to understand and relate intelligently to the work of others. Somewhat to my surprise, institutional theory has become, as my juniors would say, a "hot" topic. Work has developed, and at an accelerating pace, across a broad front, and currently engages scholars in many disciplines associated with the study of organizations. In this volume, I attempt to review and evaluate efforts underway in economics, political science, and sociology as well as in organization studies. There is enough work, and it shows sufficient variety, that no brief review can do justice to all of the developments in this intellectual arena, but I have tried to incorporate its major strands.

I began the process of attempting to get my head around institutional theory the year that I was a fellow at the Center for Advanced Study in the Behavioral Sciences (1989-1990). That halcyon setting encourages wider-ranging scholarship and symbolizes the virtue of interdisciplinary inquiry. During that year, I drafted several articles, all of which dealt with some aspect of institutional theory. Two of these (see Scott 1994b; 1994c) began the process of comparing and contrasting work on institutions across several disciplines. This volume continues that effort.

Whom to thank, or blame, for my current understanding of institutional theory? My major debt is to John Meyer, my long-term colleague and collaborator, whose cogitive resources are both rich and subtle. I struggle to understand what he is talking about, and always find it worth the effort. For both intellectual stimulation and much valued friendship, I will forever be grateful to Jim March. Other local sources of friendship and intellectual challenge include Jim Baron, Mike Hannan, Joanne Martin, Milbrey McLaughlin, Jeff Pfeffer, and Bob Sutton as well as a wide assortment of stimulating colleagues associated with the Stanford Center for Organizations Research (SCOR). Also, several recent students (most of whom are now full-fledged colleagues) helped to keep me honest and up-to-date. They include Andrew Creighton, Jerry Davis, Frank Dobbin, Stephen Mezias, Sue Monahan, David Strang, Mark Suchman, John Sutton, Ann Takata, Patricia Thornton, and Marc Ventresca.

Others not associated with Stanford have also been of great value to me as I pursued this work. I have benefited greatly from interacting in recent years with Paul DiMaggio, Neil Fligstein, Peter A. Hall, Richard Nelson, Walter (Woody) Powell, Andrew Van de Ven, Karl Weick, Oliver Williamson, Mayer Zald, and Lynne Zucker. Also important have been connections to a set of Scandinavian colleagues who challenged and contributed to my institutional learning. These include Nils Brunsson, Soren Christensen, Christian Knudsen, Helge Larsen, and Johan Olsen.

The editors for this series, David Whetten and Andy Van de Ven, have been constructive and supportive in guiding this project, and I have benefited greatly from the suggestions and comments received from three colleagues who agreed to read an earlier draft of this work. My warm thanks to Christine Oliver, Jitendra Singh, and Marc Ventresca. I also received very helpful assistance from a current doctoral student, Peter Mendel, who reviewed an early draft. To a greater extent than most of us are willing to recognize, our individual scholarship is a social product.

W. RICHARD SCOTT
STANFORD, CALIFORNIA
SEPTEMBER 1994

Preface to the Second Edition

My most significant new debt, in connection with preparing the revised edition of this book, is to all of the scholars who have contributed to the intellectual development of the field in the short time since the first edition was written. I am greatly indebted to their creativity and intelligence. Science is a social process, and knowledge a collective product.

The institutional theory of organizations has significantly advanced in the few years since the preparation of the first edition. When I was first approached by my editor, Harry Briggs, to prepare a second edition, I foolishly estimated a time frame of less than a year to complete my revisions. That year has extended to two years and a little more, not only because of the press of my other obligations and my indolence, but due to the impressive volume of new scholarship that demanded to be digested and incorporated. This field exhibits extraordinary vitality! I have tried to reflect not only the substance but the contagious energy of the recent work in this new edition.

I also must acknowledge some more specific sources of intellectual stimulation and obligation incurred on the road to this revised edition. Three sets of activities loom large.

First, in 1992, I was invited by Søren Christensen of the Copenhagen School of Business to work with him in organizing a workshop on institutions and organizations involving both European and American scholars. Invited participants presented papers in May 1993 at a conference on the beautiful island of Møn, Denmark, and because of a collegial atmosphere that stimulated constructive, lively discussions, all papers were significantly improved by the process. Yet another round of review and revision followed in which all participants served as both contributors and reviewers, and the final versions of selected papers were published by Sage (Scott and Christensen 1995b).

In addition to Søren, I want to express particular gratitude to my Scandinavian colleagues, Tom Christensen, Finn Borum, Nils Brunsson, Peter Karnøe, Christian Knudsen, Helge Larsen, Kari Lilja, Kerstin Sahlin-Andersson, Risto Tanio, and Ann Westenholz, who have provided many years of friendship and hospitality.

Second, I was a member of the Commission on Behavioral and Social Sciences and Education of the National Academy of Sciences from 1990 to 1996 and, during that time, sought to initiate activities intended to stimulate theory and research in organizational studies and applications to social problems. A primary project developed during this period was focused on evaluating the diffusion of total quality management (TQM) techniques—the most significant contemporary attempt to stimulate and institutionalize change—in organizations. The commission joined forces with the Transformation to Quality Organizations program under the auspices of the National Science Foundation to host a series of workshops in 1996 and 1997 to bring together quality researchers and organization theorists to better link theory, research, and application in this area. I co-chaired these workshops with Robert E. Cole, professor of business administration and sociology at the University of California, Berkeley, who was a member of the steering committee overseeing the foundation's research program. Again, constructive discussions resulted in improved understanding of the complexity of organizational change, and a collection of empirical studies and commentaries was published by Sage earlier this year (Cole and Scott 2000).

Without question, however, the most direct and powerful source of intellectual stimulation for me was my involvement in a research project focused on institutional change. In 1994, I received an Investigator Award in Health Policy Research from the Robert Wood Johnson Foundation, which provided support for a study of the ways in which health care organizations in the San Francisco Bay Area had participated in and responded to institutional change during the half century since World War II. To assist me with this work, I recruited three sociology doctoral students, Martin Ruef, Peter J. Mendel, and Carol Ann Caronna, who began as research assistants but, by virtue of their intelligence and energy, quickly became full-fledged research colleagues. This project allowed me to think long and hard about how to conceptualize, study, and attempt to account for institutional change and its effects on organizations. Our findings were published in *Institutional Change and Healthcare Organizations* (Scott et al. 2000), and some of our thinking is reflected more generally in this revised edition.

In addition to the insights and stimulation received from these workshops and projects, I have lectured and taught shorter and longer versions of a seminar on institutional theory during the past five years at Stanford University, Copenhagen Business School, Ecole de Paris du Management, University of Georgia, Helsinki School of Economics and Management, University of Mannheim, University of Minnesota, New York University, University of North Carolina, Northwestern University, University of Oslo, and Stockholm Center for Organization Research. All of these occasions provided opportunities to hone my ideas and arguments with the help of colleagues.

In the few years since the first edition appeared, the coherence and civility of the organizations research community at Stanford have become somewhat frayed, but its intellectual quality remains unexcelled. In the years since 1995, Stanford has lost few scholars, except to retirement, and it has been graced with notable additions including Stephen Barley, Doug McAdam, and Woody Powell. These and others help keep me intellectually alive.

All or parts of the present manuscript have been reviewed and improved thanks to the helpful comments of Mie Augier, Peter J. Mendel, Ekaterina Seryakove, and Marc Ventresca. Marquita Flemming, senior editor at Sage Publications, has been consistently supportive and helpful through all the phases from manuscript preparation to completed book.

W. RICHARD SCOTT

JULY 2000

Introduction

Institutional theory burst on the organizations scene during the mid-1970s and has generated much interest and attention. It has raised provocative questions about the world of organizations:

- Why do organizations of the same type, such as schools and hospitals, located in widely scattered locales so closely resemble one another?
- Institutions of various sorts have existed for thousands of years. What specific types of institutions are associated with the rise of organizations?
- How are we to regard behavior in organizational settings? Does it reflect the pursuit of rational interests and the exercise of conscious choice, or is behavior primarily shaped by conventions, routines, and habits?
- Why is it that the behavior of organizational participants is often observed to depart from the formal rules and stated goals of the organization?
- Why is it, if formal rules are largely ignored, that resources and energy are expended to maintain them?
- Why and how do laws, rules, and other types of regulative and normative systems arise? Do individuals voluntarily construct rule systems that then bind their own behavior?
- Where do interests come from? Do they stem from human nature or are they culturally constructed?

- Why do specific structures and practices diffuse through a field of organizations in ways not predicted by the particular characteristics of adopting organizations?
- How do differences in cultural beliefs shape the nature and operation of organizations?
- Why do organizations and individuals conform to institutions? Is it because they are rewarded for doing so, because they think they are morally obliged to obey, or because they can conceive of no other way of behaving?
- What processes relate institutions to organizations? What vehicles or carriers transmit institutional messages to organizations, and how do organizational actions and reactions affect institutions?
- If institutions work to promote stability and order, how does change occur? If institutions control and constitute individuals, how can individuals hope to alter the systems in which they are embedded?

I see the ascendance of institutional theory as simply a continuation and extension of the intellectual revolution begun during the mid-1960s, which introduced open systems conceptions into the study of organizations. Open systems theory transformed existing approaches by insisting on the importance of the wider context or environment as it constrains, shapes, penetrates, and renews the organization (see Katz and Kahn 1966; Scott 1998). First to be recognized was the technical environment—resources and task-related information—as the organization was conceived primarily as an instrumental production system, transforming inputs into outputs. Only later, during the mid-1970s, did investigators begin to recognize the significant effects on organizing associated with wider social and cultural forces: the institutional environment. Organizations were seen to be more than production systems; they were social and cultural systems.

Much of the challenge posed by this subject—to the author as well as the readers—resides in the many varying meanings and usages of the concept of institution. Being one of the oldest and most oft-employed ideas in social thought, it has continued to take on new and diverse meanings over time, much like barnacles on a ship's hull, without shedding the old. I attempt in this book to pursue three somewhat contradictory aims.

First, I seek to capture and accurately reflect the richness and diversity of institutional thought, viewed both historically and as a contemporary, ongoing project, drawing on the insights of some of the greatest minds working from the late nineteenth to the first years of the 21st century. Chapter 1 reviews the principal contributions of influential economists, political scientists, and sociologists working at the turn of the century, a heyday of institutional activity. It appears that in this early period, institutionalists in economics operated primarily as gadflies and critics on the margins of the discipline. By contrast, during this same time, institutionalists were regarded as more mainstream in both political science and in sociology. Nevertheless, during most of the twentieth century, as empiricism and positivism flourished, institutionalists in all disciplines were chased from center stage, persisting primarily in peripheral fields of study such as economic history, industrial relations, and the sociology of work. Hence, at the time when the field of organizations was established as an academic specialty, around the 1940s, institutionalists were hardly to be found. Chapter 2 relates the story of how institutional theory became connected to and developed within the area of organizations.

A second aim of the book is to provide a relatively comprehensive analytic framework so that the different conceptions of institutions and the variety of underlying assumptions and methodological approaches can be better understood. My objective is not to differentiate in order to dismiss or belittle one or another formulation but to improve our understanding of the many flavors and colors of institutionalism. The construction of the comparative framework commences in Chapter 3 and extends through Chapter 4, but its ramifications continue throughout the volume. Although I endeavor to be more rather than less inclusive, and to be relatively even-handed in my treatment of the various approaches, I have given more space and attention to those approaches associated with the "new" institutionalism in sociology. This emphasis was selected for two reasons. First, I am a sociologist by training and temperament and, hence, more comfortable with and, I hope, better able to describe and assess these perspectives. Second, these newer approaches are by definition more recently developed and, as a consequence, more in need of exposition and refinement. I devote considerable energy to interpreting obscure nascent ideas, mediating family disputes, and connecting disparate arguments.

A final objective is to review and assess the burgeoning body of empirical research that has developed in recent years to test and extend institutional arguments. As social scientists, we must be as interested in empirically evaluating theoretical arguments as in generating them. Institutional researchers have been highly active and creative in devising ways to evaluate their assertions. As was the case with the theoretical literature, I have given more coverage to the neoinstitutional sociological studies, but I have included examples of the wider range of work.

Chapters 5 through 8 present the empirical review. Surveying empirical studies also provides an opportunity to illustrate and further clarify differences in theoretical conceptions. Chapter 5 concentrates on studies of arguments concerning the origins, maintenance, and diffusion of institutions. Chapter 6 examines the processes by which society-wide systems, organizational fields, and organizational populations are institutionally structured; and Chapter 7 examines these processes at the organizational level. Chapter 8 reviews work on institutional change, focusing particularly on destructuration and restructuration processes. Institutional change received scant attention from earlier scholars but currently attracts much interest. In a concluding chapter, Chapter 9, I adopt a more individual voice, presenting my personal judgments of the intellectual gains associated with an institutional perspective; I describe efforts under way to correct earlier misdirections or remove limitations, call attention to lacunae in current work, and offer suggestions for future development.

1   Early Institutionalists

N o attempt will be made to provide a comprehensive or thorough review of early institutional theory, but to completely neglect these ideas and arguments would be inexcusable. Although much of this work differs from today's institutional agenda, all contemporary scholars draw inspiration from the efforts of the pioneers. In examining this early work, it must be recognized that contemporary students bring their own interests and concerns to the reading of these texts. As Alexander (1983) observes, "'Reading' is an important part of any theoretical strategy, and if the work in question is in any way open to varied interpretation, then it certainly will be so interpreted." (Vol. 2, p. 119). Conflicting interpretations are even more likely when the theorists in question change their views over time—so that, for example, there appears to be an "early" Durkheim and a "late" one—or when, like Weber, they simultaneously express contradictory or ambivalent views.

Somewhat arbitrarily, I sort the work into disciplinary categories—as will soon become apparent, greater divisions often exist within than between disciplinary camps—and briefly review leading contributors to institutional thought from the late nineteenth to the mid-twentieth century in economics, political science, and sociology.

Early Institutional Theory in Economics

It is well at the outset to acknowledge the lack of logical coherence in the strands of work to be examined. In many respects, the "old" institutional economics bears a stronger intellectual kinship with the "new" institutional approaches advanced by sociologists and anthropologists than to the "new" institutional economics. Conversely, the new institutional economics is more indebted to the critics of old institutional economics than to their early namesakes. The earliest institutional arguments arose in Germany and Austria in the late nineteenth century as one by-product of the famous *Methodenstreit*: the debate over scientific method in the social sciences. Drawing energy and inspiration from the earlier Romantic movement as well as from the ideas of Kant and Hegel, a collection of economists challenged the conventional canon that economics could be reduced to a set of universal laws. Led by Gustav Schmoller (1900-1904), this historical school insisted that economic processes operated within a social framework, which was in turn shaped by a set of cultural and historical forces. Historical and comparative research was required to discern the distinctive properties of particular economic systems. Moreover, Schmoller and his associates called for economics to eschew its simplistic assumptions regarding "economic man" and embrace more realistic models of human behavior. The principal defender of the classical approach in this debate was Carl Menger ([1883] 1981), the Viennese economist, who insisted on the utility of simplifying assumptions and the value of developing economic principles that were both abstract and timeless. But rather than denying the importance of broader societal institutional forces, Menger argued that institutions were themselves social phenomena in need of theoretical explanation. For this reason, Langlois (1986a) suggests that Menger "has perhaps more claim to be the patron saint of the new institutional economics than has any of the original institutionalists" (p. 5).

As in many intellectual debates, the warring factions sharpened and perfected their arguments, but neither succeeded in convincing the other. Attempts at reconciliation and synthesis occurred only among scholars of a later generation, principally in the work of Weber, to be discussed later.

Many of the ideas of the historical school were embraced and further developed by American institutional economists, a number of whom had received training in Germany. An earlier cohort working in the mid-nineteenth century did not receive much attention, but by the turn of the century, three institutional economists had become quite influential: Thorstein Veblen, John Commons, and Westley Mitchell. Although there were important differences in their views, all criticized conventional economic models for their unrealistic assumptions and inattention to historical change.

Veblen (1898) was highly critical of the underlying economic assumptions regarding individual behavior: He ridiculed "the hedonistic conception of man as that of a lightning calculator of pleasures and pain" (p. 389). Instead, Veblen (1909) insisted that much behavior was governed by habit and convention: "Not only is the individual's conduct edged about and directed by his habitual relations to his fellows in the group, but these relations, being of an institutional character, vary as the institutional scene varies" (p. 245). Indeed, Veblen (1919) defines institutions as "settled habits of thought common to the generality of man" (p. 239).

Commons (1924) similarly challenged the conventional emphasis on individual choice behavior, suggesting that a more appropriate unit of economic analysis was the *transaction*, a concept borrowed from legal analysis: "The transaction is two or more wills giving, taking, persuading, coercing, defrauding, commanding, obeying, competing, governing, in a world of scarcity, mechanisms and rules of conduct" (p. 7). The rules of conduct to which Commons ([1950] 1970) alludes are social institutions. Institutional rules were necessary to define the limits within which individuals and firms could pursue their objectives.

> To Commons, the institutions existing at a specific time represent nothing more than imperfect and pragmatic solutions to reconcile past conflicts; they are solutions that consist of a set of rights and duties, an authority for enforcing them, and some degree of adherence to collective norms of prudent reasonable behavior. (Van de Ven 1993:142)

All three institutional economists emphasized the importance of change and were critical of their colleagues for not making its examination central to their mission. Veblen embraced an evolutionary perspective and insisted that a valid economics would emphasize the role of technological change and trace the changing phases of the economy. Commons (1924) likewise stressed the centrality of change, viewing the economy as "a moving, changing process" (p. 376). Mitchell believed that conventional economics was a hindrance to understanding the nature of the business cycle, and he devoted much of his energies to studying economic change. Like all institutionalists, he was reluctant to embrace an assumption of economic equilibrium. As one of the founders of the National Bureau of Economic Research and chair of the committee that published the voluminous report, *Recent Social Trends* (President's Research Committee on Social Trends 1934), Mitchell pioneered in the collection of empirical data on the operation of the economy, insisting that economic principles should be grounded in facts as opposed to abstract deductive theories.

The American institutionalists were influenced not only by the German historical school but also by the homegrown philosophy of pragmatism as espoused by Dewey, James, and others. Their work reflected a suspicion of abstract universal principles, an interest in solving practical problems, and an awareness of the role of chance events and historical contingencies.

Jaccoby (1990) argues that the approaches offered by the early institutionalists departed from those adopted by their mainstream neoclassical colleagues in four important respects:

> *Indeterminancy versus determinancy.* Whereas the orthodox model assumed "perfect competition and unique equilibria, the institutionalists pointed to pervasive market power and to indeterminancy even under competition" (Jaccoby 1990:318).
>
> *Endogenous versus exogenous determination of preferences.* Neoclassical theorists posited individual preferences or wants whereas institutionalists argued that such preferences were shaped by social institutions, whose operation should be the subject of economic analysis.
>
> *Behavioral realism versus simplifying assumptions.* Institutional theorists argued that economists should use pragmatic and psychologically realistic models of economic motivation rather than subscribe to naive utilitarian assumptions.
>
> *Diachronic versus synchronic analysis.* Rather than assuming the "timeless and placeless" assumptions of the neoclassical theorists, institutionalists insisted that economists should ascertain "how the economy acquired its features and the conditions that cause these features to vary over time and place" (Jaccoby 1990:320).[1]

Whether or not they were correct in their accusations and assertions, the early institutional economists did not prevail: Neoclassical theory was victorious and continues its dominance up to the present time. Prior to the rise of the new institutional economics in the 1970s, only a few economists attempted to carry forward the institutionalist agenda, the best known of whom are J. A. Schumpeter, Karl Polanyi, John Kenneth Galbraith, and Gunnar Myrdal (see Swedberg 1991). Arguably, the subfields of economics most affected by the legacy of the institutional theorists are those of labor economics, which is the field in which Commons specialized; industrial relations, which focuses on broader social and political factors affecting economic structures and processes; and the economics of industry, which examines the varying configurations of industrial structures and their effects on the strategies and performance of individual firms.

Why was the impact of the early institutionalists blunted? Modern-day commentators offer several explanations. The German historical school, no doubt, overemphasized the uniqueness of economic systems and underemphasized the value of analytic theory. Even sympathetic critics acknowledge that Veblen exhibited "an explicit hostility to intellectual 'symmetry and system-building'" (Hodgson 1991:211) and that Commons's arguments were hampered by his "ideosyncratic terminology and unsystematic style of reasoning" (Vanberg 1989:343). But a more serious shortcoming was the tendency for the work to degenerate into naive empiricism and historicism. Emphasizing the importance of the particular, of time and place and historical circumstance, institutional analysis came more and more to underline "the value of largely descriptive work on the nature and function of politico-economic institutions" (Hodgson 1991:211).

Here, then, we have the principal reason why the godfather of the new institutional economics, Ronald Coase (1983), so cavalierly dismissed the old institutional economics: "Without a theory they had nothing to pass on except a mass of descriptive material waiting for a theory, or a fire" (p. 230).

The battle between the particular and the general, between the temporal and the timeless, is one that contemporary institutional theorists continue to confront.

Early Institutional Theory in Political Science

Institutional approaches dominated political science in both Europe and America during the latter half of the nineteenth and the first two decades of the twentieth century. I concentrate on the American scene. As carried out by such leading practitioners as J. W. Burgess (1902), Woodrow Wilson (1889), and W. W. Willoughby (1896, 1904), institutional analysis was grounded in constitutional law and moral philosophy. In the heavy tomes produced by these scholars, careful attention was given to the legal framework and administrative arrangements characterizing particular governance structures. Much of the work involved painstaking historical examination of the origins, controversies, and compromises producing specific regimes; some analyses were explicitly comparative, detailing how central problems or functions were variously managed by diverse governance mechanisms. But the underlying tone of the work was normative: "In the mainstream of political science, description was overshadowed by moral philosophy" (Simon 1991:57).

As depicted by Bill and Hardgrave (1981; see also Peters 1999), the institutional school that developed at the turn of the century exhibited several defining features. First, it was preoccupied with formal structures and legal systems. "Emphasis was placed upon the organized and evident institutions of government, and studies concentrated almost exclusively upon constitutions, cabinets, parliaments, courts, and bureaucracies" (Bill and Hardgrave 1981:3).

Second, the approach emphasized detailed accounts of particular political systems, resulting in *configurative description*: intricate descriptive accounts of interlinked rules, rights, and procedures (Bill and Hardgrave 1981:3). Third, the approach was conservative in the sense that it emphasized origins but not ongoing change. "Political institutions were examined in terms of an evolutionary development which found fulfillment in the immediate present. But while these institutions had a past, they apparently had no future" (p. 6). The institutions were regarded as completed products. Fourth, the work was largely nontheoretical, primary attention being given to historical reconstruction of specific institutional forms. Finally, the tone of these studies was associated more with moral philosophy and less with empirical science. These scholars devoted more attention to the explication of normative principles than to the formulation of testable propositions.

Although he acknowledges many of the same characteristics, Eckstein (1963) also insists that these early institutionalists did usher in the first crude form of positivism in political science. Unlike their own predecessors, primarily "historicists" who focused their interest on abstracted political systems derived from philosophical principles, they were looking at the real world: at hard facts. Indeed,

> Primitive, unadulterated positivism insists upon hard facts, indubitable and incontrovertible facts, as well as facts that speak for themselves—and what facts of politics are harder, as well as more self-explanatory than the facts found in formal legal codes? (Eckstein 1963:10)

In addition, these students attended to the real world in yet another sense: They placed great emphasis on formal political institutions, on charters, legal codes, and administrative rules, in part because "the nineteenth century was a great age of constitution-making" (Eckstein 1963:10).

Beginning during the mid-1930s and continuing through the 1960s, the institutionalist perspective was challenged and largely supplanted by the behavioralist approach (not to be confused with behaviorism in psychology), which attempted to sever the tie to moral philosophy and rebuild political science as a theoretically guided empirical science (see Easton 1965). More important for our concerns, the behavioralist persuasion diverted attention away from institutional structures to political behavior.

> Behaviorists argued that, in order to understand politics and explain political outcomes, analysts should focus not on the formal attributes of government institutions but instead on informal distributions of power, attitudes, and political behavior. (Thelen and Steinmo 1992:4)

Students of politics focused attention on voting behavior, party formation, and public opinion. Moreover, this reductionist shift in emphasis from rules and structures to behavior was accompanied by a more utilitarian orientation, viewing action as "the product of calculated self-interest" and taking an instrumentalist view of politics, regarding the "allocation of resources as the central concern of political life" (March and Olsen 1984:735). To study politics was to study, following the title of Lasswell's (1936) work, "Who Gets What, When, and How?"

These theoretical strands associated with behavioralism have been reinforced and deepened by the "rational revolution" arising in the 1970s and 1980s. As I discuss in later chapters, the rational choice approach, which is based on the application of economic assumptions to political behavior, has brought about fundamental changes in political science. Peters (1999) suggests that the attributes characterizing both movements, behavioralist and rational, include (a) an emphasis on rigorous and deductive theory and methodology; (b) a bias against normative, prescriptive approaches; (c) methodological individualism, or the assumptions that individuals are the only actors and that they are motivated by individual utility maximization; and (d) "input-ism," a focus on societal inputs to the political system—for example, votes, interest group pressures, money—to the exclusion of attention to the internal workings of the system, or the institutional political structures, as they may affect outcomes.

The new institutionalism in political science has developed in reaction to the excesses of the behavioralist revolution, although one major variant employs rational choice approaches to account for the building and maintenance of institutions. Current institutionalists do not call for a return to configurational history, but they do seek to re-establish the importance of normative frameworks and rule systems in guiding, constraining, and empowering social and political behavior.

Early Institutional Theory in Sociology

Sociologists have paid more constant attention to institutions than either economists or political scientists have. Although there are a number of different discernable strands with their distinctive vocabularies and emphases, we also observe continuity from the early work of Spencer and Sumner through Davis to the recent work of Friedland and Alford; from Cooley and Park through Hughes to the contemporary analyses of Friedson and Abbott; from the early efforts of Marx, Durkheim, and Weber through Parsons to DiMaggio and Powell; and from the early work on the social sources of mind and self in Mead and Schutz to the emphasis on cognitive processes and knowledge systems in Berger and Luckmann and in Meyer and Rowan.

Spencer and Sumner

Without question, the most influential conception of institutions pervading mainstream sociology throughout the twentieth century has its origins in the work of Herbert Spencer. Spencer (1876-1896) viewed society as an organic system evolving through time. Adaptation of the system to its context was achieved via the functions of specialized "organs" structured as institutional subsystems. Spencer devoted the main body of his work to a comparative study of these institutions, attempting to draw generalizations from comparing and contrasting of their operation in different societies.

Spencer's general conceptions were embraced and amplified by William Graham Sumner (1906) in his major treatise, *Folkways*. Teeming with ethnographic and historical materials, the book generated numerous hypotheses concerning the origins, persistence, and change of folkways and mores (albeit many of these have a strong biopsychological basis). For Sumner, "an institution consists of a concept (idea, notion, doctrine, interest) and a structure" (p. 53). The concept defines the purposes or functions of the institution; the structure embodies the idea of the institution and furnishes the instrumentalities through which the idea is put into action. Social evolution progresses from individual activities to folkways, to mores, to full-fledged institutions. Such institutions are *cressive*—evolving slowly through instinctive efforts over long periods of time—but institutions can also be *enacted*, the products of rational invention and intention.

Later generations of sociologists discarded the strong biological/evolutionary analogies and functional arguments devised by Spencer and Sumner but, nevertheless, recognized the centrality of institutions as a sociological focus. Thus, in his influential mid-century text on *Human Society*, Kingsley Davis (1949) defined institutions as "a set of interwoven folkways, mores, and laws built around one or more functions," adding that in his opinion, "the concept of institutions seems better than any other to convey the notion of segments or parts of the normative order" (p. 71). And every major sociological text and curriculum of the last hundred years has reflected not only the important distinction of levels (individuals, groups, communities, societies, etc.) but also the functional division of social life into spheres or arenas—kinship, stratification, politics, economics, religion, and so on—governed by

varying normative systems. The conception of institutions as func-
tionally specialized arenas persists in contemporary notions of organization "field" or "sector" (DiMaggio and Powell 1983; Scott and Meyer
1983; see Chapter 3) and is strongly reflected in the recent work of
Friedland and Alford (1991), who stress the importance for social
change of the existence of multiple, differentiated, and partially conflicting institutional spheres.

Cooley and Hughes

Cooley and his followers emphasized the interdependence of individuals and institutions, of self and social structure. Although the great
institutions—language, government, the church, laws and customs of
property and of the family—appear to be independent and external to
behavior, they are developed and preserved through interactions
among individuals and exist "as a habit of mind and of action, largely
unconscious because largely common to all the group. . . . The individual is always cause as well as effect of the institution" (Cooley [1902]
1956:313-14).

Hughes shared and developed this interdependent model. Deftly defining an institution as an "establishment of relative permanence of a
distinctly social sort" (Hughes 1936:180), he identifies their essential
elements as

> (1) a set of mores or formal rules, or both, which can be fulfilled only by (2)
> people acting collectively, in established complementary capacities or of-
> fices. The first element represents consistency; the second concert or orga-
> nization. (Hughes 1939:297)

Although institutions represent continuity and persistence, they
exist only to the extent that they are carried forward by individuals:
"Institutions exist in the integrated and standardized behavior of individuals" (Hughes 1939:319). In most of his writing, Hughes directed
attention to the institutional structures surrounding and supporting
work activities: in particular, to occupations and professions. His
studies and essays are laced with insights on the myriad ways in which
the institutional interacts with the individual: creating identities,
shaping the life course (careers), providing a license to perform otherwise forbidden tasks and a rationale to account for the inevitable

mistakes that occur when one is performing complex work (see Hughes 1958).

Empirical work developing these insights has focused more on occupations—in particular, professions—than on organizations as institutional systems constraining and empowering individual participants (see, e.g., Becker 1982; Freidson 1970; Abbott 1988). However, a number of studies examined "strong" organizational contexts, such as mental hospitals and medical schools (Becker et al. 1961; Goffman 1961). These studies emphasized "the microprocesses by which individuals attempt to limit the power of institutions," identifying "the cracks, the loopholes in social structures" that enabled patients, students, or other subordinate participants to construct meaningful selves and obtain some freedom even when confronting these "total institutions" (Fine and Ducharme 1995:125, 126).

As a sociologist studying occupations, Abbott (1992) perceives an unbroken (Midwest/Chicago) tradition linking contemporary with earlier work and wonders what is so new about the new institutionalism in sociology. The institutional tradition has been carried forward in an uninterrupted fashion by the Chicago school studying occupations and the sociology of work, but this is much less the case for research on organizations. I believe that, over a substantial period during its development, the sociology of organizations largely lost sight of, lost focus on, and gave insufficient attention to the institutional moorings of organizations.

Marx, Durkheim, Weber, Parsons

The European tradition in institutional analysis was spearheaded by Karl Marx, whose influence permeated economics and political science, as well as sociology. Although Marx inspired a diverse array of theories and political movements, the work of primary importance to institutional theory involved his struggle with and reinterpretation of Hegel, the great German idealist philosopher. Hegel viewed history as the self-realization through time of abstract ideas or spirit (*Geist*). This self-creative spirit is reflected in the objective world, which most of us mistakenly take to be the true reality. It is the task of man to overcome this alienated state, in which the world appears to be other than spirit

(Hegel [1807] 1967; Tucker 1972). Marx, famously, turned Hegel's arguments upside down.

For Marx, the materialist world is the true one, and the alienation we experience occurs because humankind is estranged from itself in existing political and economic structures. Marx, working in the early decades of the industrial revolution, saw the key structures as the economic: Productive activity had been transformed into involuntary labor. Under a capitalist system, work was no longer an expression of creative productivity; it was alienated labor. The nature and meaning of work and work relations were seen to be transformed by structures of oppression and exploitation. These structures—involving the accompanying beliefs, norms, and power relations—are the product of human ideas and activities, but they appear to be external and objective to their participants. Ideas and ideologies reflect and attempt to justify material reality, not the other way around (Marx [1844] 1972, [1845-46] 1972). Thus, in important (but historically specific) respects, Marx gave early expression to the social construction of reality.

The other two major European figures involved in establishing sociological variants of institutional analysis were Durkheim and Weber. The French sociologist Émile Durkheim was preoccupied with understanding the changing bases of social order that accompanied the industrial revolution, but, as previously noted, he appears to have modified his views over time. His early classic, *The Division of Labor in Society* (Durkheim [1893] 1949), differentiated between the *mechanical* solidarity based on shared religious beliefs that integrated traditional societies and the newly emerging *organic* solidarity associated with an advanced division of labor. Initially, Durkheim viewed this new collective order as "based on the belief that action was rational and that order could be successfully negotiated in an individualistic way"— social order as "the unintended aggregate of individual self-interest" (Alexander 1983, Vol. 3: 131, 134). But Durkheim's revised arguments led him away from an instrumentalist, individualist explanation to focus on collective, normative frameworks that supply "the noncontractual elements" of contract (Durkheim [1893] 1949, Book 1, Chapter 7).

Durkheim's mature formulation emphasizes the pivotal role played by symbolic systems—systems of belief and "collective representations"—along with shared cognitive frames and schemas, which, if not explicitly religious, have a moral or spiritual character.

There is something eternal in religion which is destined to survive all the particular symbols in which religious thought has successively enveloped itself. There can be no society which does not feel the need of upholding and reaffirming at regular intervals, the collective sentiments and the collective ideas which make its unity and its personality. (Durkheim [1912] 1961:474-75)

These systems, although a product of human interaction, are experienced by individuals as objective. Although subjectively formed, they become crystallized. They are, in Durkheim's ([1901] 1950) terms, social facts: phenomena perceived by the individual to be both external (to that person) and coercive (backed by sanctions). And, as is the case with religious systems, ritual and ceremonies play a vital role in expressing and reinforcing belief. Rituals and ceremonies enact beliefs. They "act entirely upon the mind and upon it alone" (Durkheim [1912] 1961:420), so that to the extent that these activities have impact on situations, it is through their effects on beliefs about these situations.

These symbolic systems—systems of knowledge, belief, and moral authority—are, for Durkheim, social institutions.

Institutions, Durkheim writes, are a product of joint activity and association, the effect of which is to "fix," to "institute" outside us certain initially subjective and individual ways of acting and judging. Institutions, then, are the "crystallizations" of Durkheim's earlier writing. (Alexander 1983, Vol. 2:259)

The third major European figure contributing to institutional theory was Max Weber. As I will note in more detail in Chapter 2, more contemporary analysts of institutions lay claim to Weber as their guiding genius than to any other early theorist. Although Weber did not explicitly employ the concept of institution, his work is permeated with a concern for understanding the ways in which cultural rules, ranging in nature from customary mores to legally defined constitutions or rule systems, define social structures and govern social behavior, including economic structures and behavior. For example, his justly famous typology of administrative systems—traditional, charismatic, and rational legal—describes three types of authority systems differing primarily in the types of belief or cultural systems that legitimate the exercise of authority (see Weber [1924] 1968:215; Bendix 1960; Dornbusch and Scott 1975).

That there remains much controversy as to how to characterize Weber's theoretical stance is largely because he stood at the crossroads of three major debates raging at the turn of the nineteenth century: first, that between those who viewed the social sciences as a natural science and those who argued that it was rather a cultural science; second, between idealist arguments associated with Durkheim and the materialist emphasis of Marx; and third, between the institutionalist historical school of economics and the classical interest in developing general theoretical principles. More than any other figure of his time, Weber wrestled with and attempted to reconcile these apparently conflicting ideas.

Weber argued that the social sciences differ fundamentally from the natural sciences in that, in the former but not the latter, both the researcher and the object of study attach meaning to events. For Weber ([1924] 1968), action is social "when and insofar as the acting individual attaches a subjective meaning to his behavior" (p. 4). Individuals do not mechanically respond to stimuli; they first interpret them and then shape their response. Researchers cannot expect to understand social behavior without taking into account the meanings that mediate social action. Weber employed his interpretive approach to attempt a synthesis in which both the material conditions and interests stressed by materialists such as Marx and the idealist values emphasized by Durkheim combined to motivate and guide action (see Alexander 1983, Vol. 2; and Chapter 3).

In developing his *Wirtschaftssoziologie* (economic sociology), Weber embraced the institutionalist argument that economics needs to be historically informed and comparative in its approach, but at the same time, he sided with Menger and the classicists in supporting the value of theoretical models that allowed one to abstract from specific, historically embedded systems to formulate and evaluate general arguments. Weber believed that economic sociology could bridge the chasm by attending to both historical circumstance and the development of analytic theory (Swedberg 1991, 1998). Weber suggested that by abstracting from the specificity and complexity of concrete events, researchers could create "ideal types" to guide and inform comparative studies. If researchers were careful not to mistake the ideal types for reality—for example, to insist that individuals under all conditions would behave as rational "economic men"—such models could provide useful maps to guide analysis and increase understanding of the real world (Weber [1904-1918] 1949). More precisely, "Weber views rational behavior as evolving historically, or, to phrase it differently, to Weber—unlike to today's economists—rational behavior is a variable, not an assumption" (Swedberg 1998:36).

The American sociologist Talcott Parsons also attempted to synthesize the arguments of major early theorists, in particular, Durkheim, Weber, and Freud, in constructing his voluntaristic theory of action (see Parsons 1937, 1951).[2] Like Weber, he attempted to reconcile a subjective and an objective approach to social action by emphasizing that whereas normative frameworks existed independently of a given social actor, analysts needed to take into account the orientation of actors to them. A system of action was said to be *institutionalized* to the extent that actors in an ongoing relation oriented their actions to a common set of normative standards and value patterns. As such a normative system becomes internalized, "conformity with it becomes a need-disposition in the actor's own personality structure" (Parsons 1951:37). In this sense, institutionalized action is motivated by moral rather than by instrumental concerns: "The primary motive for obedience to an institutional norm lies in the moral authority it exercises over the individual" (Parsons [1934] 1990:326). The actor conforms because of his or her belief in a value standard, not out of expediency or self-interest.

Viewed more objectively, from the standpoint of the social analyst, institutions are appropriately seen as a system of norms that "regulate the relations of individuals to each other," that define "what the relations of individuals ought to be" (Parsons [1934] 1990:327). Also, implicitly following the lead of Spencer and Sumner, Parsons developed his own abstract typology of norms oriented to the solution of the four generic problems confronting all social systems: adaptation, goal attainment, integration, and latency (maintenance of cultural patterns) (see Parsons 1951; Parsons, Bales, and Shils 1953).

Contemporary theorists note several kinds of limitations with Parsons's formulation. Alexander (1983, Vol. 4) concludes that although Parsons attempted to develop a multidimensional view of social action, his conception of institutionalization put too much weight on cultural patterns, overemphasizing the "control exerted by values over conditions" (p. 242). The importance of interests and of instrumental action and rational choice was underemphasized. DiMaggio and Powell (1991) praise Parsons for the contribution he made to the "microfoundations" of institutional theory in his attempt to understand the ways in which culture influences behavior. But they complain that his conception of culture failed to stress its existence as "an object of orientation existing outside the individual." Instead, following Freud, Parsons viewed culture as acting primarily as "an internalized element of the personality system," thus giving too much weight to the subjective in contrast to the objective view. In addition, DiMaggio and Powell (1991) argue that Parsons's analysis of culture neglected its cognitive dimensions in favor of its evaluative components: culture limited to value orientations (p. 17). Each of these emphases drew Parsons away from examining the interplay of the instrumental and the normative in social action.

Mead, Schutz, Berger and Luckmann

George Herbert Mead, like Cooley, emphasized the interdependence of self and society but gave particular attention to the role played by symbolic systems in creating both the human and the social. Meaning is created in interaction as gestures, particularly vocal gestures (language), call out the same response in self as in other; and self arises in interaction as an individual "takes on the attitudes of the other" in arriving at a self-conception (Mead 1934).

Working at about the same time as Mead, but in Vienna, Alfred Schutz also examined in detail the ways in which common meanings are constructed through interaction by individuals. However, Schutz also explored the wider "structure of the social world," noting the great variety of social relations in which we become involved. In addition to intimate, face-to-face, "Thou" relations, as well as "We" relations with people thought to be similar to ourselves, we engage in multiple "They" relations with others known only indirectly and impersonally. Such relations are only possible to the extent that we develop an "ideal type" conception that enables us to deal with these others as needed, for example, to mail a letter or to stand beside them in an elevator. These relations are based on typifications of the other and taken-for-granted assumptions as to the way the interaction will proceed. In this sense, the meanings are highly institutionalized (Schutz [1932] 1967).

Stimulated by the work of Mead but even more by that of Schutz, Berger and Luckmann (1967) redirected the sociology of knowledge away from its earlier concerns with epistemological issues or a focus on intellectual history to more mainstream sociological concerns, insisting that "the sociology of knowledge must concern itself with everything that passes for 'knowledge' in society" (p. 15). The concern is not with the validity of this knowledge but with its production, with "the social creation of reality" (p. 15). Berger and Luckmann argue that social reality is a human construction, a product of social interaction. They underscore this position in their attention to language (systems of symbols) and cognition mediated by social processes as crucial to the ways in which actions are produced, repeated, and come to evoke stable, similar meanings in self and other. They define this process as one of *institutionalization*. In contrast to Durkheim and Parsons, Berger and Luckmann emphasized the creation of shared knowledge and belief systems rather than the production of rules and norms. Cognitive frameworks are stressed over normative systems. A focus on the centrality of cognitive systems forms the foundation for the sociological version of the new institutionalism in organizations (see Chapter 2).

Concluding Comment

This brief review has attempted to identify some of the varying interests and emphases of the early institutionalists, formulations developed between 1880 up to the mid-twentieth century. As we will see, these theorists in numerous ways anticipated distinctions and insights rediscovered by later analysts. Contemporary economists, with the notable exception of economic historians, have rejected the approaches promoted by the German historical school, but some strands of the new institutionalism in economics reflect the interests of Menger and the Austrian school. Contemporary political scientists have left behind the moral philosophical roots of the early institutionalists, but a lively subset has rediscovered an interest in the historical and comparative study of political systems. An even larger collection of political scientists has adapted rational choice models devised by economists to better explain the emergence and functioning of political institutions. Contemporary sociologists continue to pursue and refine the ideas of their numerous and varied predecessors. Some continue to examine the diverse institutional spheres that make up society; others examine the ways in which individuals are empowered and constrained by shared normative systems; and still others explore the ways in which symbolic systems—cultural rules and schemas—shape and support social life.

Although there is continuity, there is also change, perhaps even progress. Most of the early work on institutions shared a common limitation: Little attention was accorded to organizations.[3] Some theorists focused their analyses on wider institutional structures—on constitutions and political systems, on language and legal systems, on kinship and religious structures—whereas others emphasized the emergence of common meanings and normative frameworks out of localized social interaction. Few, however, treated organizations themselves as institutional forms or directed attention to the ways in which wider institutions shaped collections of organizations.

Theorists in the 1940s and 1950s began to recognize the existence and importance of particular collectivities—individual organizations—entities that were distinguishable from both broader social institutions on the one hand and the behavior of individuals on the other. Later developments, in the 1970s and 1980s, called attention to the significance of organizational *forms* and organizational *fields*, and the recognition of each of these levels has stimulated much fruitful development of institutional theory and research.

Notes

1. These generalizations—particularly the first and the fourth—are less applicable to the Austrian branch of economics led by Menger and Hayek. These theorists, while insisting on the importance of making theory and of simplifying assumptions, were interested in understanding economic change and so were sympathetic to a more evolutionary approach and the study of economic processes (see Langlois 1986a). Their ideas fueled the development of evolutionary economics (see Chapter 2).

2. Camic (1992) argues that Parsons strategically selected these European predecessors—rather than American institutionalist scholars such as Veblen and Mitchell and his own teachers (Hamilton and Ayres), who shared their interests—because of the tarnished reputation of these institutional economists at the time when Parsons was constructing his theory of action. There is

a politics to selecting intellectual forebears that helps to explain why it is that some previous work is "drawn upon, while other work is overlooked" (p. 421).

Ironically, in a parallel fashion, Hall (1992) has accused sociological neoinstituionalists of failing to acknowledge Parsons (whose reputation until recently has been on the wane) as an important intellectual predecessor.

3. An essay by Znaniecki (1945) in an influential review volume edited by Gurvitch and Moore is an exception to this generalization. Taking off from Spencer's and Sumner's definition of institution, Znaniecki proposes that research on institutions ought to focus on "the comparative study of those many and diverse organized groups or associations, small and large, simple and complex" (p. 208) that provide the forms and carry out the specialized purposes of a given institutional arena. This approach anticipates by more than 25 years the concept of organizational field that emerged in the early 1980s (see Chapter 4), but it did not stimulate visible interest or related work at the time.

2 Institutional Theory
and Organizations

Although institutions were identified and analyzed quite early by social scientists, as we have seen, organizations as distinctive types of social forms did not become a focus of study until relatively recently. March (1965) dates the origins of organizational studies to the period 1937 through 1947, noting the appearance of the influential publications of Gulick and Urwick (1937), Barnard (1938), Roethlisberger and Dickson (1939), and Simon ([1945] 1997).

Early work connecting organizations and institutional arguments commenced in the 1940s. Three streams are identified. The first was stimulated by the translation into English of Weber's work on bureaucracy ([1906-1924] 1946, [1924] 1947), which aroused much interest among a collection of sociologists at Columbia University. Talcott Parsons, at Harvard, was the reigning American sociological theorist of his time; he became a second early conduit, both because he was a translator of Weber and because he was encouraged to apply his own cultural-institutional theory to organizations. James D. Thompson, the founding editor of *Administrative Science Quarterly*, a new interdisciplinary journal devoted

21

to research on organizations, invited Parsons to prepare an article for the inaugural issue in 1956. Third, Simon's pioneering work at the Carnegie Institute of Technology (now Carnegie-Mellon University) on organizational decision making was expanded in collaboration with James G. March into an influential statement about the nature of rationality in organizations.

This early work connecting institutions and organizations is reviewed in the first section of this chapter. Then, I consider the emergence of a complex of new ideas that provided the basis for the more recent, somewhat novel conception of institutions: work that laid the foundations of neoinstitutional organization theory.

Institutions and Organizations: Early Approaches

The Columbia School and Selznick's Institutional Model

Shortly after selections from Weber's seminal writings on bureaucracy were translated into English during the late 1940s, a collection of scholars at Columbia University under the leadership of Robert K. Merton revived interest in bureaucracy and bureaucratization, its sources, and the consequences for behavior in organizations (see Merton et al. 1952).[1] It is generally acknowledged that a series of empirical studies of diverse organizations carried out by Merton's students—by Selznick (1949), of the Tennessee Valley Authority (TVA); by Gouldner (1954), of a gypsum plant and mine; by Blau (1955), of a federal and a state bureau; and by Lipset, Trow, and Coleman (1956), of a typographical union—were instrumental in establishing organizations as a distinctive arena of study (see Scott 1998:9). What is less widely recognized is Merton's influence on Selznick's institutional theory of organizations.

As described below, Merton's (1936) early work on "unanticipated consequences of purposive action" was helpful to Selznick, but his analysis of bureaucratic behavior was even more directly influential. Although Merton ([1940] 1957) did not employ the term "institutionalization" in his well-known essay, "Bureaucratic Structure and Personality," he provides a lucid discussion of processes within organizations, leading officials to orient their actions around rules even "to the point where primary concern with conformity to the rules interferes with the achievement of the purposes of the organization" (p. 199). Merton depicts the multiple forces within bureaucracy producing discipline and orienting officials to a valued normative order. The strength of these pressures is such that officials are prone to follow the rules to the point of rigidity, formalism, and even ritualism. Stimulated by the arguments of Durkheim and Hughes (and Parsons), Merton ([1940] 1957) spells out his version of institutional processes within organizations:

> There may ensue, in particular vocations and in particular types of organization, the process of sanctification . . . [T]hrough sentiment-formation, emotional dependence upon bureaucratic symbols and status, and affective involvement in spheres of competence and authority, there develop prerogatives involving attitudes of moral legitimacy which are established as values in their own right, and are no longer viewed as merely technical means for expediting administration. (p. 202)

The leading early figure in the institutional analysis of organizations is Philip Selznick, whose conception of institutional processes was strongly influenced by Merton's work. His views have evolved throughout the corpus of his writings. From the beginning, Selznick (1948) was intent on distinguishing between organization as "the structural expression of rational action" (p. 25)—as a mechanistic instrument designed to achieve specified goals—and organization viewed as an adaptive organic system, affected by the social characteristics of its participants as well as by the varied pressures imposed by its environment. "Organizations," to a variable extent and over time, are transformed into "institutions."

In his earliest formulation, Selznick borrows heavily from Merton's (1936) analysis, "The Unanticipated Consequences of Purposive Social Action." Whereas some consequences of our actions occur as planned, others are unanticipated; social actions are not context-free but are constrained, and their outcomes are shaped by the setting in which they occur. Especially significant are the constraints on action that arise from "commitments enforced by institutionalization. . . . Because organizations are social systems, goals or procedures tend to achieve an established, value-impregnated status. We say that they become institutionalized" (Selznick 1949:256-57). In his later work on leadership, Selznick (1957) elaborates his views:

Institutionalization is a process. It is something that happens to an organization over time, reflecting the organization's own distinctive history, the people who have been in it, the groups it embodies and the vested interests they have created, and the way it has adapted to its environment. . . .

In what is perhaps its most significant meaning, "to institutionalize" is to *infuse with value* beyond the technical requirements of the task at hand. (pp. 16-17; emphasis in original)

As organizations become infused with value, they are no longer regarded as expendable tools; participants want to see that they are preserved. By embodying a distinctive set of values, the organization acquires a character structure, a distinctive identity. Maintaining the organization is no longer simply an instrumental matter of keeping the machinery working; it becomes a struggle to preserve a set of unique values. A vital role of leadership for Selznick, echoing Barnard (1938), is to define and defend these values.

In addition to viewing institutionalization as a process, as something "that happens to the organization over time," Selznick (1957) also treated institutionalization as a variable: Organizations with more precisely defined goals or with better developed technologies are less subject to institutionalization than those with diffuse goals and weak technologies.

Contrasting Selznick's with Merton's conception, both emphasized quite similar processes of value commitments to procedures extending beyond instrumental utilities. However, whereas Selznick focused on commitments distinctive to the developing character of a specific organization, Merton stressed commitments associated with characteristics of bureaucratic (rational-legal) organizations generally. Selznick's approach calls for depicting a "natural history" of a specific organization, a description of the processes by which, over time, it develops its distinctive structures, capabilities, and liabilities. He himself studied the evolution of the TVA, noting how its original structures and goals were transformed over time by the commitments of its participants and the requirements imposed by powerful constituencies in its environment (Selznick 1949; see also Chapter 4). Selznick's students conducted similar case studies of the transformation of organizational goals: in the Women's Christian Temperance Union (WCTU) (Gusfield 1955), a community college (Clark 1960), a voluntary hospital (Perrow 1961), and the YMCA (Zald and Denton 1963). In all of these studies, the official goals of the organization are shown to differ from—to mask—the "real" objectives, which had been transformed in interaction with interests both internal and external to the organization. As Perrow (1986:159) notes, Selznick's institutional school tends to produce an exposé view of organizations: Organizations are not the rational creatures they pretend to be but vehicles for embodying (sometimes surreptitious) values.

Another of Selznick's students, Arthur Stinchcombe (1968), has built on Selznick's formulation, making more explicit the role of agency and power. Stinchcombe defines an institution as "a structure in which powerful people are committed to some value or interest" (p. 107), emphasizing that values are preserved and interests are protected only if those holding them possess and retain power. Institutionalization connotes stability over time, and Stinchcombe's analysis attempts to identify the ways in which power holders are able to preserve their power. Stinchcombe (1968) asserts, "By selection, socialization, controlling conditions of incumbency, and hero worship, succeeding generations of power-holders tend to regenerate the same institutions" (p. 111).

Merton and Selznick laid the basis for a process model of institutions; Merton described processes operating in all or most bureaucratic organizations influencing officials toward overconformity, whereas Selznick focused on processes within particular organizations giving rise to a distinctive set of value commitments. Stinchcombe elaborated the mechanisms used by powerful actors to perpetuate their interests and commitments.

Parsons's Institutional Approach

Talcott Parsons ([1956] 1960a) applies his general cultural-institutional arguments to organizations primarily by examining the relation between an organization and its environment, the ways in which the value system of an organization is legitimated by its connections to "the main institutional patterns" in "different functional contexts" (p. 20). Although in most of his writing, as noted in Chapter 1, Parsons stressed the subjective dimension of institutions, whereby individual actors internalize shared norms so that they become the basis for the individual's action, in his analysis of organizations, Parsons ([1934] 1990) shifts attention to what he terms the objective dimension: "a system of norms defining what the relations of individuals [or organizations] ought to be" (p. 327).

Parsons ([1956] 1960a) argues that these wider normative structures serve to legitimate the existence of organizations but, "more specifically, they legitimize the main functional patterns of operation which are necessary to implement the values" (p. 21). Schools receive legitimacy in a society to the extent that their goals are connected to wider cultural values, such as socialization and education, and to the extent that they conform in their structures and procedures to established "patterns of operation" specified for educational organizations. Note that in some respects, this argument replicates at the organizational level Parsons's discussion of institutionalization at the individual level, because it focuses on the individual unit's—whether a person's or an organization's—orientation to a normative system. Organizations operating in different functional sectors are legitimated by differing values, exhibit different adaptive patterns, and are governed by different codes and normative patterns. Moreover, value systems are stratified within a society such that organizations serving more highly esteemed values are thought to be more legitimate and are expected to receive a disproportionate share of societal resources (Parsons 1953).

Parsons finds yet another use for the concept of institution. He argues that organizations tend to become differentiated vertically into three somewhat distinctive levels or layers: the technical, concerned with production activities; the managerial, concerned with control and coordination activities and with procurement of resources and disposal of products; and the institutional, concerned with relating the organization to the norms and conventions of the community and society. Every organization is a subsystem of "a wider social system which is the source of the 'meaning,' legitimation, or higher-level support which makes the implementation of the organization's goals possible" (Parsons [1956] 1960b:63-64). Parsons's typology of organizational levels was subsequently embraced by Thompson (1967), and it has been widely employed. Moreover, in discussing the "points of articulation" between the three system levels, Parsons ([1956] 1960b) notes that they are characterized by "a qualitative break in the simple continuity of line authority" because "the functions at each level are qualitatively different" (pp. 65-66). His discussion thus anticipates the recognition by later analysts that some structural elements are "loosely coupled" or "decoupled" (see Weick 1976; Meyer and Rowan 1977).

Unlike Selznick's formulation, Parsons's theoretical work on organizations did not stimulate much empirical research. A few students, such as Georgopoulos (1972), employed Parsons's general conceptual scheme and described the importance of institutional underpinnings for specific types of organizations, but in general, Parsons's insights were not so much built on as rediscovered by later theorists.

The Carnegie School

Political scientist Herbert Simon developed his theory of administrative behavior to counteract and correct conventional economic theories that made heroic, unreasonable assumptions about individual rationality. Simon was among the first theorists to link the limits of individual cognitive capacity with the features of organizational structure. In his classic *Administrative Behavior*, Simon ([1945] 1997) described how organizational structures work to simplify and support decision making of individuals in organizations, allowing them to achieve higher levels of consistent and "boundedly rational" behavior than would otherwise be possible. In accepting organizational membership, individuals are expected to adopt organizational value premises as a guide for their decisions; factual premises—beliefs about means-ends connections—are also commonly supplied, in the form of organizational rules, procedures, and routines (Simon [1945] 1997, Chapter 5). Behavior is rational in organizations because choices are constrained, and individuals are guided by rules.

Together with March, Simon developed his arguments concerning the ways in which organizations shape the behavior of participants by developing "performance programs" to guide routine behavior and "search programs" to follow when confronting unusual tasks. March and Simon (1958) argue that, in many circumstances, "search and choice processes are very much abridged. . . . Most behavior, and particularly most behavior in organizations, is governed by performance programs" (pp. 141-42), which are preset routines that provide guidance to individuals confronted by recurring demands. Such routines greatly reduce the discretion of most participants so that they both make fewer choices and are more circumscribed in the choices they do make. Value assumptions, cognitive frames, rules, and routines—these are the ingredients that lead individuals to behave rationally. Indeed, "the rational individual is, and must be, an organized and institutionalized individual" (Simon [1945] 1997:111).

March and Simon's arguments, albeit among the earliest, remain among the most influential and clearest statements of the microfeatures and functions of neoinstitutional forms (see DiMaggio and Powell 1991:15-26).

Foundations of Neoinstitutional Theory

We have arrived at the point in our history when the ideas that have come to be recognized as neoinstitutional theory appeared. As we will see, these ideas do not represent a sharp break with the past, although there are new emphases and insights. I begin by briefly reviewing the proximate sources and founding conceptions linking neoinstitutional theory and organizations in economics, political science, and sociology. Then, in Chapter 3, I attempt a more analytic review of current theory, noting areas of consensus and dispute.

Neoinstitutional Theory in Economics

Many diverse lines of work contribute to the mixture of ideas fueling neoinstitutional theory in economics. It is instructive, and rather ironic, that the newer economic work "reflects less the ideas of the early institutionalists than it does those of their opponents" (Langlois 1986a:2). Most neoinstitutional economists seek not to replace orthodox economic theory with the study of multiple and diverse institutional conditions but rather to develop an economic theory of institutions.

In his influential review, Langlois (1986a) incorporates within neoinstitutional economics the contributions of Simon (discussed above), a focus on transaction cost and property rights inspired by Coase (1937) (with a slight nod to Commons), the modern Austrian school as influenced by Hayek (1948), the work of Schumpeter ([1926] 1961) on innovation, and evolutionary theory as developed by Nelson and Winter (1982). Three more or less common themes underlie and link these contributions (see Langlois 1986a; Knudsen 1993):

1. A broader conception of the economic agent is embraced, replacing the assumption of maximizing within a set of known alternatives.

How broad a view is taken varies greatly among the identified schools. In his work on transaction costs, Williamson embraces Simon's conception of bounded rationality, whereas the Austrian and evolutionary theorists use an even more expansive view that includes rule-based or procedural rationality.

> 2. The focus is on the study of economic processes rather than on the purely logical study of equilibrium states, and it is recognized that economic systems evolve over time reflecting, in part, learning by the agents.

Conventional economics devotes the lion's share of its resources to the study of various types of economic systems that have attained an equilibrium (stable and well-coordinated behavior), but little attention is paid to the question of how a state of equilibrium came into being. Ad hoc "stories" are generated about how stability may have been achieved, but these are only tacked on to the formal model (see Knudsen 1993). Neoinstitutional economists are interested in developing and testing these process arguments. Rather than treating institutions mainly as exogenous variables affecting economic behavior, the newer scholarship considers how institutions affecting economic transactions arise, are maintained, and are transformed. Game theorists have also become interested in these questions.

> 3. The coordination of economic activity is not simply a matter of market-mediated transactions, but involves many other types of institutional structures that are, themselves, important topics of study.

In addition to the role of governmental systems, among the most important of these institutional structures are those embedded in organizations.

It is not possible here to consider in detail all of the specific approaches associated with these themes (for reviews, see Hodgson 1993, 1994; Mäki, Gustafsson, and Knudsen 1993), but two of the more influential contributions will be briefly described.

Transaction Cost Economics

One branch of neoinstitutional economics is concerned with the rule and governance systems that develop to regulate or manage economic exchanges. These systems occur at many levels, from macro-regimes at the international level to understandings governing micro-exchanges between individuals. Accounting for the emergence and change of trading regimes among societies has been of primary interest to economic historians (e.g, North 1990), industry systems have been examined by industrial organization economists (e.g., Stigler 1968), and studies of the sources of organizational forms are being conducted by a growing set of organizational economists. Although all of this work is properly regarded as institutional economics, it is the latter work, focusing on firm-level structures, that is especially identified with the new institutionalism in economics.

By consensus, the pioneer theorist inaugurating this approach was Ronald Coase (1937), whose article, "The Nature of the Firm," asks why some economic exchanges are carried out within firms under a governance structure involving rules and hierarchical enforcement mechanisms rather than being directly subject to the price mechanism in markets. Coase suggests that the reason must be that "there is a cost of using the price mechanism," namely "the costs of negotiating and concluding a separate contract for each exchange transaction which takes place in a market" (p. 389). Because of these *transaction costs,* firms arise.

This insight lay fallow: In Coase's (1972) own words, his article was "much cited and little used" until it was resurrected in the 1970s by Oliver Williamson, who pursued its development by adding conditions and elaborations. Williamson argued that transaction costs increase as a function of two paired conditions: when individual rationality, which is bounded (cognitively limited), is confronted by heightened complexity and uncertainty; and when individual opportunism—some actors' propensity to lie and cheat—is coupled with the absence of alternative exchange partners. Under such conditions, exchanges are likely to be removed from the market and brought within an organizational framework or, if the exchanges are already inside an organization, more elaborate controls are likely to be developed (Williamson 1975, 1985). Williamson extends Coase's arguments by pushing them beyond the market versus firm comparison to consider a wide variety of "governance systems" ranging from markets to hybrid organizational forms, such as franchising or alliance arrangements; to hierarchical structures, such as unified firms and multidivisional corporations (Williamson 1985, 1991).[2]

Thus, the Williamson variant of new institutional economics focuses primarily on the meso-analytic questions of "the comparative efficacy with which alternative generic forms of governance—markets, hybrids, hierarchies—economize on transactions costs" rather than on more macro questions regarding the origins and effects of the "institutional rules of the game: customs, laws, politics" (Williamson 1991:269), the latter issues being left to economic historians and sociologists (see also Williamson 1994).

Although Williamson stretches conventional economics to take seriously the effects of varying institutional contexts, or governance structures, on economic behavior, unlike earlier economic institutionalists, he has remained firmly within the neoclassical tradition. Hodgson (1994) underlines the point:

> Like the work of other new institutionalists, Williamson's is constructed in atomistic and individualistic terms because its elemental conceptual building block is the given, "opportunistic" individual. He does not consider the possibility that the preference functions of the individual may be molded by circumstances, such as the structure and culture of the firm, or that this phenomenon may be significant in analyzing or understanding such institutions. (p. 70)

In addition, Williamson shows little interest in the processes by which varying governance structures arise or are transformed. His explanation for a structure is more often constructed as a functionalist one, "explaining" the choice of a given form by pointing to its consequences (see Knudsen 1993; see also Chapter 5).

By contrast, other economists, such as Douglass North, have developed approaches that incorporate assumptions much more similar to those embraced by the turn-of-the-century economic institutionalists. As noted, North focuses on a higher level of analysis, examining the origins of cultural, political, and legal frameworks and their effects on economic forms and processes. As an economic historian, his focus is on development and change rather than on comparative statics (North 1989, 1990). And, although he attends to transaction costs in his analysis of economic systems, he is more prone to treat them as dependent variables, subject to the effects of wider institutional frameworks, than as independent variables to explain differences among actors' choice of governance mechanisms (see Hirsch and Lounsbury 1996).

Evolutionary Economics

A second, important addition to neoinstitutional economic theory has been developed by Nelson and Winter (Winter 1964; Nelson and Winter 1982). Their evolutionary economics distantly echoes the interests of Veblen but is more solidly based on Schumpeter's ([1926] 1961) ideas on innovation and on Alchian's (1950) arguments that economic agents such as firms are subject to adaptation and selection processes. Nelson and Winter embrace an evolutionary theory of the firm analogous to biology, in which a firm's "routines" are argued to be the equivalent of genes in a plant or animal. Routines are made up of the conscious and tacit knowledge and skills held by participants who carry out organizational tasks. To survive, a firm must be able to reproduce and modify its routines in the face of changing situations.

Nelson and Winter (1982) locate their arguments at the industry or organizational population level of analysis to develop a theory of economic change processes (p. 36). Their concern is to examine the ways in which competitive processes operate among firms so that those whose routines are best adapted to current conditions flourish whereas those with less adequate routines falter. A dynamic model of accumulating knowledge and capabilities is developed to displace the static model of orthodox economics. Firms are viewed as historical entities, their routines being "the result of an endogenous, experience-based learning process" (Knudsen 1995:203). Moreover,

> It is quite inappropriate to conceive of firm behavior in terms of deliberate choice from a broad menu of alternatives that some external observer considers to be "available" opportunities for the organization. The menu is not broad, but narrow and idiosyncratic; it is built into the firm's routines, and most of the "choosing" is also accomplished automatically by those routines. (Nelson and Winter 1982:134)

Nelson and Winter do not themselves employ the term *institution* in their arguments, but it is quite clear that their conception of organizational routines can be treated as one mode of institutionalized behavior. Implicitly, as Langlois (1986a) suggests, their view of institution is one of "regularities of behavior understandable in terms of rules, norms, and routines" (p. 19). Note that Nelson and Winter embrace a much broader conception of factors shaping behavior and structure in organizations than do transaction-cost economists. Also, their approach strongly favors a process orientation rather than one of comparative statics.

In sum, there are important differences among contemporary institutional economists in the nature of their assumptions and the focus of their analytic attention. However, it is unquestionably the case that the new institutional economics is dominated currently by scholars who cling to the neoclassical core of the discipline while struggling to broaden its boundaries.

Neoinstitutional Theory in Political Science

As described in Chapter 1, neoinstitutionalism in political science may be viewed, at least in part, as a reaction to the behavioralist emphasis that dominated the field at mid-century. In a situation that somewhat resembles the instance of economics, the new institutionalists in political science and political sociology have grouped themselves into two quite distinct camps: the historical and the rational choice theorists.[3] The two perspectives differ along several dimensions.

Historical Institutionalism

The historical institutionalists, in many respects, harken back to the turn-of-the-century institutional scholars who devoted themselves to the detailed analysis of regimes and governance mechanisms. Members of this camp include March and Olsen (1984, 1989), Krasner (1988), Hall (1986), Skocpol (1985), and Zysman (1983). Institutions are viewed as including "both formal structures and informal rules and procedures that structure conduct" (Thelen and Steinmo 1992:2). Historical scholars emphasize that political institutions are not entirely derivative from other social structures, such as class, but have independent effects on social phenomena; that social arrangements are not only or even primarily the result of aggregating individual choices and actions; that many structures and outcomes are not planned or intended but rather are the consequence of unanticipated effects and constrained choice; and that history is not usually "efficient"—a process "that moves rapidly to a unique solution" (March and Olsen 1984:737)—but one that is much more indeterminate and context-dependent.

The historical group takes a social-constructionist position that assumes "that capabilities and preferences, that is, the very nature of the actors, cannot be understood except as part of some larger institutional framework" (Krasner 1988:72; see also Chapter 3). Individual preferences are not stable and often result from choices, rather than preceding or determining them. Institutions construct actors and define their available modes of action; they constrain behavior, but they also empower it. Analysis from this perspective is aimed at providing a detailed account of the specifics of institutional forms because they are expected to exert strong effects on individual behavior, structuring agendas, attention, preferences, and modes of acting.

These analysts attempt to show that political systems are not neutral arenas within which external interests compete but rather complex forms that generate independent interests and advantages and whose rules and procedures exert important effects on whatever business is being transacted. The structure of political systems, such as the state, matters (see Skocpol 1985). In accounting for the origins of these structures, the approach is primarily that of historical reconstruction. Although individuals build these structures, there is no assurance that they will produce what they intend. Current choices and possibilities are constrained and conditioned by past choices (see Skowronek 1982).

Rational Choice Theory

The second camp consists of the rational choice theorists (also termed *positive theory*) and includes such scholars as Moe, Shepsle, and Weingast. These analysts view institutions as governance or rule systems, arguing that they represent rationally constructed edifices established by individuals seeking to promote or protect their interests. The approach represents an extension of the neoinstitutional work in economics—including the transaction-cost approach of Williamson and the work of agency theorists such as Alchian and Demsetz (1972)—and its application to the study of political systems. Tullock (1976), an early advocate of importing economic models to explain political behavior, argues that "voters and customers are essentially the same people. Mr. Smith buys and votes; he is the same man in the supermarket and the voting booth" (p. 5; see also Buchanan and Tullock 1962). Moe (1984) enumerates the major elements making up the paradigm adopted from the economists as including

> the contractual nature of organizations; markets vs. hierarchies, transactions costs, the rationality of structure, individualistic explanation, and economic methods of analysis. Standard neoclassical notions—optimization, marginality, equilibrium—are often central to work in this new tradition. (p. 750)

Political theorists recognize that economic models developed to account for economic organizations require modification if they are to be applied to political systems. But they also insist that many of the basic questions are parallel, including, Why do public organizations exist, and how are we to account for their varying forms and governance mechanisms? How can elected political officials, as principals, control their bureaucratic agents? What are the effects of political institutions on political and social behavior? As Peters (1999) observes, "Within this approach, institutions are conceptualized largely as sets of positive (inducements) and negative (rules) motivations for individuals, with individual utility maximization providing the dynamic for behavior within the models" (p. 45).

Rational choice theorists recognize that "in the reality of politics, social choices are not chaotic. They are quite stable." They are stable because "of the distinctive role that institutions play." Thus, the task becomes to understand this role and, "more fundamentally, to determine where these institutions come from in the first place" (Moe 1990a:216). The general argument embraced by these theorists is that "economic organizations and institutions are explained in the same way: they are structures that emerge and take the specific form they do because they solve collective action problems and thereby facilitate gains from trade" (pp. 217-18).

Theorists disagree as to what is distinctive about political institutions. Weingast (1989) argues that politics differs from markets in that in the former, actors cannot simply engage in market exchange but must make decisions under some framework such as majority rule. Shepsle (1989) suggests that the most important task of political systems is to "get property rights right": to establish rule systems that will promote efficient economic organizations. Moe (1990a) argues that political decisions are distinctive in that they are "fundamentally about the exercise of public authority" (p. 221), which entails access to unique coercive powers. These and related researchers have attempted to account for the distinctive powers of congressional committees (Shepsle and Weingast 1987) and the inefficiency of governmental bureaucracies (Moe 1990a, 1990b) as rational solutions to collective problems.

An important arena of application for both historical and rational choice theorists has been that of international relations. Rational models view nation-states as self-interested actors attempting to maximize their own advantage in dealing with other nations. Rules are accepted when they lower the transaction costs of a participant and/or decrease the overall level of uncertainty (Rittberger 1993; Hasenclever, Mayer, and Rittberger 1997). Historical institutionalists, such as Krasner (1983) and Keohane (1989), emphasize the important independent effects of the emergence of cooperative norms among participating nations. In addition, as Keohane (1989) points out, the "institutions do not merely reflect the preferences and power of the units constituting them; the institutions themselves shape those preferences and that power" (p. 382; see also Kahn and Zald 1990).

Thus, although both historical institutionalists and rational choice theorists agree on the importance of institutions in political life, important differences in assumptions and perspectives remain. Rational choice theorists are more likely to stress the micro-foundations of institutions, asking how institutions are devised to solve collective action problems experienced by individuals. Historical institutionalists are more likely to emphasize a macro perspective, tracing the evolution of an institutional form and asking how it affects individual preferences and behavior. Preferences are more likely to be treated by rational choice theorists as stable properties of actors, whereas for historical institutionalists, preferences are thought to be more problematic, emergent from the situation (endogenous) and context-specific. And the two camps are attracted to different sets of problems. Historical institutionalists "begin with empirical puzzles that emerge from observed events or comparisons"; rational choice theorists are more likely to be attracted to "situations in which observed behavior appears to deviate from what the general theory predicts" (Thelen 1999:374). Finally, rational choice theorists give central place to the concept of equilibria and view institutions as central mechanisms in sustaining this condition, whereas historical institutionalists, like their nineteenth-century counterparts, are more interested in historical change than in equilibrium: the factors producing political and economic change broadly viewed as structured institutional change (see Orren and Skowronek 1994).

Thelen (1999) cites evidence of convergence in the perspectives of the two camps in recent years, and Scharpf (1997) suggests that each approach is incomplete and proposes that in the long run, they can be combined into a more complete explanation. At the present time, however, they remain relatively distinct approaches, more independent than overlapping in perspective and assumptions and more competitive than cooperative in demeanor.

Neoinstitutional Theory in Sociology

Sociological scholars have ranged rather widely in assembling the principal ingredients making up neoinstitutional approaches to organizational sociology. They have drawn on developments in cognitive and cultural theory in the neighboring disciplines of social psychology and anthropology, as well as on their home-grown subdiscipline, ethnomethology.

Theoretical Roots

Cognitive theory. Simon's work on decision making in organizations paralleled developments in social psychology, as this field of study—both its psychological and sociological sides—experienced the cognitive revolution. During the 1940s and 1950s, the stimulus-response (S-R) approach began to be revised to include attention to the participation of an active organism (S-O-R) (see Lewin 1951). Early research concentrated on how the state of the organism, as defined by various motivational and emotional variables, affected perception, selective attention, and memory. Gradually, however, a concern with such "hot" cognition began to be superseded by attention to the effects of "cool" factors influencing everyday information-processing and problem-solving behaviors.

> The idea of the human organism as an information processor became popular. The mind came to be viewed by many as a computerlike apparatus that registered the incoming information and then subjected it to a variety of transformations before ordering a response. (Markus and Zajonc 1985:141)

The question became, What types of software provide the programs and transformation rules for these processes?

The programs individuals use to select and process information are variously labeled schemas, frames, or inferential sets. These terms refer broadly to cognitive structures ranging from worldviews to specific filing systems for classifying and ordering data (see Jones and Davis 1965; Neisser 1976). Extensive research by psychologists over the past three decades has shown that these cognitive frames enter into the full range of information-processing activities, determining what information will receive attention; how it will be encoded; how it will be retained, retrieved, and organized into memory; and how it will be interpreted, thus affecting evaluations, judgments, predictions, and inferences (for an extensive review, see Markus and Zajonc 1985). In related work, Schank and Abelson (1977) introduced the concept of *script:* behavior patterns and sequences called up by specific roles or situations.

Psychologists have long vacillated between positions that regard individuals as basically competent, rational beings and views emphasizing cognitive biases and limitations. The general impact of recent cognitive theory and research has been to emphasize the shortcomings of individuals as information processors and decision makers.[4]

Tversky and Kahneman (1974) pioneered in the identification of a number of specific types of biases likely to cause mistakes in assessing information and reaching conclusions.[5] These and related problems were generalized by Nisbett and Ross (1980) into two common sources of inferential error: (a) a tendency to overuse simplistic strategies and fail to use the logical and statistical rules that guide scientific analysis and (b) a "tendency to attribute behavior exclusively to the actor's dispositions and to ignore powerful situational determinants of the behavior" (p. 31).

Even though their views have stressed the intellectual limitations of individuals, cognitive psychologists have recognized that individuals do participate actively in perceiving, interpreting, and making sense of their world. By contrast, until fairly recently, sociologists have tended to give primacy to the effects of contextual factors, viewing individuals as more passive, prone to conform to the demands of their social systems and roles. Identity theory has emerged as a corrective to this oversocialized view by giving renewed attention to an active and reflexive self that creates, sustains, and changes social structures (see Rosenberg 1979;

Stryker 1980; Burke and Reitzes 1981). Similar issues are addressed by structuration theory, which is discussed in Chapter 4.

Phenomenology and cultural studies. The literature on culture is vast, and theoretical emphases have varied over the years. Without attempting to reflect the complexities, it is possible to identify a few fundamental changes in conceptualizations of culture that provided important stimulation to the development of new approaches to institutions.

One of the important developments involved a shift away from a more diffuse definition of culture as encompassing the entire way of life of a people to a focus on its semiotic functions. Clifford Geertz (1973), one of the leading cultural theorists in anthropology, nicely captures this emphasis: "Believing, with Max Weber, that man is a social animal suspended in webs of significance he himself has spun, I take culture to be these webs . . . culture consists of socially established structures of meaning" (pp. 5, 12). Phenomenology, which began as a branch of philosophy, was incorporated into social science by scholars such as Schutz and Berger, who "stressed the in-depth exploration of the meanings associated with symbols" (Wuthnow 1987:42).

A second change involved a movement away from an early focus on shared norms and values as, for example, in the work of Durkheim and Parsons, to an emphasis on shared knowledge and belief systems. Behavior is shaped not only by attention to rules and the operation of norms but also by common definitions of the situation and strategies of action. As noted in Chapter 1, attention to cognitive frames and cultural frameworks rather than to normative systems is one of the major criteria defining neoinstitutional theory in sociology (see DiMaggio and Powell 1991:15-18).

Another development challenges the unitary conception of culture as internally consistent across groups and situations to recognize that cultural conceptions often vary: beliefs are held by some but not by others. Persons in the same situation can perceive the situation quite differently, both in terms of what is and what ought to be. Cultural beliefs vary and are frequently contested, particularly in times of social disorganization and change (Martin 1992; Swidler 1986; DiMaggio 1997).

Yet another important shift in emphasis involves the recognition that symbols exist not only as internalized beliefs but also as external

frameworks. Early work in sociology, for example, symbolic interactionism, treated beliefs as primarily internalized and subjective. By
contrast, the types of data preferred by the new cultural scholars "are
more readily observable kinds of behavior"—such as verbal utter-
ances, rituals, codified bodies of knowledge and cultural artifacts—
"rather than [those] locked away in people's private ruminations"
(Wuthnow 1987:56). Such approaches direct attention away from the
internalized, subjective nature of culture and treat symbols as real, objective phenomena.[6] This emphasis is particularly apparent in Berger
and Luckmann's (1967) conceptualization of the construction of common meaning systems. They stress three "moments" or phases:

> *Externalization*—the production, in social interaction, of symbolic structures
> whose meaning comes to be shared by the participants;
>
> *Objectification*—the process by which this production "comes to confront him as a
> facticity outside of himself," as something "out there," as a reality experienced
> in common with others;

and only then comes

> *Internalization*—the process by which the objectivated world is "retrojected into
> consciousness in the course of socialization" (pp. 60-61).

As noted in Chapter 1, Berger and Luckmann (1967) define this three-
phase process as one of institutionalization. Institutions are symbolic
systems that are "experienced as possessing a reality of their own, a reality that confronts the individual as an external and coercive fact"
(p. 58). A more recent manifestation of this external emphasis is a concern with the "production of culture": an examination of the ways in
which cultural items are produced, distributed, selected, and institutionalized (see Hirsch 1972; Becker 1982; Griswold 1992).

Finally, a limitation long present in the approach to culture taken by
many sociologists is the assumption that culture is subordinate in interest and importance to social structure. The distinction between social structure, which is made up of regularities in social behavior and
relationships, and culture, which is made up of symbolic systems, is
one of long standing. Although the distinction is useful, sociologists

have tended to privilege social structure over symbolic systems in their accounts of behavior. The new cultural arguments stress the independent effects of cultural systems.

These and related developments in cultural anthropology and sociology fueled the emergence of neoinstitutionalism in sociology generally and organization studies in particular.[7]

Ethnomethodology. Closely related to phenomenology is the subfield of ethnomethodology. One of its pioneering figures, Harold Garfinkel (1974), coined the term, corresponding to usage in cultural anthropology, to refer to the "common-sense knowledge" of how to operate within some social arena, developed and acquired by its participants. *Ethno* stresses the local, indigenous production of knowledge; *methodology,* that the knowledge involves distinctions and rules necessary for conducting the work at hand.

Researchers within this tradition primarily studied the behavior of employees in organizations or other types of participants, such as jurors, engaged in some collective task. The questions posed by these researchers were: How do such individuals "make sense" of the situations they confront? and How do they, collectively, construct the rules and procedures that allow them to cope with everyday demands? Detailed participant observation studies were conducted—in police stations, welfare agencies, and psychiatric clinics, among other sites—to elicit these institutionalized understandings (see Garfinkel 1967; Cicourel 1968; Zimmerman 1969).

As DiMaggio and Powell (1991) emphasize, ethnomethodologists challenged and supplemented Parsons's model by stressing the cognitive rather than the evaluative-normative components of behavior; and they confronted the neoclassical economic model of decision making by emphasizing the tacit, routine nature of choice in organizational settings.

These, then, were the ideas and themes that came together during the 1950s and 1960s to seed the development of neoinstitutional theory in sociology. Although, as noted, some of these ideas were being developed in and applied to organizations by ethnomethodologists, they did not penetrate the mainstream of organizational studies until the 1970s.

Neoinstitutional Theory and
Organizations: Founding Conceptions

An important early attempt to introduce neoinstitutional arguments to the study of organizations was made by David Silverman (1971), who proposed an action theory of organization. Silverman attacked prevailing models of organization, including contingency arguments and Parsons's and Selznick's structural-functional views, as being overly concerned with stability, order, and system maintenance. Drawing on the work of Durkheim, Schutz, Berger and Luckmann, and Goffman, Silverman proposes a phenomenological view of organizations that focuses attention on meaning systems and the ways in which they are constructed and reconstructed in social action. Silverman (1971) contrasts his action approach with the prevailing systems view:

> The Systems approach tends to regard behaviour as a reflection of the characteristics of a social system containing a series of impersonal processes which are external to actors and constrain them. In emphasizing that action derives from the meanings that men attach to their own and each other's actions, the Action frame of references argues that man is constrained by the way in which he socially constructs his reality. (p. 141)

Drawing on the insights of Durkheim, Silverman argued that meanings not only operate in the minds of individuals but are also objective "social facts" residing in social institutions. The environment of an organization needs to be conceptualized not only as a supply house of resources and target of outputs but also as a "source of meanings for the members of organisations" (p. 19).

Silverman's critique and attempted redirection of organizational theory had more impact in European than in U.S. circles (see Salaman 1978; Burrell and Morgan 1979).[8] A subsequent effort to introduce the new institutional arguments into organizational sociology proved to be much more influential. Two seminal articles appearing in the same year introduced neoinstitutional theory into the sociological study of organizations. Articles by Meyer and Rowan (1977) and by Zucker (1977), like Silverman's work, built primarily on Durkheim's and, especially, Berger and Luckmann's conception of institutions.

Meyer and Rowan (1977) embrace the view of institutions as complexes of cultural rules. But not any and all cultural rules are supportive of organizations. Again, following Berger's lead (see Berger, Berger, and Kellner 1973), Meyer and Rowan stress the importance of beliefs that are rationalized: stated in ways that specify the design of procedures to attain specific objectives. The engines of rationalization include the professions, nation-states, and the mass media, whose efforts support the development of larger numbers and more types of organizations. Organizations are not simply the product of increasing technical sophistication, as had long been argued, or even of increasingly complex relational patterns; they also result from the increasing rationalization of cultural rules that provide an independent basis for their construction. Meyer and Rowan emphasize the impact on organizational forms of changes in the wider institutional environment.

Whereas Meyer and Rowan developed the macro side of the argument, Zucker (a student of Meyer) emphasized the "micro-foundations" of institutions (see Zucker 1991). She stressed the power of cognitive beliefs to anchor behavior: "social knowledge, once institutionalized, exists as a fact, as part of objective reality, and can be transmitted directly on that basis" (Zucker 1977:726).

Other influential contributions, by DiMaggio and Powell (1983) and by Meyer and Scott ([1983b] 1992), developed the macro (environmental) perspective, which has become the dominant emphasis in sociological work. DiMaggio and Powell distinguished three important mechanisms—coercive, mimetic, and normative—by which institutional effects are diffused through a field of organizations, and they emphasized structural isomorphism (similarity) as an important consequence of both competitive and institutional processes. And Meyer and Scott suggested that although all organizations are shaped by both technical and institutional forces, some types of organizations are more strongly influenced by one than the other. Both sets of authors identified the organizational "field" or sector as a new level of analysis particularly suited to the study of institutional processes. Organizational fields help to bound the environments within which institutional processes operate.

In sociology, as in political science, investigators have emerged who embrace a rational choice approach to social institutions. Their assumptions and approaches are quite similar to those already described as operating in political science. Although their number and influence are considerably smaller in sociology than in either economics or political science, they include a number of prominent sociologists, such as

Coleman (1990), Hechter (1987; Hechter, Opp, and Wippler 1990), and Nee (1998). As Coleman (1994) notes, these theorists embrace the "principle of actor maximization"—some in the stronger sense, others in the weaker, bounded rationality sense—as the "source of deductive power of rational choice theory." But, unlike neoclassical economics, they replace the "assumption of a perfect market with social structures, sometimes regarded as endogenous, and other times as exogenous, which carries individual actions into systemic outcomes" (p. 167). And, at least some of these analysts allow for the effects of "context-bound rationality within which individual interests and group norms develop" (Brinton and Nee 1998:xv).

Concluding Comment

Beginning in the 1940s with the emergence of organizations as a recognized field of study, scholars began to connect institutional arguments to the structure and behavior of organizations. These approaches both built on and departed from the work of earlier institutional theorists. Institutional arguments began to be connected to organizational studies through the work of Merton and his students, particularly Selznick, of Parsons, and of Simon and March.

The work that has come to be labeled neoinstitutional theory assumes quite varied guises across the social sciences. The main thrust of economic approaches embraces orthodox rationality (or slightly broadened) assumptions but seeks to apply economic arguments to account for the existence of organizations and institutions. Williamson's development of transaction-cost analysis exemplifies this approach to organizations. Political science seems split into two factions, the one applying rational choice economic models to political systems, and the other embracing a historical view of the nature of institutions and emphasizing their broad effects in constructing interests and actors.

Neoinstitutional approaches in sociology build on a loosely constructed framework of ideas stemming from cognitive psychology, cultural studies, phenomenology, and ethnomethodology. The newer conceptual models emphasize cognitive over normative frameworks and have focused primary attention on the effects of cultural belief systems operating in the environments of organizations rather than on intra-organizational processes.

In the next chapter, I shift from a historical to an analytic approach. I begin with an attempt to develop an integrated model of institutions, drawing on and encompassing much of the contemporary work of the type just reviewed. I then identify several dimensions along which contemporary theories differ as they consider the relation of institutions and organizations. The chapter concludes with a consideration of two continuing bases of controversy.

Notes

1. Translations of some of Weber's important essays were made by Hans H. Gerth and C. Wright Mills (Weber [1906-1924] 1946), who were both at Columbia University and members of the circle of scholars gathered around Merton. The other important early translators were A. M. Henderson and Talcott Parsons (Weber [1924] 1947).

2. A related line of theory and research, *agency theory*, also addresses the proper design of control structures to deal with the motivation and control of agents, those hired to assist the principal, the person expected to be the prime beneficiary of the collective work (see Alchian and Demsetz 1972; Jensen and Meckling 1976; Pratt and Zeckhauser 1985). Dealing with a problem common to all organizations, this approach focuses on the design of appropriate control and incentive systems to manage various kinds of work.

3. Peters (1999) identifies six institutional perspectives existing within political science, including normative, rational choice, historical, empirical, international, and societal. This typology, in my view, gives too much weight to differences in methodology and/or topic.

4. It is to counteract such cognitive limitations that, according to March and Simon (Simon [1945] 1997; March and Simon 1958), organizations develop performance programs and search routines, as previously described.

5. Their work has also been extensively used by those economists embracing the assumption of bounded rationality.

6. For this reason, phenomenologists such as Schutz and Bellah define themselves as "symbolic realists."

7. Informative reviews of cultural sociology are provided by Wuthnow et al. (1984), Wuthnow (1987), and DiMaggio (1990, 1997).

8. In his subsequent work, Silverman (1972; Silverman and Jones 1976) shifted his focus toward a more micro, ethnomethodological emphasis, examining the multiple meanings and rationalities associated with participants' phenomenological accounts of their common situation (see Reed 1985).

3 Constructing an Analytic Framework I

THREE PILLARS OF INSTITUTIONS

To an institutionalist, knowledge of what has gone before is vital information. The ideas and insights of our predecessors provide the context for current efforts and the platform on which we necessarily craft our own contributions. However, in this chapter and the next, I shift from a primarily historical to an analytic approach to identify and examine more closely the diverse strands that make up contemporary institutional theory. I begin with a broad definition of institutions that encompasses most contemporary views. Then, I indicate the issues and distinctions that create disagreements. The main work of the chapter is taken up by my attempt to identify three analytical elements that compose institutions. Each element is important, and all of them may work in combination, but because they operate through distinctive mechanisms and processes, I emphasize their differences in my discussion.

Having introduced the principal conceptions around which my analysis will be conducted, I bravely but briefly consider their philosophical underpinnings. Varying definitions of institutions call up somewhat different conceptions of the nature of social reality and social order. Similarly, the institutional definitions relate to varying conceptions of how actors make choices: the extent to which actors are rational and what is meant by this concept. These issues, although too complex to fully explore, are too important to ignore.

The companion chapter, Chapter 4, completes the presentation of the analytical framework and associated issues. I begin by examining what types of institutional beliefs and rules support the development of organizations. I then briefly describe the concept of *structuration*, which can assist us in the effort to reconcile institutional constraints with individual agency. Finally, I describe a set of diverse carriers that transport institutions, identifying the multiple levels at which institutional analysis takes place.

Chapters 3 and 4 should be taken as a prolegomena to the more empirically based discussions in the chapters to follow. They introduce concepts that will be employed and preview controversies and issues that will be encountered as we review developments in institutional theory and research since the 1970s (in Chapters 5 through 8).

Defining Institutions

Let us begin with the following omnibus conception of institutions:

- Institutions are social structures that have attained a high degree of resilience.
- Institutions are composed of cultural-cognitive, normative, and regulative elements that, together with associated activities and resources, provide stability and meaning to social life.
- Institutions are transmitted by various types of carriers, including symbolic systems, relational systems, routines, and artifacts.
- Institutions operate at multiple levels of jurisdiction, from the world system to localized interpersonal relationships.
- Institutions by definition connote stability but are subject to change processes, both incremental and discontinuous.

This is a dense conception containing a number of ideas that I will unpack, describe, and elaborate in this chapter and the next.

In this conception, institutions are multifaceted, durable social structures, made up of symbolic elements, social activities, and material resources. Institutions exhibit distinctive properties: They are relatively resistant to change (Jepperson 1991). They tend to be transmitted across generations, to be maintained and reproduced (Zucker 1977). As Giddens (1984) states, "Institutions by definition are the more enduring features of social life. . . giving 'solidity' [to social systems] across time and space" (p. 24).

Institutions exhibit these properties because of the processes set in motion by regulative, normative, and cultural-cognitive elements. These elements are the building blocks of institutional structures, providing the elastic fibers that resist change, and I examine the distinctive nature and contribution of each element in a subsequent section of this chapter.

Although rules, norms, and cultural beliefs are central ingredients of institutions, the concept must also encompass associated behavior and material resources. Although an institutional perspective gives heightened attention to the symbolic aspects of social life, we must also attend to the activities that produce and reproduce them. Rules, norms, and meanings arise in interaction, and they are preserved and modified by human behavior. To isolate meaning systems from their related behaviors is, as Geertz (1973) cautions, to commit the error of

> locking cultural analysis away from its proper object, the informal logic of actual life. . . . Behavior must be attended to, and with some exactness, because it is through the flow of behavior—or, more precisely, social action—that cultural forms find articulation. . . . Whatever, or wherever, symbol systems "in their own terms" may be, we gain empirical access to them by inspecting events, not by arranging abstracted entities into unified patterns. (p. 17)

Similarly, for Berger and Luckmann (1967), institutions are "dead" if they are only represented in verbal designations and in physical objects. All such representations are bereft of subjective reality "unless they are ongoingly 'brought to life' in actual human conduct" (p. 75).

Sociological theorists Giddens (1979, 1984) and Sewell (1992) underline the importance of including material resources in any conception of social structure so as to take into account asymmetries of power.

Rules and norms, if they are to be effective, must be backed with sanctioning power. Conversely, those possessing power in the form of excess resources seek authorization and legitimation for its use. And cultural beliefs, or schemas in Sewell's formulation, to be viable, must relate to resources:

> Schemas not empowered or regenerated by resources would eventually be abandoned and forgotten, just as resources without cultural schemas to direct their use would eventually dissipate and decay. (p. 13)

The Giddens/Sewell formulation usefully stresses the "duality" of social structure, encompassing both idealist and material features of social life and highlighting their interdependence, as I discuss in Chapter 4.

Many treatments of institutions emphasize their capacity to control and constrain behavior. Institutions impose restrictions by defining legal, moral, and cultural boundaries setting off legitimate from illegitimate activities. But it is essential to recognize that institutions also support and empower activities and actors. Institutions provide guidelines and resources for acting as well as prohibitions and constraints on action.

Although institutions function to provide stability and order, they themselves undergo change, both incremental and revolutionary. Thus, our subject must include not only institutions as a *property* or state of an existing social order, but also institutions as *process*, including the processes of institutionalization and deinstitutionalization (see Tolbert and Zucker 1996). Scholars increasingly attend not only to how institutions arise and are maintained but also to how they undergo change.

Institutions ride on various conveyances and are instantiated in multiple media. These institutional *carriers* vary in the processes they employ to transmit their messages. In addition, institutions operate at multiple *levels,* from the world system to interpersonal interaction. I examine these diverse carriers and levels in Chapter 4.

Important differences exist among the various schools of institutional scholars, as is apparent from our review of previous work. In my view, the most consequential dispute centers on which institutional elements are accorded priority.

The Three Pillars of Institutions

Regulative systems, normative systems, cultural-cognitive systems—each of these elements has been identified by one or another social theorist as a vital ingredient of institutions. The three elements form a continuum moving "from the conscious to the unconscious, from the legally enforced to the taken for granted" (Hoffman 1997:36). One possible approach would be to view all of these facets as contributing, in interdependent and mutually reinforcing ways, to a powerful social framework, one that encapsulates and exhibits the celebrated strength and resilience of these structures. In such an integrated conception, institutions appear, as D'Andrade (1984) observes, to be overdetermined systems: "overdetermined in the sense that social sanctions plus pressure for conformity, plus intrinsic direct reward, plus values, are all likely to act together to give a particular meaning system its directive force" (p. 98).

Although such an inclusive model has its strengths, it also masks important differences. The definition knits together three somewhat divergent conceptions that need to be differentiated. Rather than pursuing the development of a more integrated conception,[1] I believe more progress will be made at this juncture by distinguishing among the several component elements and identifying their different underlying assumptions, mechanisms, and indicators.[2] By employing a more analytical approach to these arguments, we can identify important underlying theoretical fault lines that transect the domain.

Consider Table 3.1. The columns contain the three elements—three pillars—identified as making up or supporting institutions. The rows define some of the principal dimensions along which assumptions vary and arguments arise among theorists emphasizing one element over the others. This table will serve as a guide as I consider each element.

The Regulative Pillar

In the broadest sense, all scholars underscore the regulative aspects of institutions: Institutions constrain and regularize behavior. Scholars more specifically associated with the regulatory pillar are distinguished by the prominence they give to explicit regulatory processes:

Table 3.1   Three Pillars of Institutions

	Pillar		
	Regulative	*Normative*	*Cultural-Cognitive*
Basis of compliance	Expedience	Social obligation	Taken-for-grantedness Shared understanding
Basis of order	Regulative rules	Binding expectations	Constitutive schema
Mechanisms	Coercive	Normative	Mimetic
Logic	Instrumentality	Appropriateness	Orthodoxy
Indicators	Rules Laws Sanctions	Certification Accreditation	Common beliefs Shared logics of action
Basis of legitimacy	Legally sanctioned	Morally governed	Comprehensible Recognizable Culturally supported

rule-setting, monitoring, and sanctioning activities. In this conception, regulatory processes involve the capacity to establish rules, in-
spect others' conformity to them, and, as necessary, manipulate sanctions—rewards or punishments—in an attempt to influence future
behavior. These processes may operate through diffuse informal mechanisms, involving folkways such as shaming or shunning activities, or
they may be highly formalized and assigned to specialized actors, such
as the police and courts.

Economists, including economic historians, are particularly likely to
view institutions as resting primarily on the regulatory pillar. The economic historian Douglass North (1990), for example, features rule systems and enforcement mechanisms in his conceptualization.

> [Institutions] are perfectly analogous to the rules of the game in a competi-
> tive team sport. That is, they consist of formal written rules as well as typi-
> cally unwritten codes of conduct that underlie and supplement formal rules
> . . . the rules and informal codes are sometimes violated and punishment is
> enacted. Therefore, an essential part of the functioning of institutions is the
> costliness of ascertaining violations and the severity of punishment. (p. 4)

This emphasis may stem in part from the character of the customary objects studied by economists. They are likely to focus attention on the behavior of individuals and firms in markets and other competitive situations, where contending interests are more common and, hence, explicit rules and referees more necessary to preserve order. Economists view individuals and organizations that conform to rules as pursuing their self-interests, as behaving instrumentally and expediently. The primary mechanism of control, employing DiMaggio and Powell's (1983) typology, is coercion.

Force, fear, and expedience are central ingredients of the regulatory pillar, but they are often tempered by the existence of rules, whether in the guise of informal mores or formal rules and laws. As Weber ([1924] 1968) emphasized, few if any rulers are content to base their regime on force alone; all attempt to cultivate a belief in its legitimacy. Hence, powerful actors may sometimes *impose* their will on others, based on the use or threat of sanctions. Or they may provide *inducements* to secure compliance: For example, many federal programs lack programmatic authority but secure local cooperation by supplying funds designated to support specific programs. The most common case, however, involves the use of *authority*, in which coercive power is legitimated by a normative framework that both supports and constrains the exercise of power (see Scott 1987). The regulative and normative pillars can be mutually reinforcing.

Recent work in economics emphasizes the costs of regulation. Agency theory stresses the expense and difficulty entailed in accurately monitoring performances relevant to contracts, whether implicit or explicit, and in designing appropriate incentives (see Pratt and Zeckhauser 1985; Milgrom and Roberts 1992). Although, in some situations, agreements can be monitored and mutually enforced by the parties involved, in many circumstances, it is necessary to vest the enforcement machinery in a third party expected to behave in a neutral fashion. Economic historians view this as an important function of the state. Thus, North (1990) argues,

> Because ultimately a third party must always involve the state as a source of coercion, a theory of institutions also inevitably involves an analysis of the political structure of a society and the degree to which that political structure provides a framework of effective enforcement. (p. 64)

North (1990) also calls attention to problems that can arise because "enforcement is undertaken by agents whose own utility functions influence outcomes" (i.e., third parties who are not neutral) (p. 54). This possibility is stressed by many historical institutionalists, such as Skocpol (1985); they argue that the state develops its own interests and operates somewhat autonomously from other societal actors. In this and other ways, attention to the regulative aspects of institutions creates renewed interest in the role of the state: as rule maker, referee, and enforcer.

Law and society theorists point out that analysts should not conflate the coercive functions of law with its normative and cognitive dimensions. Rather than operating in an authoritative and exogenous manner, many laws are sufficiently controversial or ambiguous that they do not provide clear prescriptions for conduct. In such cases, law is better conceived as an occasion for sense making and collective interpretation, relying more on cultural-cognitive and normative than coercive elements for its effects (see Suchman and Edelman 1997).

In sum, there is much to examine in understanding how regulative institutions function and how they interact with other institutional elements. Through the work of agency and game theorists at one end of the spectrum and law and society theorists at the other, we are reminded that laws do not spring from the head of Zeus nor norms from the collective soul of a people; rules must be interpreted and disputes resolved; incentives and sanctions must be designed and will have unintended effects; surveillance mechanisms are required but will prove to be fallible, not foolproof; and conformity is only one of many possible responses by those subject to regulative institutions.

A stable system of rules, either formal or informal, backed by surveillance and sanctioning power, is one prevailing view of institutions.

The Normative Pillar

A second group of theorists sees institutions as resting primarily on a normative pillar (again, see Table 3.1). Emphasis here is placed on normative rules that introduce a prescriptive, evaluative, and obligatory dimension into social life. Normative systems include both values and norms. *Values* are conceptions of the preferred or the desirable, together with the construction of standards to which existing structures or behavior can be compared and assessed. *Norms* specify how things should be done; they define legitimate means to pursue valued ends. Normative systems define goals or objectives (e.g., winning the game, making a profit) but also designate appropriate ways to pursue them (e.g., rules specifying how the game is to be played, conceptions of fair business practices).

Some values and norms are applicable to all members of the collectivity; others apply only to selected types of actors or positions. The latter give rise to *roles:* conceptions of appropriate goals and activities for particular individuals or specified social positions. These beliefs are not simply anticipations or predictions but prescriptions—normative expectations—of how the specified actors are supposed to behave. The expectations are held by other salient actors in the situation and so are experienced by the focal actor as external pressures. Also, and to varying degrees, they become internalized by the actor. Roles can be devised formally. For example, in an organizational context, particular positions are defined to carry specified rights and responsibilities and to have varying access to material resources. Roles can also emerge informally as, over time through interaction, differentiated expectations develop to guide behavior.

Normative systems are typically viewed as imposing constraints on social behavior, and so they do. But, at the same time, they empower and enable social action. They confer rights as well as responsibilities, privileges as well as duties, licenses as well as mandates. In his essays on the professions, Hughes (1958) reminds us how much of the power and mystique associated with these types of roles comes from the license they are given to engage in "forbidden" or fateful activities: conducting intimate physical examinations or sentencing individuals to prison or to death.

The normative conception of institutions was embraced by most early sociologists—from Durkheim through Parsons and Selznick—perhaps because sociologists tended to focus attention on those types of institutions, such as kinship groups, social classes, religious systems, and voluntary associations, where common beliefs and values are more likely to exist. Moreover, the normative conception continues to guide and inform much contemporary work by sociologists and political scientists on organizations. For example, March and Olsen (1989) embrace a primarily normative conception of institutions:

The proposition that organizations follow rules, that much of the behavior in an organization is specified by standard operating procedures, is a common one in the bureaucratic and organizational literature. . . . It can be extended to the institutions of politics. Much of the behavior we observe in political institutions reflects the routine way in which people do what they are supposed to do. (p. 21)

Although their conception of rules is quite broad, including cultural-cognitive as well as normative elements—"routines, procedures, conventions, roles, strategies, organizational forms, and technologies . . . beliefs, paradigms, codes, cultures, and knowledge" (p. 22)—their focus remains on social obligations:

> To describe behavior as driven by rules is to see action as a matching of a situation to the demands of a position. Rules define relationships among roles in terms of what an incumbent of one role owes to incumbents of other roles. (March and Olsen 1989:23)

Indicators of the presence and strength of normative systems vary by level of analysis. Within organizations, analysts such as Selznick (1949) have examined changing goals (values) and interpersonal constraints on behavior. At broader levels, researchers have studied the rules and conventions promulgated by trade and professional associations (see Stern 1979; Starr 1982).

Theorists embracing a normative conception of institutions emphasize the stabilizing influence of social beliefs and norms, which are both internalized and imposed by others. For early normative theorists such as Parsons, shared norms and values were regarded as *the* basis of a stable social order. And, as Stinchcombe (1997) has eloquently reaffirmed, institutions are widely viewed as having moral roots:

> The guts of institutions is that somebody somewhere really cares to hold an organization to the standards and is often paid to do that. Sometimes that somebody is inside the organization, maintaining its competence. Sometimes it is an accrediting body, sending out volunteers to see if there is really any algebra in the algebra course. And sometimes that somebody, or his or her commitment is lacking, in which case the center cannot hold, and mere anarchy is loosed upon the world. (p. 18)

The Cultural-Cognitive Pillar

A third set of institutionalists, principally anthropologists such as Geertz and Douglas and sociologists such as Berger and Meyer and Zucker, stress the centrality of cultural-cognitive elements of institutions: the shared conceptions that constitute the nature of social reality and the frames through which meaning is made (again, see Table 3.1). Attention to the cultural-cognitive dimension of institutions is the major distinguishing feature of neoinstitutionalism within sociology.

These institutionalists take seriously the cognitive dimensions of human existence: Mediating between the external world of stimuli and the response of the individual organism is a collection of internalized symbolic representations of the world. "In the cognitive paradigm, what a creature does is, in large part, a function of the creature's internal representation of its environment" (D'Andrade 1984:88). Symbols—words, signs, gestures—have their effect by shaping the meanings we attribute to objects and activities. Meanings arise in interaction and are maintained and transformed as they are employed to make sense of the ongoing stream of happenings. Emphasizing the importance of symbols and meanings returns us to Max Weber's central premise. As noted in Chapter 1, Weber regarded action as social only to the extent that the actor attaches meaning to the behavior. To understand or explain any action, the analyst must take into account not only the objective conditions but also the actor's subjective interpretation of them.

As discussed in Chapter 2, the new cultural perspective focuses on the semiotic facets of culture, treating them not simply as subjective beliefs but also as symbolic systems perceived to be objective and external to individual actors. As Berger and Kellner (1981) summarize, "Every human institution is, as it were, a sedimentation of meanings or, to vary the image, a crystallization of meanings in objective form" (p. 31). The hyphenated label *cognitive-cultural* recognizes that internal interpretive processes are shaped by external cultural frameworks. As Douglas (1982) proposes, we should "treat cultural categories as the cognitive containers in which social interests are defined and classified, argued, negotiated, and fought out" (p. 12).

For cultural-cognitive theorists, compliance occurs in many circumstances because other types of behavior are inconceivable; routines are followed because they are taken for granted as "the way we do these things." Social roles are given a somewhat different interpretation by cultural as opposed to normative theorists. Rather than stressing the force of mutually reinforcing obligations, cultural theorists point to the power of templates for particular types of actors and scripts for action. For Berger and Luckmann (1967), roles arise as common understandings develop that particular actions are associated with particular actors.[3]

> We can properly begin to speak of roles when this kind of typification occurs in the context of an objectified stock of knowledge common to a collectivity of actors. . . . Institutions are embodied in individual experience by means of roles. . . . The institution, with its assemblage of "programmed" actions, is like the unwritten libretto of a drama. The realization of the drama depends upon the reiterated performance of its prescribed roles by living actors. . . . Neither drama nor institution exist empirically apart from this recurrent realization. (pp. 73-75)

Differentiated roles can and do develop in localized contexts as repetitive patterns of action gradually become habitualized and objectified, but it is also important to recognize the operation of wider institutional frameworks that provide prefabricated organizing models and scripts (see Goffman 1974, 1983). Meyer and Rowan (1977) and DiMaggio and Powell (1983) emphasize the extent to which wider belief systems and cultural frames are imposed on or adopted by individual actors and organizations.

At the intra-organizational level, researchers have examined the development of common scripts (Barley 1986) and common beliefs (Kunda 1992) as indicators of cultural-cognitive systems. At the organizational field level, researchers have employed discourse analysis and other types of content-analytic techniques to assess meaning systems (e.g., Deephouse 1996; Hoffman 1997).

A cultural-cognitive conception of institutions stresses the central role played by the socially mediated construction of a common framework of meaning.[4]

The Three Pillars and Legitimacy

"Organizations require more than material resources and technical information if they are to survive and thrive in their social environments. They also need social acceptability and credibility" (Scott et al.

2000:237). Sociologists employ the concept of legitimacy to refer to these conditions. Suchman (1995b) provides a helpful definition of this central concept: "*Legitimacy* is a generalized perception or assumption that the actions of an entity are desirable, proper, or appropriate within some socially constructed system of norms, values, beliefs, and definitions" (p. 574). Legitimacy is a generalized rather than an event-specific evaluation and is "possessed objectively, yet created subjectively" (p. 574). The socially constructed systems to which Suchman refers are, of course, institutional frameworks. And, consistent with the preceding discussion, each of the three pillars provides a basis for legitimacy, albeit a different one.

In a resource-dependence or social exchange approach to organizations, legitimacy is typically treated as simply another kind of resource. However, from an institutional perspective, legitimacy is not a commodity to be possessed or exchanged but a condition reflecting perceived consonance with relevant rules and laws, normative support, or alignment with cultural-cognitive frameworks. Moreover, unlike material resources or technical information, legitimacy is not an input to be combined or transformed to produce some new and different output, but a symbolic value to be displayed in a manner such that it is visible to outsiders (see Scott 1998:211).

Berger and Luckmann (1967) describe legitimacy as evoking a "second order" of meaning. In their early stages, institutionalized activities develop as repeated patterns of behavior that evoke shared meanings among the participants. The legitimation of this order involves connecting it to wider cultural frames, norms, or rules. "Legitimation 'explains' the institutional order by ascribing cognitive validity to its objectivated meanings. Legitimation justifies the institutional order by giving a normative dignity to its practical imperatives" (pp. 92-93). In a parallel vein, Weber ([1924] 1968) argues that power becomes legitimated as authority to the extent that its exercise is supported by prevailing social norms, whether traditional, charismatic, or bureaucratic (see also Dornbusch and Scott 1975). And, emphasizing the cultural-cognitive dimension, Meyer and I propose that "organizational legitimacy refers to the degree of cultural support for an organization" (Meyer and Scott 1983a:201).

This "vertical" dimension entails the support of significant others: various types of authorities—cultural as well as political—who are empowered to confer legitimacy. Who these authorities are varies from time to time and place to place but, in our time, agents of the state and professional and trade associations are often critical for organizations. Certification or accreditation by these bodies is frequently employed as a prime indicator of legitimacy (Dowling and Pfeffer 1975; Ruef and Scott 1998). In complex situations, individuals or organizations may be confronted by competing sovereigns. Actors confronting conflicting normative requirements and standards typically find it difficult to take action because conformity to one undermines the normative support of other bodies. "The legitimacy of a given organization is negatively affected by the number of different authorities sovereign over it and by the diversity or inconsistency of their accounts of how it is to function" (Meyer and Scott 1983a:202).

There is always the question as to whose assessments count in determining the legitimacy of a set of arrangements. Many structures persist and spread because they are regarded as appropriate by entrenched authorities, even though their legitimacy is challenged by other, less powerful constituencies. Martin (1994), for example, notes that salary inequities between men and women are institutionalized in American society, even though the disadvantaged groups perceive them to be unjust and press for reforms. Legitimate structures may, at the same time, be contested structures.

Stinchcombe (1968) asserts that, in the end, whose values define legitimacy is a matter of concerted social power:

> A power is legitimate to the degree that, by virtue of the doctrines and norms by which it is justified, the power-holder can call upon sufficient other centers of power, as reserves in case of need, to make his power effective. (p. 162)

Although power certainly matters in supporting legitimacy processes, as in other social activities, power is not the absolute arbiter. Entrenched power is, in the long run, helpless against the onslaught of opposing power allied with more persuasive ideas.

The three pillars elicit three related but distinguishable bases of legitimacy (see Table 3.1).[5] The regulatory emphasis is on conformity to rules: Legitimate organizations are those established by and operating in accordance with relevant legal or quasi-legal requirements. A normative conception stresses a deeper, moral base for assessing legitimacy. Normative controls are much more likely to be internalized than are regulative controls; and the incentives for conformity are, hence, likely to include intrinsic as well as extrinsic rewards. A cultural-cognitive view stresses the legitimacy that comes from adopting a common frame of reference or definition of the situation. To adopt an orthodox structure or identity to relate to a specific situation is to seek the legitimacy that comes from cognitive consistency. The cultural-cognitive mode is the "deepest" level because it rests on preconscious, taken-for-granted understandings.

The bases of legitimacy associated with the three elements are different and may, sometimes, be in conflict. A regulative view would ascertain whether the organization is legally established and whether it is acting in accord with relevant laws and regulations. A normative orientation, stressing moral obligations, may countenance actions departing from "mere" legal requirements. Many professionals adhere to normative standards that compel them to depart from the rule-based requirements of bureaucratic organizations. And whistle-blowers claim that they are acting on the basis of a higher authority when they contest organizational rules or the orders of superiors. Street gangs may be widely recognized in urban America, signifying that they provide a culturally constituted mode of organizing to achieve specified ends, and they are regarded as legitimate ways of organizing by their members. Although many members of the community may readily recognize gangs, and their structures may be widely reproduced, they are often treated as illegal forms by police and other regulative bodies, and they frequently lack the normative endorsement of established community and societal authorities.

What is taken as evidence of legitimacy varies by which elements of institutions are privileged.

Basic Assumptions Associated With the Three Pillars

Although the differences among analysts emphasizing one or another element are partly a matter of substantive focus, they are also associated with more profound differences in underlying philosophical assumptions. Although it is not possible here to do full justice to the complexity and subtlety of these issues, I attempt to depict the differences in broad outline. Two matters are particularly significant: differences among analysts in their ontological assumptions—assumptions concerning

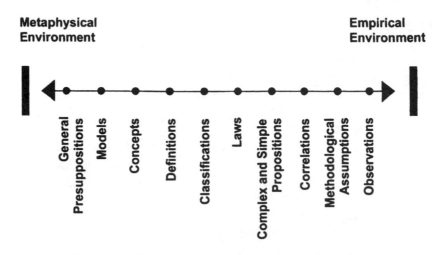

Figure 3.1. The Scientific Continuum and Its Components
SOURCE: Alexander (1983, Volume 1, p. 3). Reprinted with permission of the author.

the nature of social reality—and differences among them in the extent and type of rationality invoked in explaining behavior.

Regulative and Constitutive Rules

Truth and Reality

To examine the ontological assumptions underlying the varying conceptions of institutional elements, I believe it is necessary to begin by clarifying one's epistemological assumptions: How do we understand the nature of scientific knowledge? My position in these debates has been greatly influenced by the formulation advanced by Jeffrey C. Alexander (1983), who provides a broad, synthetic examination of the nature and development of theoretical logic in modern sociological thought. Following Kuhn (1970), Alexander adopts a "postpositivist" perspective, viewing science as operating along a continuum stretching from the empirical environment, on the one hand, to the metaphysical environment, on the other (See Figure 3.1).

At the metaphysical end reside the most abstract general presuppositions and models associated with more theoretical activity. At the empirical end, one finds observations, correlations, and empirical propositions. The continuum obviously incorporates numerous types of statements, ranging from the more abstract and general to the more specific and particular. But, more important, the framework emphasizes that, although the mix of empirical and metaphysical elements varies, *every point on the continuum is an admixture of both elements.* "What appears, concretely, to be a difference in types of scientific statements—models, definitions, propositions—simply reflects the different emphasis within a given statement on generality or specificity" (Alexander 1983, Vol. 1:4).

The postpositivist conception of science emphasizes the fundamental similarity of the social and physical sciences: Both are human attempts to develop and test general statements about the behavior of the empirical world. It rejects both a radical materialist view, which espouses that the only reality is a physical one, and also the idealist (and postmodernist) view that the only reality exists in the human mind. It also usefully differentiates reality from truth, as Rorty (1989) observes:

> We need to make a distinction between the claim that the world is out there and the claim that truth is out there. To say that the world is out there, that it is not our creation, is to say, with common sense, that most things in space and time are the effects of causes which do not include human mental states. To say that truth is not out there is simply to say that where there are no sentences there is no truth, that sentences are elements of human languages, and that human languages are human creations. (pp. 4-5)

Social Reality

Although the physical and social sciences share important basic features, it is essential to recognize that the subject matter of the social sciences is distinctive. In John Searle's (1995) terminology, portions of the real world, although they are treated as "epistemically objective" facts in the world, "are facts only by human agreement." Their existence is "observer-relative": dependent on observers who share a common conception of a given social fact (pp. 1, 11, 13). Social reality is an important subclass of reality.[6]

Social institutions refer to types of social reality that involve the collective development and use of both regulative and constitutive rules. *Regulative rules* involve attempts to influence "antecedently existing activities;" constitutive rules "create the very possibility of certain activities" (Searle 1995:27). *Constitutive rules* take the general form: X counts as Y in context C; for example, an American dollar bill counts as legal currency in the United States. "Institutional facts exist only within systems of constitutive rules" (p. 28). In general, as the label implies, scholars embracing the regulative view of institutions focus primary attention on regulative rules; cultural-cognitive scholars stress the importance of constitutive rules. They, thus, differ in their ontological assumptions or, at least, in the ontological level at which they work.

Constitutive rules operate at a deeper level of reality creation, involving the devising of categories and the construction of typifications: processes by which "concrete and subjectively unique experiences . . . are ongoingly subsumed under general orders of meaning that are both objectively and subjectively real" (Berger and Luckmann 1967:39). Such processes are variously applied to things, to ideas, to events, and to actors. Games provide a ready illustration. Constitutive rules construct the game of football as consisting of things such as goal posts and the gridiron and events such as "first downs" and "off-sides" (see D'Andrade 1984). Similarly, other types of constitutive rules result in the social construction of actors and associated capacities and roles; in the football context, the creation of quarterbacks, coaches, and referees. Regulative rules define how the ball may legitimately be advanced or what penalties are associated with what rule infractions. Thus, cultural-cognitive theorists amend and augment the portrait of institutions crafted by regulative theorists. Cultural-cognitive theorists insist that games involve more than rules and enforcement mechanisms: They consist of socially constructed players endowed with differing capacities for action and parts to play. Constitutive rules construct the social objects and events to which regulative rules are applied.

Such processes, although most visible in games, are not limited to these relatively artificial situations. Constitutive rules are so basic to social structure, so fundamental to social life, that they are often overlooked. In our liberal democracies, we take for granted that individual people have interests and capacities for action. It seems natural that there are citizens with opinions and rights, students with a capacity to learn, fathers with rights and responsibilities, and employees with aptitudes and skills. But all of these types of actors—and a multitude of others—are social constructions; all depend for their existence on constitutive frameworks, which, although they arose in particular interaction contexts, have become reified in cultural rules that can be imported as guidelines into new situations (see Berger and Luckmann 1967; Gergen and Davis 1985).

Moreover, recognition of the existence of such constitutive processes provides a view of social behavior that differs greatly from lay interpretations or even from those found in much of social science. As Meyer, Boli, and Thomas (1987) argue:

> Most social theory takes actors (from individuals to states) and their actions as real, a priori, elements. . . . [In contrast] we see the "existence" and characteristics of actors as socially constructed and highly problematic, and action as the enactment of broad institutional scripts rather than a matter of internally generated and autonomous choice, motivation, and purpose. (p. 13)

In short, as constitutive rules are recognized, individual behavior is often seen to reflect external definitions rather than (or as a source of) internal intentions. The difference is nicely captured in the anecdote reported by Peter Hay (1993):

> Gertrude Lawrence and Noel Coward were starring in one of the latter's plays when the production was honored with a royal visit. As Queen Elizabeth entered the Royal Box, the entire audience rose to its feet. Miss Lawrence, watching from the wings, murmured: "What an entrance!" Noel Coward, peeking on tip-toe behind her, added "What a part!" (p. 70)

The social construction of actors also defines what they consider to be their interests. The stereotypic "economic man," which rests at the heart of much economic theorizing, is not a reflection of human nature but a social construct that arose under specific historical circumstances and is maintained by particular institutional logics associated with the rise of capitalism (see Heilbroner 1985).[7] From the cultural-cognitive perspective, interests are not assumed to be "natural" or outside the scope of investigation: They are not treated as exogenous to the theoretical framework. Rather, they are recognized as varying by institutional context and as requiring explanation.

The social construction of actors is not limited to people: Collective actors are similarly constituted and come in a wide variety of forms. We, naturally, will be particularly interested in the nature of those institutional processes at work in the constitution of organizations. We begin the discussion of this topic in the next chapter.

Rational and Reasonable Behavior

Theorists make different assumptions regarding how actors make choices: what logics determine social action. As discussed in Chapter 1, Weber defined social action to emphasize the importance of the meanings individuals attach to their own and others' behavior. For Weber and many other social theorists, "the central question that every social theory addresses in defining the nature of action is whether or not—or to what degree—action is rational" (Alexander 1983, Vol. 1:72). The key question is, however, how is rationality to be defined? Institutional theorists propose a wide range of answers.

At one end of the spectrum, a neoclassical economic perspective embraces an atomist view that focuses on an individual actor engaged in maximizing behavior, guided by stable preferences and possessing complete knowledge of the possible alternatives and their consequences. Game-theory analysts typically adhere rather closely to this lean model of the rational actor (see, e.g., Schotter 1986). Embracing a somewhat broader set of assumptions, neoinstitutional analysts in economics and rational choice theorists in political science (e.g., Williamson 1985; Moe 1990a) use a model such as Simon's ([1945] 1997) bounded rationality, which presumes that actors are "intendedly rational, but only boundedly so" (p. 88). These versions relax the assumptions regarding complete information and utility maximization as the criteria of choice, while retaining the premise that actors seek "to do the best they can to satisfy whatever their wants might be" (Abell 1995:7). Institutional theorists employing these and related models of individual rational actors are more likely to view institutions primarily as regulative frameworks. Actors construct institutions to deal with collective action problems—to regulate their own and others' behaviors—and they respond to institutions because the regulations are backed by incentives and sanctions.

A benefit of these models is that rational choice theorists have "an explicit theory of individual behavior in mind" when they examine motives for developing and consequences attendant to forming institutional structures (Peters 1999:45; see also Abell 1995). Economic theorists argue that, although their assumptions may not be completely accurate, "many institutions and business practices are designed as if people were entirely motivated by narrow, selfish concerns and were quite clever and largely unprincipled in their pursuit of their goals" (Milgrom and Roberts 1992:42).

From a sociological perspective, a limitation of employing an overly narrow rational framework is that it "portrays action as simply an adaptation to material conditions"—a calculus of costs and benefits—rather than allowing for the "internal subjective reference of action," which opens up potential for the "multidimensional alternation of freedom and constraint" (Alexander 1983, Vol. 1:74). Rather than positing a lone individual decision maker, the sociological version embraces an "organicist rather than an atomist view" such that "the essential characteristics of any element are seen as outcomes of relations with other entities" (Hodgson 1994:61). Actors in interaction constitute social structures, which, in turn, constitute actors. The products of prior interactions—norms, rules, beliefs, resources—provide the situational elements that enter into individual decision making (see the discussion of structuration in Chapter 4).

A number of terms have been proposed for this broadened view of rationality. As usual, Weber anticipated much of the current debate by distinguishing among several variants of rationality, including *Zweckrationalität*—action that is rational in the instrumental, calculative sense—and *Wertrationalität*—action that is inspired by and directed toward the realization of substantive values (Weber [1924] 1968:24; see also Swedberg 1998:36). The former focuses on means-ends connections; the latter on the types of ends pursued. Although Weber himself was inconsistent in his usage of these ideal types, Alexander suggests that they are best treated as analytic distinctions, with actual rational behavior being seen as involving an admixture of the two types. All social action involves some combination of calculation and orientation toward socially defined values.[8]

A related distinction has been proposed by March (1981), who differentiates between a logic of instrumentalism and a logic of appropriateness (see also March and Olsen 1989; March 1994). An *instrumental* logic asks, What are my interests in this situation? A logic of *appropriateness* asks, Given my role in this situation, what is expected of me? This conception stresses the normative pillar where choice is seen to be grounded in a social context and to be oriented by a moral framework that takes into account one's relations and obligations to others in the situation. A logic of appropriateness replaces, or sets limits on, individualistic instrumental behavior.

Cultural-cognitive theorists emphasize the extent to which behavior is informed and constrained by the ways in which knowledge is constructed and codified. The construction of social reality is seen as ongoing continuously but also as providing models, schemas, and scripts to orient and guide current decision making. At the micro-level, DiMaggio and Powell (1991) propose that these insights provide the basis for what they term a theory of practical action. This conception departs from a "preoccupation with the rational, calculative aspect of cognition to focus on preconscious processes and schema as they enter into routine, taken-for-granted behavior" (p. 22). At the same time, it eschews the individualistic, asocial assumptions associated with the narrow rational perspective to emphasize the extent to which individual choices are governed by normative rules and embedded in networks of mutual social obligations.

Langlois (1986b) proposes that the model of an intendedly rational actor needs to be supplemented by a model of the actor's situation that includes relevant social institutions. Institutions provide an informational-support function, serving as "interpersonal stores of coordinative knowledge" (p. 237). Such common conceptions enable the routine accomplishment of highly complex and interdependent tasks, often with a minimum of conscious deliberation or decision making. Analysts are enjoined to "pay attention to the existence of social institutions of various kinds as bounds to and definitions of the agent's situation" (p. 252). Langlois encourages us to broaden the neoclassical conception of rational action to encompass reasonable action, a conception that allows actors to "prefer more to less all things considered," but also allows for "other kinds of reasonable action in certain situations" including rule-following behavior. Social action is always grounded in social contexts that specify valued ends and appropriate means; action acquires its very reasonableness from taking into account these social rules and guidelines for behavior.

In sum, contemporary theorists not only select different pillars to support their versions of institutional structure, but these pillars themselves are constructed from varying types of ontological rules and make different assumptions about how best to account for social behavior.

Concluding Comment

Although it is possible to combine the insights of economic, political, and sociological analysts into a single, complex, integrated model of an institution, I believe it is more useful at this point to recognize the differing assumptions and emphases that accompany the models currently guiding inquiry into these phenomena. Three contrasting models of institutions are identified—the regulative, the normative, and the cultural-cognitive—although it is not possible to associate any of the disciplines uniquely with any of these proposed models. The models are differentiated such that each identifies a distinctive basis of compliance, mechanism of diffusion, type of logic, cluster of indicators, and foundation for legitimacy claims.

Although at a superficial level it appears that social analysts are merely emphasizing one or another of the multiple facets of institutional arrangements, a close examination suggests that the models are aligned with quite profound differences in the assumptions made about the nature of social reality and the ways in which actors make choices in social situations. Two sources of continuing controversy are identified. First, analysts disagree as to whether to attend primarily to regulative rules as formative of institutions or instead to give primacy to constitutive rules, which create distinctive types of actors and related modes of action. Second, institutions have become an important combat zone in the broader, ongoing disputation within the social sciences centering on the utility of rational choice theory for explaining human behavior. Are we to employ a more restricted, instrumental logic in accounting for the determinants and consequences of institutions, or is it preferable to posit a broader, more socially embedded logic? There is no sign of a quick or easy resolution to either of these debates.

Notes

1. This integrated model of institutions is elaborated in Scott (1994c).
2. Not all analysts share this belief. In a rather abrasive critique of an earlier presentation of this argument (*Institutions and Organizations,* 1st ed.), Hirsch (1997:1704) points out that my approach runs the risk of enforcing a "forced-choice" selection of one element as against another, rather than recognizing the reality that all institutional forms are composed of multiple elements. Such is not my intent. I willingly accede to the multiplex nature of institutional reality while insisting on the value of identifying analytic concepts that, I believe, will aid us as we attempt to sort

out the contending theories. Far from wishing to "rule out" or "discourage inter-pillar communication" or to make the "cross-fertilization of ideas unusual and unlikely," as Hirsch (p. 1709) alleges, my intent in constructing this analytic scheme is to encourage and inform such efforts.

3. Schutz ([1932] 1967) analyzes this process at length in his discussion of "the world of contemporaries as a structure of ideal types" (pp. 176-207).

4. Another candidate for an institutional pillar is cathetic or emotional elements. Both Durkheim and Parsons emphasize the importance of emotion-laden attachments to practices or relations, which provide not only a motivational basis but a kind of logic of action: behavior guided by "habits of the heart" (see Bellah et al. 1985). D'Andrade (1984) also stresses that meaning systems have an evocative as well as a cognitive aspect. Such systems evoke not only ideas but feelings and desires, and the latter no less than the former are part of the cultural meaning of symbols. Hochschild (1983) and Van Maanen and Kunda (1989) have empirically examined the development of norms governing the expression of emotion in work and other social settings.

5. Related typologies of the varying bases of legitimacy have been developed by Stryker (1994, 2000) and by Suchman (1995b).

6. Searle's framework is, hence, a moderate version of social constructionism. This more conservative stance is signaled by the title of his book, *The Construction of Social Reality,* which differs markedly from the broader interpretation implied by the title of Berger and Luckmann's book, *The Social Construction of Reality.*

7. As succinctly phrased by the economic historian Shonfield (1965): "Classical economics, which was largely a British invention, converted the British experience ... into something very like the Platonic idea of capitalism" (p. 71).

8. Famously, Weber ([1906-1924] 1946) captured this combination of ideas and interests in his "switchman" metaphor:

> Not ideas, but material and ideal interests directly govern men's conduct. Yet very frequently the "world images" that have been created by "ideas" have, like switchmen, determined the tracks along which action has been pushed by the dynamics of interests. (p. 280)

4 Constructing an Analytic
Framework II

CONTENT, AGENCY,
CARRIERS, AND LEVELS

In Chapter 3, three institutional elements were defined, and differences were described related to each regarding motivation for compliance, enforcement mechanisms, logic, types of indicators, and bases of legitimacy and social order. Building on this framework, the present chapter examines the content of institutional rules conducive to organizational development, considers the relation of agency to institutions, and describes varying types of carriers and levels of analysis used by institutional analysts.

Institutional Content and Organizations

Institutions of one type or another can be traced back to the earliest stages of the history of humankind, whereas organizations as we know them are a relatively recent development. Clearly, then, all institutional frameworks are not conducive to organizational growth and sustenance. Numerous social theorists have attempted to specify what types of institutional forms are likely to give rise to formal organizations.[1]

Early views placed more emphasis on regulatory and normative structures. Weber ([1924] 1968) stressed the emergence of a "legal order" consisting of a "system of consciously made rational rules" that support "instrumentally rational" action (pp. 24, 953-54). Parsons (1951; Parsons, Bales, and Shils 1953) devoted much attention to detailing the value orientations and normative systems that support the development of more instrumental and impersonal social forms. His typology of *pattern variables*—basic value dimensions giving rise to different kinds of action orientations and supporting structures—identified universalism (versus particularism), affective neutrality (versus affectivity), achievement (versus ascription), and specificity (versus diffuseness) as normative orientations conducive to the rise of organizations.

Later theorists emphasized the cultural-cognitive systems supporting organizations. Ellul ([1954] 1964) notes the emergence of a "technicist" mentality that encourages analytic approaches and the development of systematic, instrumental rules to pursue specific objectives. Berger, Berger, and Kellner (1973) describe the novel states of consciousness that accompany the emergence of technology and bureaucracy, including mechanisticity, reproducibility, orderliness, and predictability. And Meyer (1983) depicts the cultural elements that underlie the creation of formal organizations as including "definable purposes," "culturally defined means-ends relationships or technologies," a view of things and people as "resources," and the presumption that a "unified sovereign" exists that gives coherence to collective actors (pp. 265-67).

What all of these arguments have in common is that they embody a *rationalized* conception of the world. Purposes are specified and then rule-like principles are devised to govern activity. Rationalization involves "the creation of cultural schemes defining means-ends relationships and standardizing systems of control over activities and actors" (Scott and Meyer 1994:3). Some of the principles, like the laws of mechanics, have an empirical base; others, like legal frameworks, are rooted in a logical or philosophical structure. All such rationalized beliefs support the rise of organizations.

Institutional scholars argue that rationalization also entails the creation of entities—identifiable social units—endowed with interests and having the capacity to take action. In the modern world, commencing with social processes associated with the Enlightenment, three categories of actors have been accorded primacy: individuals, organizations, and societies, the latter in the guise of the nation-state (see Meyer, Boli, and Thomas 1987). James S. Coleman (1974, 1990, chap. 20) provides a valuable historical-analytic account of the emergence of organizations as significant collective actors, as they were accorded legal rights, capacities, and resources independent of those held by their individual participants.[2] Coleman employs changes in the law, not as causal factors, but as significant indicators of the growing independence of these new corporate forms as they became recognized to be legal entities in the eyes of the law. Pedersen and Dobbin (1997) propose that this process was fueled primarily by the growth of a scientific ethos, which created abstract and general categories to classify and enumerate, first, the biological and physical universe and, subsequently, the social world. The rapid advance of commensuration—"the measurement of characteristics normally represented by different units according to a common metric" (Espeland and Stevens 1998:315)—allowed the counting and measuring of all manner of material and social objects.

Professionals, initially from the engineering sciences (Shenhav 1995, 1999), attempted to tame the exotic, multiple, idiosyncratic instances of enterprise and fostered the emergence of, on the one hand, the generic category *organization* accompanied by its universal handmaiden, *management*, and, on the other hand, the differentiation of recognizable subtypes: for example, schools, hospitals, public agencies, and nonprofit or for-profit corporations. The development of such templates or archetypes, as well as the specification of their structural characteristics, utilities, capabilities, and identities, takes place over many years, but once these are established, the templates can provide cultural models for the rapid molding of other similar forms. This professional project—of treating all manner of collectivities as part of a more generic form, organization, and of identifying meaningful subtypes—was later embraced and, necessarily, reinforced by the emergence of an academic discipline devoted to the pursuit of organizational studies.

The socially constructed characteristics of both people and collective actors, such as firms, vary over time and place (see Hollingsworth and Boyer 1997). Institutional rules in the West have accorded greater individual autonomy and independence to social actors, both people and firms, compared to related rules in East Asian societies. Thus, whereas "the United States has institutionalized competitive individualism in its market structure," Asian economies "are organized through networks of [interdependent and less autonomous] economic actors that are believed to be natural and appropriate to economic development" (Biggart and Hamilton 1992:472). Relations among people or firms that Western eyes would view as involving nepotism or collusion are normal, inevitable, and beneficial to Eastern observers.

In general, regulative and normative theorists give more attention to the examination of regulative rules and tend to treat constitutive rules as background conditions. Thus, for example, neoinstitutionalist economists and political scientists will inquire into the activities of a firm or agency and consider what kinds of structural arrangements or procedures are associated with specified behaviors, such as improved productivity. By contrast, economic historians and historical political scientists give much more attention to the origin of general types of social actors (e.g., "jobber, importer, factor, broker, and the commission agent"; Chandler 1977:27) or organizational archetypes (e.g., joint-stock companies, multidivisional firms, and nonprofit forms), or to changes in property or political rights. Similarly, neoinstitutional sociologists are more apt to focus on changes over time in the types of actors involved or in the cultural rules establishing the logics of practice within a particular organizational context (e.g., Fligstein 1990; Scott et al. 2000). Scholars attending to constitutive rules insist that much of the coherence of social life is due to the creation of categories of social actors, both individual and collective, and to associated ways of acting. Note that one methodological consequence of this different focus is that scholars focusing on regulative processes are more apt to examine similar types of organizations cross-sectionally or over shorter time periods (often assuming equilibrium conditions), whereas scholars focusing on more constitutive processes embrace longer time periods or use comparative designs.

Agency and Institutions

Throughout the history of social science, there has existed a tension between those theorists who emphasize structural and cultural constraints on action and those who emphasize the ability of individual actors to "make a difference" in the flow of events. This is a version of the ancient antinomy between freedom and control. Obviously, the thrust of institutional theory is to account for continuity and constraint in social structure, but that need not preclude attention to the ways in which individual actors take action to create, maintain, and transform institutions.

Early neoinstitutional scholars, such as Meyer and Rowan (1977) and DiMaggio and Powell (1983), tended to emphasize the ways in which institutional mechanisms constrained organizational structures and activities. However, more recent work (which I review in subsequent chapters), including that of both DiMaggio (1988, 1991) and Powell (1991), gives more attention to the ways in which both individuals and organizations innovate, act strategically, and contribute to institutional change (see Oliver 1991; Christensen et al. 1997).

Many theoretical frameworks treat freedom and constraint as opposing ideas, requiring us to "take sides": to privilege one social value or the other. Fortunately, recent developments in sociological theory allow us to see both as interrelated, compatible processes. In particular, the work of Anthony Giddens (1979, 1984) on *structuration* has provided a productive framework for examining the interplay between these forces.

Although it is a rather infelicitous word, *structuration* is the term coined by Giddens to remind us that social structure involves the patterning of social activities and relations through time and across space. Social structures only exist as patterned social activities, incorporating rules and resources, that are reproduced over time. Giddens (1984) envisions what he terms the "duality of social structure," recognizing it to be both product and platform of social action. Social structures exhibit a dual role in that they are "both the medium and the outcome of the practices they recursively organize" (p. 25). Individual actors carry out practices that are simultaneously constrained and empowered by existing social structure. In Giddens's model, social structures are made up of rules—"generalized procedures applied in the enactment/reproduction of social life" (p. 21)—and resources—objects, both human and nonhuman, "that can be used to enhance or maintain power" (Sewell 1992:9). Institutions are those types of social structures that involve more strongly held rules supported by more entrenched resources. Institutional practices are "those deeply embedded in time and space" (Giddens 1984:13).

Structuration theory views actors as creating and following rules and using resources as they engage in the ongoing production and reproduction of social structures. Actors are viewed as both knowledgeable and reflexive, capable of understanding and taking account of everyday situations and of routinely monitoring the results of their own and others' actions. Agency refers to an actor's ability to have some effect on the social world, altering the rules or the distribution of resources. The presence of agency presumes a nondeterminant, voluntaristic theory of action: "to be able to 'act otherwise' means being able to intervene in the world, or to refrain from such intervention, with the effect of influencing a specific process or state of affairs" (Giddens 1984:14). All actors, both individual and collective, possess some degree of agency, but the amount of agency varies greatly among actors as well as among types of social structures. Agency itself is socially structured.

The basic theoretical premise underlying the concept of agency is strongly aligned with the phenomenological assumptions that undergird sociological versions of neoinstitutional thought. Between the context and the response is the interpreting actor. Agency resides in "the interpretive processes whereby choices are imagined, evaluated, and contingently reconstructed by actors in ongoing dialogue with unfolding situations" (Emirbayer and Mische 1998:966).

Structuration theory joins with numerous other theoretical arguments to support a more proactive role for individual and organizational actors, as well as a more interactive and reciprocal view of institutional processes. For example, to view behavior as oriented to and governed by rules need not imply that behavior is either "unreasoned" or automatic. March and Olsen (1989) insist that rules must be both selected—often more than one rule may be applicable—and interpreted, or adapted to the demands of the particular situation. Weick (1979, 1995) emphasizes that understandings and scripts not only guide actions but also emerge out of them, and that collective symbols are as likely to be used to justify past behaviors as to guide current ones. Newer versions of role and cultural theory view individuals as playing an active part, using existing rules and social resources as a cultural "tool kit" for constructing strategies of action (Swidler 1986). Analysts have posited a "politics of identity" in which individuals or organized groups create goals, identities, and solidarities that provide meaning and generate ongoing social commitments (Aronowitz 1992; Calhoun 1991; Somers and Gibson 1994). And they increasingly recognize the

Table 4.1   Institutional Pillars & Carriers

| | *Pillars* | | |
Carriers	*Regulative*	*Normative*	*Cultural-Cognitive*
Symbolic systems	Rules, Laws	Values, Expectations	Categories, Typifications, Schema
Relational systems	Governance systems, Power systems	Regimes, Authority systems	Structural isomorphism, Identities
Routines	Protocols, Standard operating procedures	Jobs, Roles, Obedience to duty	Scripts
Artifacts	Objects complying with mandated specifications	Objects meeting conventions, standards	Objects possessing symbolic value

extent to which organizational participants do not always conform to conventional patterns but respond variably, sometimes creating new ways of acting and organizing.

Varying Carriers

Institutions, whether regulative, normative, or cultural-cognitive elements are stressed, are embedded in various types of repositories or carriers (see Jepperson 1991:150). I identify four types: symbolic systems, relational systems, routines, and artifacts.[3] These distinctions are largely orthogonal to the three pillars, permitting us to cross-classify them. (See Table 4.1.) Theorists vary not only in which elements they favor but in which carriers they emphasize.

Symbolic Systems

Culture is one of the most widely used and least-well defined concepts in the social sciences (Archer 1988). The usage employed here includes the more conventional notions of rules and values, as well as the newer conceptions of culture discussed in Chapter 2, those stressing symbolic schemata that include models, classifications, representations, and logics (Jepperson and Swidler 1994:361). All can be examined as social phenomena external to any particular actor but also as subjective, internalized cognitive frames and beliefs. In his analysis of social structures, Bourdieu (1977) places great importance on the internalization of cultural rules. His concept of habitus refers to the existence of a "system of lasting and transposable dispositions which, integrating past experiences, functions at every moment as a matrix of perceptions, appreciations, and actions" (p. 95) allowing individuals to structure their behavior within situations. Symbolic systems vary in their degree of institutionalization. Although neoinstitutionalists give particular attention to the role of symbolic processes in promoting order and stability, as Jepperson (1991) correctly insists, institutions should not be equated with symbolic effects. Symbolic systems vary in the extent to which they exhibit uniformity and promote consistency of action. Swidler (1986), for example, argues that whereas in "settled" times, "culture accounts for continuities . . . organizing and anchoring patterns of action," in times of change, culture functions more like a tool kit providing repertoires "from which actors select different pieces for constructing lines of action" (pp. 277, 278).

As the entries in Table 4.1 suggest, which symbolic systems emphasized vary depending on which elements of institutions are given prominence. Cognitive theorists will stress the importance of categories, distinctions, and typifications; normative theorists will accent shared values and normative expectations; and regulative theorists point to the role played by conventions, rules, and laws. The development of standards and standardization processes constitutes a clear instance of institutionalized normative and cultural carriers. As Brunsson (1998) notes, "Standards constitute a particular kind of rules: they are explicit and they are, at least formally, voluntary. . . . Standards are a kind of general advice directed at many" (p. 3; see also Brunsson and Jacobsson 2000). Loya and Boli (1999) elaborate,

[Standardization] embodies the principles of universalism, rationality, and homogenization to an extreme degree. . . . The standards bodies champion voluntary participation and rational decision making, and they have far too few resources to impose their standards on lower-level organizations, but the standards they adopt become obligatory and are routinely enforced by states, industry groups, and individual firms. These lower-level actors find it virtually impossible to reject standards because doing so is seen as irrational—they would be limiting their access to world markets and technologies to a fatal degree. (pp. 192-93)

Symbolic systems may exist in the wider environment at the societal or even the world system levels, or they may be more restricted in their jurisdiction, applying only to specific organizations or subsystems of organizations. Although it is conventional among macro scholars to characterize such systems as operating in the organization's environment (see Meyer and Scott [1983b] 1992; Zucker 1987), it is important to recognize that these systems are carried in the minds of individuals. They exist not only as "widely held beliefs" in the wider environment or as laws that organizational actors need to take into account, but also as ideas or values in the heads of organizational actors. Indeed, attending to this connection is one of the vital ways in which institutional analysis can help to link the work of micro and macro organizational scholars.

Relational System Carriers

Institutions can also be carried by relational systems. Such systems are carriers that rely on patterned expectations connected to networks of social positions: role systems. Again, the systems constrain and empower the behavior of actors at the same time that they are reproduced and transformed by this behavior.

Rules and belief systems are coded into positional distinctions and roles; relational systems incorporate or instantiate institutional elements. As with cultural carriers, some relational arrangements are widely shared across many organizations, creating structural isomorphism (similar forms) or structural equivalence (similar relations among forms). Other forms may be distinctive to a particular organization, embodying localized belief systems and creating what Selznick (1957) termed a unique organizational "character structure."

As with cultures, the aspects of relational structures that are emphasized depend on which elements of institutions are featured. Cognitive theorists stress structural isomorphism. Cognitive typifications are often coded into organizational structures as differentiated departments and roles. For example, codified knowledge systems support the development of differentiated academic departments in universities. Normative and regulatory theorists are apt to view relational systems as governance systems, emphasizing either the normative (authority) or the coercive (power) aspects of these structures. Such governance systems are viewed as creating and enforcing codes, norms, and rules and as monitoring and sanctioning the activities of participants. The new institutional economists, such as Williamson, emphasize relational systems erected to exercise governance as the principal carriers of institutional forces.

Routines as Carriers

Institutions may also be embodied in—or carried by—structured activities in the form of habitualized behavior and routines. Routines are carriers that rely on patterned actions that reflect the tacit knowledge of actors: deeply ingrained habits and procedures based on inarticulated knowledge and beliefs.

Rather than privileging cultural systems, many early institutionalists viewed habitualized action, routines, standard operating procedures, and similar patterned activities as the central features of institutions. March and Simon (1958) identified repetitive "performance programs" as the central ingredient accounting for the reliability of organizations. And, more recently, evolutionary theorists, such as Nelson and Winter (1982), point to the stabilizing role played by participants' skills and organizational routines: activities involving little or no conscious choice and behavior governed by tacit knowledge and skills of which the actor may be unaware. Viewing routines as the "genes" of organizations, Winter (1990) points out that they range from "hard"— activities encoded into technologies—to "soft"—organizational routines such as airplane inspection or fast-food procedures—but all involve "repetitive patterns of activity" (pp. 274-75). These patterns include a broad range of behaviors, extending from standard operating procedures and skill sets of individual employees to "organizational activity bundles such as jobs, assembly lines, airline reservations systems, accounting principles, or rules of war" (Miner 1991:773). Such routines underlie much of the stability of organizational behavior, accounting for both reliable performance and organizational rigidities.

Artifacts as Carriers

Anthropologists have long recognized the importance of material culture or artifacts created by human ingenuity to assist in the performance of various tasks. Earlier forms were often as primitive as shaped rocks and sticks, but more recent artifacts include complex technologies, embodied in both hardware and software. Organizational students of technology earlier treated these features as a unidirectional and deterministic influence affecting organizational structure and behavior (see, e.g., Woodward 1958; Blau et al. 1976). Later theorists reacted by emphasizing the socially constructed nature of technology and the extent to which its effects are mediated by situational factors and interpretive processes (Bijker, Hughes, and Pinch 1987).

Orlikowski (1992) usefully proposes that artifacts and technology can be examined within the same theoretical framework devised by Giddens (1984) to accommodate structure and action. Viewing artifacts as an instance of structuration allows analysts to recognize that such inventions are, on the one hand, products of human action, but also that "once developed and deployed," they become reified and appear "to be part of the objective, structural properties" of the situation (Orlikowski 1992:406). This perspective is often obscured from participants and analysts because the actors and actions that create the new instruments may be removed in time and space from those that employ them to accomplish work. Analysts focusing on artifact creation are better able to see the multiple possibilities: the path selected versus the "roads not taken"; analysts focusing on artifact use see primarily the constraints imposed by the design selected on those who employ it. Although such differences do exist, they should not obscure the extent to which users interact with and modify the meaning and use of artifacts. As Orlikowski (1992) observes,

> While we can expect a greater engagement of human agents during the initial development of a technology, this does not discount the ongoing potential for users to change it (physically and socially) throughout their interaction with it. In using a technology, users interpret, appropriate, and manipulate it in various ways. (p. 408)

Barley (1986) provides an instructive empirical study of the deployment of identical technologies, CT scanners, by radiological departments in two community hospitals, examining the ways and extent to which the technologies were associated with somewhat divergent changes in the decision making and power structure of the departments (see Chapter 8).

Artifacts, like other carriers, can be viewed as associated with, and affected by, each of the three pillars. The design and construction of some artifacts and technologies are mandated by regulative authorities, often in the interests of safety. Modern societies contain a wide range of agencies that oversee product quality, ranging from those that attempt to ensure the reliability of atomic plants to those that set performance and safety standards for commercial aircraft and passenger cars. Technologies are also shaped by and embody normative processes. Trade and industrial groups often convene to set standards for a wide range of machines and technical equipment, as discussed above. Such agreements serve to ensure compatibility, and they can serve to create excess value for participants to the extent that many players adopt the standard (Katz and Shapiro 1985). And artifacts can embody and represent particular constellations of ideas. Indeed, the symbolic freight of some objects can outweigh their material essence, for example, the significance of the bread and wine in the communion service or the goal posts in the football match.

As with the other types of carriers, artifacts work at various levels, some being relatively limited in their deployment and use across time and space, some being used more widely by particular types of organizations or industries, whereas others, such as telephones and computers, border on the ubiquitous.

These arguments and distinctions suggest some of the many ways in which organizations are deeply embedded in institutional contexts. A given organization is supported and constrained by institutional forces. Also, a given organization incorporates with its own boundaries a multitude of institutionalized features, in the form of cultures, relational systems, routines, and artifacts. It is, hence, appropriate to speak of the extent to which organizational components or features are institutionalized. These views are shared by all, or by the great majority of institutional theorists. That subset endorsing a cultural-cognitive perspective adds an additional, even more fateful assertion: The very concept of an organization as a special-purpose, instrumental entity is itself a product of institutional processes: constitutive processes that define the capacities of collective actors, both generally, and as specialized subtypes.

This version of institutional theory, in particular, tends to subvert or undermine the conventional distinction between organization and environment. Organizations are penetrated by environments in ways not envisioned by many theoretical models.

Varying Levels of Analysis

One of the principal ways in which the several varieties of institutional theory differ is in the level at which they are applied. Levels identified differ greatly in terms of whether the investigator is focusing on more micro or more macro phenomena. The key underlying dimension is the scope of the phenomena encompassed, whether measured in terms of space, time, or numbers of people affected. For institutions, level may be usefully operationalized as the range of jurisdiction of the institutional form. Given the complexity and variety of social phenomena, any particular set of distinctions will be somewhat arbitrary. Nevertheless, for our purposes, it is useful to identify six categories: the levels of *world system, society, organizational field, organizational population, organization,* and *organizational subsystem.* Most of these six levels are widely employed and recognizable to social analysts; all are of interest to students of organizations. Perhaps the least familiar, yet the level of most significance to institutional theory, is that of the organizational field. Following DiMaggio and Powell (1983), an *organization field* refers to

> those organizations that, in the aggregate, constitute a recognized area of institutional life: key suppliers, resource and product consumers, regulatory agencies, and other organizations that produce similar services or products. (p. 148)

Hirsch (1985) has proposed the closely related concept of *industry system,* and Meyer and I have proposed that of *societal sector* (Scott and Meyer [1983] 1991). All of these conceptions build on the more conventional concept of *industry,* a population of organizations operating in the same domain as indicated by the similarity of their services or products. But added to this focal population are those other and different organizations that critically influence their performance, including exchange partners, competitors, funding sources, and regulators. Fields are bounded by the presence of shared cultural-cognitive or normative frameworks or a common regulatory system so as to "constitute a recognized area of institutional life":

> The notion of field connotes the existence of a community of organizations that partakes of a common meaning system and whose participants interact more frequently and fatefully with one another than with actors outside of the field. (Scott 1994a:207-8)

An example of an organizational field would be an educational system comprising a set of schools (focal population) and related organizations, such as district offices and parent-teacher associations. Given the definition of field, it is apparent that this conception provides a level at which institutional forces are likely to be particularly salient.[4]

The other level of analysis somewhat distinctive to organizational research and often employed in institutional studies is that of the population. *Organizational populations* are defined as a collection or aggregate of organizations that are "alike in some respect"; in particular, they are "classes of organizations that are relatively homogeneous in terms of environmental vulnerability" (Hannan and Freeman 1977:166) Newspaper companies or trade unions are examples of organizational populations.

Nevertheless, to reiterate, all six levels are of interest to those who study organizations. And, as with the notion of carriers, the levels distinction is orthogonal to and can be cross-classified with the set of institutional elements. (See Table 4.2.) The entries in Table 4.2 refer to theorists whose work has pursued one or another institutional element at the specified levels. (Most of these studies are reviewed in more detail in subsequent chapters.)

Beginning with scholars examining the operation of regulative processes at differing levels, North and Thomas (1973) have examined how the institution of property rights and associated state-regulatory apparatus developed in the Western world during the fifteenth through the seventeenth centuries. Skocpol (1979) examined differences in the organization and operation of the state as it affected the course of revolutions occurring in France, Russia, and China. Analysts such as Schmitter (1990) and Campbell and Lindberg (1991) have examined the varying governance mechanisms at work in different societal sectors or industries. Barnett and Carroll (1993a) have studied the effects on

Table 4.2   Institutional Pillars and Varying Levels: Illustrative Theorists

	Pillar		
Level	*Regulative*	*Normative*	*Cultural-Cognitive*
World system	North and Thomas 1973	Krasner 1983	Meyer 1994
Societal	Skocpol 1979	Parsons 1953, 1960a	Dobbin 1994b
Organizational field	Campbell and Lindberg 1991 Schmitter 1990	Mezias 1990	DiMaggio 1991
Organizational population	Barnett and Carroll 1993a	Singh, Tucker, and House 1986	Carroll and Hannan 1989
Organization	Williamson 1975, 1985, 1991	Selznick 1949	Clark 1970
Organizational subsystem	Shepsle and Weinsgast 1987	Roy 1952 Burawoy 1979	Zimmerman 1969

the development of the population of early telephone companies of various regulatory policies pursued by state and federal authorities. Williamson (1975, 1985, 1991) has developed his markets and hierarchies framework to explain the emergence of varying types of organizational forms to govern and reduce the costs of economic transactions. And Shepsle and Weingast (1987) have studied the institutional foundations of committee power in Congress.

Turning to theorists emphasizing normative elements, Krasner (1983) and colleagues have examined the circumstances surrounding the development of common normative frameworks or regimes at the international level. Parsons (1953) has described differences in value systems and normative frameworks at the societal level and their consequences for organizations. Mezias (1990) has studied changes in normative beliefs regarding financial reporting requirements for corporations occasioned by the actions of state agents and professional accounting societies. Singh, Tucker, and House (1986) have examined the effects on survival rates, in a population of voluntary social service organizations, of being certified by public agencies. Selznick (1949) studied the ways in which procedural requirements became "infused with value" in the TVA. And Roy (1952) and Burawoy (1979) examined the institutionalization of normative frameworks regarding production and restriction of output among workers in the machine shop of a manufacturing plant.

And, among those scholars examining cultural-cognitive conceptions of institutional processes, Meyer (1994) examines processes operating at the level of the world system, giving rise to institutions. Dobbin (1994b) has studied the varying cultural belief systems that underlie societal policies affecting railway systems in the United States, England, and France. Working at the level of the organization field, DiMaggio (1991) has studied the cultural belief systems constructed to support artistic organizations, such as museums in the United States. Carroll and Hannan (1989) employ data on the density or prevalence of newspapers—viewed as an indicator of the taken-for-grantedness of this form—to examine its effects on the growth rates of newspapers in selected U.S. cities. At the organization level, Clark (1970) has examined the distinctive cultural values cultivated by a set of elite colleges and their effects on organizational viability. And Zimmerman (1969), working at the subsystem level, has described the development of typifications and routines among intake workers in a social welfare agency.

More generally, as illustrated in Figure 4.1, it is possible to associate various schools or types of work with different locations in the property space created by the cross-classification of pillars and levels. Most of the neoinstitutional work conducted by sociologists in the recent period is guided by the combination of a cultural-cognitive emphasis and attention to the macro levels: processes operating at a transorganizational level. Moreover, this work stresses cultural carriers—widespread beliefs, professional norms—but also attends to the impact of macro structural carriers such as international organizations, the state, and trade and professional associations.

Organizational ecologists have directed attention to the organizational population level of analysis and, in their recent work, have appropriated institutional arguments to account for the density dynamics of organizational populations. The familiar slow take-off and then more rapid growth rate has been interpreted by Carroll and Hannan (1989) as reflecting the increasing cognitive legitimacy of a form. (See Chapter 6.)

Attention to cognitive elements at the organization or organizational subsystem level has largely been provided by the ethnomethodologists

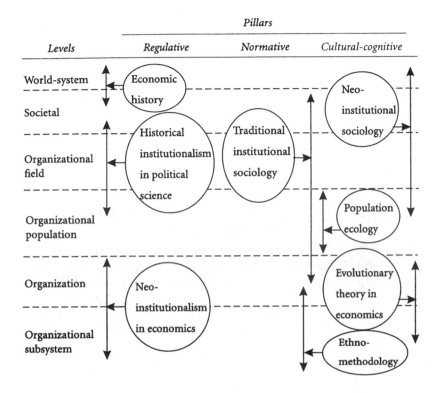

Figure 4.1. Institutional Pillars and Varying Levels: Illustrative Schools

and by students of corporate culture (see Martin 1992; Trice and Beyer 1993). The ethnomethodologists, along with some evolutionary economists, focus on habits and skills and so attend more closely to activities as carriers of institutions at the organizational and suborganizational levels (see Turner 1974). Those who examine corporate culture, of course, give primacy to cultural carriers.

The traditional institutional approach in sociology—work associated with Hughes, Parsons, and Selznick—is defined by a focus on normative elements and attention to levels ranging from the individual organization to the society. This approach is very much alive and well and continues to be emphasized by such scholars as Brint and Karabel (1991) and Padgett and Ansell (1993). Both the cultural and relational carriers are emphasized in this approach.

Economists and political scientists are most likely to emphasize the regulative view of institutions. Economic historians focus on the macro levels, examining the origins and functions of transnational and national rules and enforcement mechanisms that are developed to regulate economic behavior of firms and individuals. Historical institutionalists in both sociology and political science emphasize the study of regulatory regimes and governance mechanisms that operate at the societal and industry level. And the new institutionalists in economics, along with the rational choice theorists in political science, focus primarily on regulatory processes operating at the organizational or suborganizational level. The economic historians and historical institutionalists emphasize cultural and relational carriers, whereas the new institutional economists emphasize primarily relational carriers.

We discover, then, substantial differences among current schools aligned with the new institutionalism. Sociologists pursuing this line of work emphasize a cognitive conception, cultural carriers, and macro forces. By contrast, neoinstitutional economists and most political scientists stress a regulative conception, relational carriers, and a micro focus. Rather different perspectives to be sharing the same label!

Concluding Comment

Organizations have arisen and gained prominence in part because of the development of distinctive cultural logics that endeavor to rationalize the nature of the physical and social world. Valued ends are to be pursued systematically by codified, formalized means; and organizations are viewed as providing appropriate social entities to promote such projects. As such beliefs become more widespread and invade ever more arenas of social life, organizations become ubiquitous vehicles of collective action.

Whereas institutional conceptions underline the sources of social stability and order, the structuration framework advanced by Giddens enables us simultaneously to theorize and examine the sources of both social order and social change. These and related conceptions increasingly guide developments in institutional theory and research.

To complement the concept of elements or pillars, two other distinctions are introduced in an attempt to recognize the variety of forms and processes exhibited by institutions, as well as the great variety of scholarly approaches currently in use. First, institutions are viewed as varying in their mode of carrier or host. Institutions may be borne by symbols, relational structures, routines, and artifacts. Second, institutions are described as capable of operating at, or having jurisdiction over, differing levels. Some are restricted to operating within organizational subunits whereas others function at levels as broad as that of world systems. The variety of possible carriers through which institutions work, together with the multiple levels at which they operate, helps to account for why they receive so much attention and why they generate so much confusion and inconsistency among their observers.

Notes

1. Other theorists have called attention to the role played by technological innovations and associated developments, such as labor specialization, in the role of organizational forms (see Kerr et al. 1964; Rosenberg and Birdzell 1986; for a review, see Scott 1998, Chapter 7).

2. Krasner (1988) and Meyer and colleagues (Meyer et al. 1997) provide an institutional perspective on the emergence of nation-states.

3. Jepperson (1991:150) identifies a somewhat different set of carriers: cultures, regimes, and organizations.

4. Bourdieu (1988) has developed a related but more general conception of *social field*, which is not restricted to organizations. In Bourdieu's conception, all societies contain an assemblage of fields governed by distinctive values and logics. Fields are, in part, structured by *habitus:* dispositional orientations shared by agents within the field. Bourdieu views a field as a "relational configuration" contained in a patterned system of forces. "A field is simultaneously a space of conflict and competition" in which "participants vie to establish a monopoly over the species of capital effective in it" (Bourdieu and Wacquant 1992:17).

5 Institutional Construction,
Maintenance, and Diffusion

The concerted efforts to revive interest in institutional analysis and
to connect these arguments to organizations began in the mid-
1970s. Not surprisingly, most of the early statements were primarily
theoretical, employing evidence in only a casual and illustrative manner. It was not long, however, before various types of empirical investi-
gations began to appear. Their numbers have steadily increased, so that
by now, a substantial amount of research relevant to the testing and
elaboration of institutional arguments has been produced. Most of this
work treats institutional frameworks as given and asks how they affect
organizational structures and functions. That is, in most of the empirical literature, institutions are treated as independent variables, and the
studies are directed to examining their effects on some organizational
entity or process, the units ranging from trans-societal systems to organizational subunits. This focus is understandable because students of
organizations are primarily interested in assessing whether and to what
extent institutional systems affect individual organizations or collections of organizations. If such influences cannot be demonstrated,

there would be little incentive for these analysts to pursue the related questions regarding the sources of institutions and the causes of institutional change and persistence.

Chapters 6 and 7 describe and discuss this more extensive literature on the ways in which institutional systems relate to organizational fields, populations, and organizations. The current chapter considers the question of institutional determinants: how institutions arise and achieve stability, legitimacy, and adherents. We consider here, then, two types of questions: How are institutions created? and How are institutions maintained and diffused? An important, related question—how do institutions lose credibility and undergo change?—is deferred to Chapter 8.

Before addressing any of these questions, however, we call attention to a distinction between process and variance approaches that cuts across the full range of studies of institutions, affecting what questions are asked and what methods are employed. Although it is not restricted to institutional analysis, this distinction is especially evident in current efforts to explain institutional emergence and change.

Variance and Process Approaches to Explaining Institutions

In an important early article on the subject, Zucker (1977) observed that "institutionalization is both a process and a property variable" (p. 728). That is, for some purposes, we treat an institution as an entity, as a cultural or social system characterized by one or more features or properties. On other occasions, we are interested in institutionalization as a process, as the growth (or decline) over time of cultural-cognitive, normative, or regulative elements capable, to varying degrees, of providing meaning and stability to social behavior.[1] Although the two views are obviously closely related, our modes of analysis tend to privilege one or the other, and the theoretical frameworks and methodologies we employ are also likely to vary, as Mohr (1982) has emphasized (see also Scott 1994b).[2]

Lawrence Mohr (1982) differentiates between variance and process theories. *Variance theories*, associated with viewing institutions as entities, examine their characteristics; treat them as abstract variables, either independent or dependent; and attempt to establish their causal relations to other variables. Precursor (independent) variables are seen as a necessary and sufficient condition for determining the values of outcome (dependent) variables. Although precursor variables obviously predate outcome variables, the time ordering among these precursor variables themselves is viewed as immaterial to the outcome. Variance theories address the question, Why did the observed effect happen? They attempt to identify what factors were associated with the observed characteristics of the phenomena of interest.

By contrast, *process theories* deal with "a series of occurrences of events rather than a set of relations among variables" (Mohr 1982:54; see also Van de Ven and Huber 1990). In process theories, time is of the essence, in particular, the time ordering of the contributory events. "In a process analysis, events are represented as taking place sequentially in real time" (Langlois 1986a:7). Often, a sequence of events—for example, those leading up to the French Revolution—does not lend itself to multivariant analysis, as Alford (1998) emphasizes:

> Attempts to reconceptualize these unique sequences of events as instances of a general class of phenomena ("revolutions," "regime transformations"....) in order to be able to classify their attributes as "variables" and thus incorporate them into multivariate arguments may miss their essential features *and* their unique social consequences. Systematic statements of empirical covariation are of course important, but they do not replace a complex description and explanation of a particular historical totality. (p. 45; emphasis in original)

A process approach addresses the question, How did the observed effects happen? This approach assumes that "history matters," that how things occur influences what things happen (see Zald 1990).

Although history always matters in the sense that effects follow causes in temporal succession, David (1985) argues that some historical processes matter more than others. For example, some technologies, for idiosyncratic reasons, gain an initial advantage over others that allows them to prevail even in the face of superior technologies. Such outcomes are regarded as path dependent and are of particular interest to social scientists because they can result in "locked in" structures that may be demonstrably inferior to (less efficient than) alternative options. And sociological institutionalists point out that specific conditions present at the time of the founding of some new social arrangement (for example, new types of organization) enable some solutions but foreclose others (see Thelen 1999; Chapter 8).

Process theories vary in their degree of formalization. Most often, a process argument is a historical account: a narrative frequently consisting of "stage-naming" concepts that provide a description of a sequence of events. Economists refer to such explanations, rather pejoratively, as "storytelling" (Knudsen 1993). Explanations of particular institutions can easily become historicist, favoring "interpretations that stress the complexity, uniqueness, and contingency of historical events" (Kiser and Hechter 1991:10). Most sociologists struggle to avoid such restricted explanations, seeking to preserve some degree of generality in their theoretical approaches. Currently, the most popular approach in contemporary historical sociology involves *inductive generalism,* the examination of one or more cases employed to generate and assess historically limited explanations (Kiser and Hechter 1991). Such analyses attempt to develop or to apply general theories, recognizing that the generalizations are relative—and may be limited—to a certain type of context or set of conditions (Skocpol 1984:376).

Another approach to developing more systematic process accounts of historical processes is the *narrative* approach, a methodology that has close affinities to institutional theory. Czarniawska (1997) suggests that the "narrative mode of knowing consists in organizing experience with the help of a scheme assuming the intentionality of human action" (p. 18). She proposes that all societies have a repertoire of legitimate stories that individuals employ, in varying combinations, both to make sense of and to provide guidelines for ongoing actions. Organizational life is viewed as a drama—"patterns of action" held in place by "legitimate interpretations of why things should be done this or some other way" (p. 24)—and the behavior of individual participants is examined as autobiography. Identities, both organizational and individual, are constructed in conversations using texts involving institutionalized meanings, metaphors, and templates. Czarniawska illustrates her approach by examining a number of contested changes within Swedish public agencies.

More rigorous and highly formalized approaches attempt to specify explicitly the nature of the probabilistic process that connects events with outcomes (see Lave and March 1975). Game theorists such as Schotter (1986) and Sugden (1986) have developed mathematical models of the processes by which rule systems or sets of conventions evolve from repeated game situations played by rational actors; the models are typically assessed through experiments or computer simulations. And economic historians such as Arthur (1988) have employed Markov models to depict path-dependent processes related to institution building and institutional change. Abbott (1990) has pioneered in the development of sequence methods that enable the investigator to identify characteristic patterns in sequences of social events.

It is possible for a single study to combine both variance and process approaches in its design. Indeed, many of the best studies attempt to capitalize on the strengths of each approach by presenting both historical accounts (e.g., case studies) and a multivariant analysis. In addition, some of the newer quantitative techniques succeed in combining variance and processes approaches. For example, in *event history* methods, variables are identified, but the analysis procedures take into account both changes in the values of independent and dependent variables and the timing of such changes (see Tuma, Hannan, and Groeneveld 1979; Tuma and Hannan 1984).

Creating Institutions

It is somewhat arbitrary to distinguish the processes involved in creating institutions from those employed to change them. Institutions do not emerge in a vacuum; they always challenge, borrow from, and, to varying degrees, displace prior institutions. The difference lies largely in the investigator's focus. If attention is directed primarily to the processes and conditions giving rise to new rules and associated practices, then we have a study of institutional creation. However, if the analyst examines how an existing set of beliefs, norms, and practices comes under attack, undergoes delegitimation, or falls into disuse, to be replaced by new rules, forms, and scripts, we have a study of institutional change. The former interests are reviewed here; the latter, in Chapter 8.

The analysis of institutional processes appears to vary significantly by what types of elements are invoked. Those examining regulative elements are more likely to be methodological individualists and to assume that individuals construct their rules and requirements by some kind of deliberative or calculative process. Pros and cons are weighed, cause and effect evaluated and argued, and considered choices are made. Majorities or authorities rule. Analysts examining institutions made up of normative elements are more likely to posit a more organic process, as moral imperatives evolve and obligatory expectations develop in the course of repeated interactions. Cultural-cognitive institutions appear by even more ephemeral processes. Particularly in early accounts, shared understandings, common meanings, and taken-for-granted truths seem to have no parents, no obvious sources.

Although there are differences in institutional processes, these characterizations, on reflection, are oversimplied and can be misleading. Consider regulative rules. If they appear rational and transparent, this reflects the extent to which certain types of social settings and procedures have been constructed to be—are institutionalized to serve as—seats of collective authority. A full analysis of regulatory rule making would examine the constitutive roots of the specific governance apparatus: the development of the forums, the evolution of rules for decision making and for selecting participants, and the "back-stage" activities (the fodder of political scientists) that enter into the creation of laws and legal rulings. Similarly, norms may evolve through interaction, but they can also be rationally crafted. Professional bodies and trade associations often create and amend their normative frameworks and standards via more conscious and deliberative processes. As with regulatory authorities, some social groups are endowed with special prerogatives allowing them to exercise moral leadership in selected arenas. Cognitive elements also result from both more and less rational choice processes and may be produced by inchoate collective interactions or by highly institutionalized cultural authorities. Folkways are produced by the former; scientific truths by the latter.

Suchman (1995a) provides an illuminating general discussion of conditions giving rise to new institutional arrangements. He suggests that the impetus for institutional creation is the development, recognition, and naming of a recurrent problem to which no existing institution provides a satisfactory repertoire of responses. These cognitive processes can be viewed as giving rise to collective sense-making activities (Weick 1995), as actors attempt to understand and diagnose the problem and propose what are, at the outset, various ad hoc solutions. Once these responses have been "generalized into solutions," it may be possible for the participants to engage in "a more thoroughgoing 'theorization' of the situation—in other words, to formulate general accounts of how the system works and, in particular, of which solutions are appropriate in which contexts" (Suchman 1995a:43). Solutions generated in one context may then diffuse to other situations regarded as similar. Note the extent to which Suchman's discussion maps onto and builds from Berger and Luckmann's (1967) general formulation of institutionalization.

The foregoing description is meant to be sufficiently abstract to be applicable to any level of analysis, from the organizational subsystem to the world system. Suchman (1995a) proposes that the question of where institutions arise—at what level—is determined by "where in the social structure particular shared understandings arise" (p. 41). That is, this question is to be settled empirically, by observing the locus of the social processes at work.

I turn now to describe briefly several studies depicting the creation of institutional forms. The studies include both process and variance approaches and are ordered by level of analysis, proceeding from the macro to the micro. The accounts also vary in terms of their relative emphasis on regulative, normative, and cultural-cognitive elements and in terms of the assumptions made regarding the rationality of the actors.

Selected Studies of Institutional Creation

World-System–Level Studies

One of the most wide-ranging and well-known studies of this type at the world-system level is the historical (process) account provided by North and Thomas (1973) of "the rise of the Western world." These economic historians argue that economic growth will not occur unless there are mechanisms that closely align social and private rates of return. Individuals will be motivated to undertake socially desirable activities only if they provide private benefits that exceed private costs. This situation, in turn, requires that appropriate property rights be established and enforced. The need for such regulatory institutions, however, does not guarantee their development. Creating such structures is costly. Since the rise of the nation-state, governments have assumed responsibility for enforcing property rights; however, the interests and fiscal needs of rulers may encourage them to establish and enforce agreements that do not promote economic growth. Hence, "we have no guarantee that productive institutional arrangements will emerge" (North and Thomas 1973:8).

North and Thomas (1973) review historical evidence from the high Middle Ages to the beginning of the eighteenth century, noting developments in the political economy of Europe that advanced or depressed economic growth. They examine a number of cases and draw on a variety of historical materials, but their most detailed discussion contrasts political and economic developments during the period 1500 through 1700 in England, the Netherlands, Spain, and France. They conclude that by the beginning of the eighteenth century, "a structure of property rights had developed in the Netherlands and England which provided the incentives necessary for sustained growth" (p. 157). In England, for example, Tudor kings early became dependent on political support from the House of Commons, which was increasingly dominated by the rising merchant class, and political compromises pressed on the rulers resulted in expanded markets, both internal and colonial. By contrast, French kings developed methods of taxation that did not require them to extend markets, eliminate hereditary land tenure, or challenge the power of guilds and monopolies to secure adequate revenue to support army and court. The interests of the fledgling bourgeoisie were not recognized or protected.

Even though their particular interpretation of history has not gone unchallenged (see, e.g., Wallerstein 1979), North and Thomas do provide a careful examination of ruling elites located in contrasting historical conditions who made choices that gave rise to markedly different institutional arrangements regulating economic activity.

Field-Level Studies

Dezalay and Garth (1996) provide a detailed historical (process) account of the creation of an institutional framework at the international level for resolving disputes between businesses in different countries: transnational commercial arbitration rules and practice. Although their scope is international, they focus on the creation of a specific organizational field. Their history depicts the construction of an international legal field: the gradual and conflictful development of an arena with defined boundaries, central players, and accepted ground rules for dispute resolution.

The focus of their history is the transformation that begins to occur in the 1970s, as an elite "club" of "grand old men" centered in Paris confronts increased demand for arbitration services fostered by burgeoning international trade and globalization. This demand brings into the arena a new generation of "technocrats" housed in corporate law firms in the United States. The delicate transition is negotiated by the International Chamber of Commerce, which succeeds in transferring the legitimacy of the former elite to an expanding set of arbitrators in a classic instance of increased bureaucratization and rationalization of the field. Personal charisma is gradually replaced by routinized, impersonal, specialized expertise. Maintaining legitimacy is essential for the continued success of arbitration if it is "to provide a basis to govern matters that involve powerful economic and political entities" (Dezalay and Garth 1996:33).

Dezalay and Garth (1996) provide a finely nuanced account of "the contests through which the field and the markets of arbitration are constituted" (p. 41). Although all participants are depicted as attempting to pursue their respective interests, the tale told is not one of rational design but of improvisation, conflict, and compromise.

DiMaggio's (1991) study of the efforts by professionals to create the cultural conditions that would support the development and maintenance of art museums during the late nineteenth century in America is also cast at the organizational field level, but it is limited to a single society.[3] In his process account, DiMaggio gives primary attention to cultural-cognitive aspects of the professional project: the creation of distinctions between high and low forms of art, and the creation of and selection among cultural models for constituting art museums as distinctive types of organizations. Struggles are depicted among contending factions and between the interests of new types of professionals—curators, art historians, acquisition experts—and those of museum managers. Philanthropic foundations, specifically the Carnegie Corporation, are shown to play a pivotal role as they work to advance the interests of the new museum professionals. DiMaggio asserts that agency and interests are more apparent when the focus is on the creation of new institutional arrangements rather than the routine operation of existing ones.[4]

Population-Level Studies

Shifting to the population level, institutional construction concerns primarily the creation of new organizational *forms*. In his now-classic discussion of organizations and social structure, Stinchcombe (1965) identified organizational forms as an important topic of study and pointed out that organizational foundings of the same type tend to be concentrated in particular historical periods. Moreover, because new organizations must rely on existing ideas, technologies, and social routines, organizations take on a character—are *imprinted* by their institutional environment—so as to reflect the historical conditions of their origin. Finally, these differences, although they reflect the somewhat arbitrary conditions of their birth, tend to persist over time. Organizational forms exhibit substantial inertia. Stinchcombe assembled data on differences in the labor force composition of varying industries to illustrate this effect, demonstrating that industries founded in different periods tended to exhibit differing labor force characteristics and that these differences were maintained over long time periods.

These insights have provided an important touchstone for both population ecologists and institutional theorists. Ecologists are necessarily concerned with the problem of identifying meaningful organizational forms. After all, it is difficult to enumerate organizational populations if their identification is problematic. Theorists like McKelvey (1982) have proposed broad taxonomies, but most ecological scholars use a more pragmatic approach that focuses on identifying similarities in key properties, such as stated goals, hierarchical forms, and core technologies (see Hannan and Freeman 1989).

Institutionalists Greenwood and Hinings (1993) stress the cognitive dimension in their attempt to identify distinctive organizational forms or archetypes, which they define as "a set of structures and systems that consistently embodies a single interpretive scheme" (p. 1055). Although they emphasize the importance of environmental niches associated with distinctive patterns of resource usage, ecologists also increasingly recognize that organization forms and the boundaries between them are institutionally defined and constructed. Although the differences involved may have their origins in technologies, in the characteristics of clients served, or in resources consumed, particular arrangements come to be seen as the "natural" way to carry out certain types of activities. Institutionalizing processes ensue,

> transforming arbitrary differences into differences with real social consequences. In this sense, nominal classifications become real classifications. They become real in their consequences when they serve as bases for successful collective action, when powerful actors use them in defining rights and access to resources, and when members of the general population use

them in organizing their social worlds. Thus, the clarity of a set of boundaries is not a permanent property of a set of classifications. Rather, the real-
ism of distinction among forms depends on the degree of institutionalization that has occurred. (Hannan and Freeman 1989:57)

In the following section, we consider the way in which ecologists measure degree of institutionalization.

Mohr and Guerra-Pearson (forthcoming) illustrate the application
of such arguments in their study of the emergence of differentiated
populations of welfare organizations in New York City during the period 1888 to 1907 (see also Mohr 1994).[5] They suggest that differentiation in these populations occurred along three axes: the sorts of sta-
tuses recognized and the merit they were accorded, the kinds of social
needs or problems identified, and the kinds of solution repertoires recognized. Client differentiation was driven by power struggles surrounding these three socially constructed dimensions.

Organizational forms are significant because they provide the containers
into which these three dimensions of institutional life are poured and they
provide the empirical foundations around which conflicts over how these
three primitive institutional elements will be combined are negotiated and
struggled over. (Mohr and Guerra-Pearson forthcoming)

The researchers examined data from city directories at the turn of
the century and, with the use of multidimensional scaling techniques,
were able to map changes over time in the coherence of organizational
boundaries as selected forms came to be seen as preferred ways of organizing specified services.

As another example of a study of institutional construction at the
population level, Suchman (1995a, in press) combines process and
variance approaches in his study of the creation of organizational forms
for semiconductor firms in California's Silicon Valley. Creating a new
organization requires not only resources but also ideas or models on
how to organize. Conventional histories celebrate the role of Stanford
University engineers in providing the designs and early material resources
for start-up companies (see, e.g., Saxenian 1994). Although acknowl-
edging this contribution, Suchman (forthcoming) lays the groundwork
for a "genetics of organization" that examines both the flows of operational resources and of "constitutive information," including "available

routines, rules, and taken-for granteds." He outlines an organizational *genetics*, concerned with the development and preservation of distinctive species or forms, to supplement organizational ecology, which focuses on competition among existing species or types of organizations. In established organizational fields, most new organizations are "reproducer" rather than "innovative" forms because they largely copy routines and competencies from existing organizations (Aldrich 1999:80). But when fields are in their early stages of development, organizations cannot simply copy successful recipes. Under such circumstances, Suchman suggests, a process of *compilation* may be employed whereby information intermediaries, such as consultants or lawyers, observe existing, relatively heterogenous practices and attempt to distill a core set of organizing principles. In his process account, Suchman (1994) describes how lawyers and venture capitalists in the Silicon Valley functioned as deal makers, linking clients with various transactional partners, and as counselors, formulating and disseminating standardized solutions to recurrent problems.[6]

Shifting to a variance approach, Suchman (1995a) analyzes data on 108 venture capital–financing contracts from two Silicon Valley venture capital funds. Such contracts bring together the venture capitalists, lawyers, and entrepreneurs in the crucial founding event, constituting the structure of relations between these parties as they jointly form the start-up company. The contracts were coded along numerous dimensions, and these scores were then used to calculate measures of contractual standardization as an indicator of increasing institutionalization. Suchman's analysis reveals that standardization was strongly correlated to both date of filing and location of the law firm that drafted the contract. In general, standardization of contracts was greater the later in the time period they were filed and the closer the location of the law firm drafting the contract was to the core of the Silicon Valley.

Organization-Level Studies

Oliver Williamson embraces (boundedly) rational choice assumptions and employs a variance rather than a process approach. As discussed in Chapter 2, he has developed an explanatory framework within which economic agents are expected to devise or select those governance forms that will minimize transaction costs. He leaves to economic historians and sociologists the tasks of accounting for the characteristics of *institutional environments*—the "background conditions" including property rights, norms, customs, and similar frameworks—focusing rather on the "mechanisms of governance," which he sees as the central focus of the economics of organizations (Williamson 1994:79-80). Designers of organizational governance arrangements must take into account these wider institutional conditions when fashioning their structures, and, over time, their choices feed back to affect environmental conditions, including institutional environments.

Walker and Weber (1984) test Williamson's arguments that transactions involving higher uncertainty and greater asset specificity (specialized skills or machinery) would be more likely to be produced rather than purchased by a firm. That is, organizational designers will elect to have such tasks governed by the firm's hierarchy rather than by the market. Their study of 60 "make or buy" decisions within a division of a large automobile company found results generally consistent with these predictions, although, unexpectedly, the researchers found that comparative production costs had a larger impact on these decisions than did transaction costs.[7]

Studies by Armour and Teece (1978) and by Teece (1981) attempt to empirically evaluate Williamson's arguments regarding the relation between a firm's governance structure and its economic performance. Following Chandler's (1962) early insights and historical research, Williamson (1975) had argued that firms adopting a multidivisional (M-form) structure would be more capable of separating strategic from operational decision making, allocating capital among divisions, and monitoring divisional performance. Armour and Teece study a sample of diversified firms in the petroleum industry and find that those firms adopting the M-form structure performed better financially. Teece (1981) extends the test to evaluate the performance of pairs of firms matched by size and product line in 20 industries. The performance of the firm first adopting the M-form (the "lead" firm) was compared with that of the matched firm for two time periods. Again, the results confirmed the hypotheses.

Williamson, in concert with other practitioners of the new institutional economics, argues, in effect, that managers will attempt to design the boundaries and the governance structures of their firms so as to economize on transaction costs. This emphasis, as David (1992) observes, assumes that these institutional arrangements represent "presently efficient solutions to resource allocation problems" and that "institutional arrangements are perfectly malleable" (pp. 2-3). Such assumptions are at odds with those held by most sociologists and economic historians, who stress the effect of past events on present institutions and the likelihood that these structures will resist change. Williamson also employs functional explanations in accounting for changes in organizational governance structures (see Granovetter 1985). Such explanations attempt to account for the existence and maintenance of a given social structure by noting what functions it performs to assist adaptation. To be valid, such explanations need to specify the causal feedback loop by which the forces maintaining the structure are selected and reinforced, although most analysts are content to argue "as if" rather than to demonstrate such connections (see Stinchcombe 1968; Elster 1983).

Like Williamson, Terry Moe focuses on the level of the individual organization. He has been particularly inventive in applying rational choice perspectives to the design of public agencies. Adopting the perspective of institutional economists, Moe views organizations primarily as governance systems, emphasizing regulatory elements. Moe (1990a) points out that governmental structures differ from those in the private sector in that, unlike the world of voluntary exchange, "people can be forced to [give up resources involuntarily] by whoever controls public authority" (p. 221). The legitimate use of coercive power distinguishes public from private authorities. The problem confronted by political actors in democratic systems is that, although they can use their power to design institutional arrangements that serve their interests, the possibility exists that opposing parties will come to power and employ the same instruments to serve their own ends. To deal with this problem of the uncertainty of political control, Moe argues, public authorities restrict the discretion of agencies and envelop them in detailed rules and procedures.

> Obviously, this is not a formula for creating effective organizations. In the interests of political protection, agencies are knowingly burdened with cumbersome, complicated, technically inappropriate structures that undermine their capacity to perform their jobs well. Nor, obviously, is this a formula for effective hierarchical control by democratic superiors. Insulationist devices are called for precisely because those who create public bureaucracy *do not want* a truly effective structure of democratic control. (Moe 1990a:228; emphasis in original)

These pathologies are particularly likely to develop in political systems based on the separation of power, such as the United States, compared to parliamentary systems, such as the United Kingdom.

The "politics of structural design" become even more perverse in situations where Congress and the White House are controlled by opposing parties. Moe (1989) provides a detailed process account of the creation of the Consumer Product Safety Commission, an agency created when Richard Nixon, a Republican, was president and was compelled to work with a Democratic Congress. Consumer interests, allied with those of Congress, were successful in their struggle to create an independent agency separate from cabinet departments, which were viewed as overly conservative. Strict procedural rules were imposed to ensure that the agency would attend to consumer interests. However, business interests, with the support of the administration, made sure that ample provision was made for their input and review of all pending decisions and that enforcement powers were not vested in the commission but in an independent agency, the Justice Department. The initial design of the agency reflected the contending interests of the parties, and subsequent modifications were governed by the shifting political power of consumer versus business interests.

Philip Selznick, like Moe, also examined the design of a public agency. However, in his well-known account of the evolution of the Tennessee Valley Authority (TVA), Selznick (1949) eschews a rational choice framework, as he depicts processes that undermine rational design. He provides a historical account of the development over time of a distinctive ideology and set of normative commitments on the part of TVA officials. As I noted in reviewing Selznick's views in Chapter 2, his approach describes how the original structure and goals of this innovative government corporation were transformed over time by the commitments of its participants to the means of action. In Selznick's (1957) work, to institutionalize is "to infuse with value beyond the technical requirements of the task at hand" (p. 17), as intrinsic worth is accorded to a structure or process that originally possessed only instrumental value. Although Selznick thus emphasizes normative beliefs and values in his analysis, he also attends to the importance of cognitive features of organizations. His discussion of the role played by grassroots ideology in framing decisions and garnering support from important constituencies is central to his argument (see Selznick 1996).

Selznick's approach focuses on internal relations, especially on informal structures rather than on formal structures, and on the immediate environment of the organization rather than on more general cultural rules or characteristics of the wider organizational field (see DiMaggio and Powell 1991). The carriers of institutionalized values are relational structures, in particular, informal structures and co-optative relations linking the organization with salient external actors, both individual and collective.[8]

Selznick's argument stresses the importance of power processes: the vesting of interests in informal structures and the co-optation of external groups who acquire internal power in return for their support. His analysis of the TVA examines the ways in which particular constituencies, such as the agricultural interests on whom the organization was dependent, were able to modify agency programs in ways that compromised its conservation program. And, as discussed in Chapter 2, Stinchcombe's (1968) amplification of Selznick's arguments stresses the ways in which power is used to perpetuate these interests and values over time.

Diane Vaughn (1996) weaves together many of the same kinds of arguments to account for the continued use of a flawed design by Morton Thiokol engineers and the fateful decision by NASA officials to launch the Challenger missile. Her richly detailed historical account of the organizational routines, both technical and decision making, that led up to the disaster depicts the development of a culture within which "signals of potential danger" were "repeatedly normalized by managers and engineers alike" (p. xiii). Although production pressures played an important role, these pressures themselves "became institutionalized and thus a taken-for-granted aspect of the worldview that all participants brought to NASA decision-making venues" (p. xiv.).

Selznick's interest in organizations that become defined by their commitments to distinctive values has been pursued by a new generation of researchers interested in organizational identity. Defined as a commitment to values that are "central, enduring, and distinctive," *organizational identity* provides participants with a core set of normative and cultural-cognitive elements around which to craft their narratives and sense-making activities (see Albert and Whetten 1985; Whetten and Godfrey 1999).

Interpersonal-Level Studies

Axelrod (1984) employs the "prisoner's dilemma" situation to examine the conditions under which individuals who pursue their own self-interest in the absence of a central authority will evolve norms of cooperation. The prisoner's dilemma involves a situation in which two players make one of two choices: cooperation (*c*) or noncooperation (*n*). The payoff matrix is such that if both players opt for *c*, then both receive an intermediate reward; if both select *n*, they receive a low reward; but if one player selects *c*, when the other selects *n*, the former (sucker) receives no reward whereas the latter (exploiter) receives a high reward. Players are not allowed to exchange any type of information other than their choices, and the game is played over a number of trials. The challenge for each player is to provide incentives and encourage the formation of norms to induce the partner to cooperate. However, the knowledge of each player is limited, and any normative structure that develops must be fashioned incrementally.

In a novel design, Axelrod (1984) invited other game theorists from many disciplines to compete in a computer tournament to select the best game strategy by submitting a program that embodies rules to select the cooperative or noncooperative choice on each move. Such a program provides a complete process description of the sequence of decisions during the course of the encounter. Of the 14 strategies submitted, the most successful was the "tit for tat" decision rule, a strategy that starts with a cooperative choice and thereafter selects whatever the other player did on the previous move. This simple strategy provided the best payoff to the player adopting it under a wide range of simulated conditions. Axelrod (1984) summarizes its virtues:

> What accounts for TIT FOR TAT's robust success is its combination of being nice, retaliatory, forgiving, and clear. Its niceness [never initiating noncooperation] prevents it from getting into unnecessary trouble. Its retaliation discourages the other side from persisting whenever defection is tried. Its forgiveness helps restore mutual cooperation. And its clarity makes it intelligible to the other player, thereby eliciting long-term cooperation. (p. 54)

Although it may be argued that the prisoner's dilemma is "just a game," it encapsulates an important dilemma built into many real-world situations, from the school yard to international diplomacy. It is to cope with such situations that security regimes and similar types of institutions develop (see Krasner 1983; Mares and Powell 1990). A particularly important element of the conditions supporting the rise of stable cooperative norms is that "the future must have a sufficiently large shadow" (Axelrod 1984:174). The anticipation of future interaction provides an important stimulus to evoke norms of reciprocity; indeed, such norms are argued to undergird the stability of much ongoing economic and social behavior, making it less necessary for parties to resort to such expensive alternative regulatory structures as the legal system and police force (see Macaulay 1963).

Comparative Comments and a Concluding Observation

The studies briefly summarized differ in a number of important respects. They are organized by level of analysis but also vary in assumptions made about rationality of actors and salience of institutional elements. Among the various studies reviewed, Moe and Williamson assume a higher level of rational choice exercised by actors in designing institutional arrangements. In these studies, actors are assumed to be pursuing their individual interests armed with substantial knowledge of alternatives and their relation to consequences. Hence, the critical questions are when and why it is in an actor's self-interest to construct and maintain institutional structures that will govern not only others' but one's own behavior. Other theorists embrace a less restrictive conception of rationality, assuming that although individuals attempt to pursue their interests, they do so with imperfect knowledge and intelligence. Errors in judgment occur, and unintended consequences result. Rather than conceiving of institutions as "sets of predesigned rules," these theorists are more apt to see them as "unplanned and unintended regularities (social conventions) that emerge 'organically'" (Schotter 1986:118). Among the studies reviewed, North and Thomas and Axelrod best exemplify these assumptions.

Although analysts in all of the studies presume that participants have interests and examine the processes by which contending interests are resolved, researchers such as Dezalay and Garth, DiMaggio, Mohr, Selznick, and Suchman view such interests not simply as pre-existing but also as constructed in the course of the interaction and negotiation processes.

With respect to institutional elements, North and Thomas, Moe, and Williamson place primary emphasis on regulatory structures. Axelrod, Dezalay and Garth, Selznick, and Vaughn attend largely to normative elements, although the latter three studies also consider cultural-cognitive elements. Suchman and DiMaggio highlight the role of cultural-cognitive processes of institutional creation.

A concluding comment is warranted on institutional creation. Most extant theory and research emphasizes a "demand-side" view of institutional formation. It is argued that institutions come into existence because players perceive problems requiring new approaches. Participants are motivated by their discomfort in ongoing situations to devise or borrow new and different rules and models. John Meyer proposes that institutional creation is also driven by "supply-side" processes.

Meyer's (1994) arguments are developed primarily at the world system level but are applicable to other levels. He suggests that certain types of actors, particularly those in the sciences and professions, occupy institutionalized roles that enable and encourage them to devise and promote new schemas, rules, models, routines, and artifacts. They see themselves as engaged in the great project of rationalization whereby more and more arenas of social life are brought under the "rubric of ideologies that claim universal applicability" (p. 42). The adoption of these generalized principles and procedures is promoted as evidence of modernization, regardless of whether local circumstances warrant or local actors need or want these developments. At the international and societal levels, general rules and principles are promulgated by professional associations and a wide range of nongovernmental organizations (see Boli and Thomas 1997, 1999); at the level of the organizational field, organizational population, and individual organization, the carriers and promoters include foundations, management schools, accounting and auditing firms, and consulting companies (see DiMaggio and Powell 1983).

Maintaining and Diffusing Institutions

Maintaining Stability

The concept of institution connotes stability and persistence. Is stability problematic? Once an institutional structure is in place, is there anything else to be said? A good many students of organizations assume that institutionalization is an absorbing state and, once completed, requires no further effort at maintenance. Simon ([1945] 1997), for example, describes a number of reasons for the persistence of behavioral patterns once established. He emphasizes, in particular, cognitive patterns: "The activity itself creates stimuli that direct attention toward its continuance and completion" (p. 106). Such individual-level, attention-directing processes also act to decrease the individual's sensitivity to external stimuli. Organizational ecologists also assume that stability or, in their terms, *inertia*, is a normal state for organizations. Inertia is the product of such organization-level processes as sunk costs, vested interests, and habitualized behavior, shored up by the external constraints imposed by contractual obligations to exchange partners and regulatory regimes (see Hannan and Freeman 1984, 1989). Change is assumed to be both difficult and dangerous for organizations.

Other theorists, however, argue that persistence cannot be taken for granted. Zucker (1988b), for example, suggests that entropy—"a tendency toward disorganization in the social system" (p. 26)—is the more normal condition. Things—structures, rules, routines—tend to fall apart. She argues, as a corollary, that deinstitutionalization is prevalent and has many roots. (These are considered in Chapter 7.) Persistence is seen to be tenuous and problematic. Theorists such as Giddens (1984) take an intermediate position. He emphasizes the extent to which the persistence of rules, norms, and beliefs requires actors to actively monitor ongoing social activities and continuously attend to maintaining the linkages with the wider social-cultural environment. Structure persists only to the extent that actors are able to continuously produce and reproduce it.

In my reading, most institutional scholars accord little attention to the issue of institutional persistence, and those who do disagree over what mechanisms underlie stability. In particular, the underlying conception of institution—whether cultural-cognitive, normative, or regulative—affects views of maintenance mechanisms. Cultural-cognitive theorists tend to emphasize the important role played by unconscious, taken-for-granted assumptions defining social reality. Jepperson (1991), for example, insists that the hallmark of an institution is its capacity for automatic maintenance, for self-restoration. Institutional mechanisms are those requiring no conscious mobilization of will or effort. Similarly, Zucker (1977) argues, "Internalization, self-reward, or other intervening processes need not be present to ensure cultural persistence because social knowledge once institutionalized exists as a fact, as part of objective reality, and can be transmitted directly on that basis" (p. 726).

To evaluate this claim, Zucker conducted an experimental study of institutions to assess the extent to which the degree of institutionalization was observed to affect the extent of uniformity, maintenance, and resistance to change exhibited by subjects. Her study used the classic Sherif (1935) stimuli, asking subjects to evaluate the amount of apparent movement by a stationary light in a darkened room. Extent of institutionalization was manipulated by instructions given to the subjects. To create lower levels of institutionalization, the subject was told only that the other person (a confederate) was "another person"; to create intermediate levels, the subject was told that she and her coworker (the confederate) were both "members of an organization," but their positions were unspecified; and to create higher levels of institutionalization, the subject was told that she and her coworker were both participants in an organization, and the coworker (confederate) was given the title of "Light Operator." Zucker (1977) reasons,

> Settings can vary in the degree to which acts in them are institutionalized. By being embedded in broader contexts where acts are viewed as institutionalized, acts in specific situations come to be viewed as institutionalized. Indicating that a situation is structured like situations in an organization makes the actors assume that the actions required of them by other actors in that situation will be . . . more regularized and that the interaction will be more definitely patterned than if the situation were not embedded in an organizational context. Any act performed by the occupant of an office is seen as highly objectified and exterior. When an actor occupies an office, acts are seen as nonpersonal and as continuing over time, across different actors. (pp. 728-29)

Note the extent to which Zucker's experiment is built on a cultural-cognitive conception of institutionalization. The only factor manipulated to account for the behaviors of subjects was their cognitive framing of the situation, including their own identity with it. No sanctions or other types of regulative controls or normative pressures were involved in producing the observed effects.

Zucker found that the extent of institutionalization exhibited the expected effects: Subjects working in more institutionalized (organization-like) conditions were more likely to transmit the standards they had learned in an initial series of trials (with the confederate supplying the standard) to a new naive subject; to maintain their standards over time (subjects were asked to return one week later to perform the same type of activity); and to resist attempts to change their judgments (having adopted the confederate's standard in the initial period, subjects were exposed to a second confederate who attempted to alter the standard). Zucker shows that in ongoing social systems, transmission of beliefs and practices to new actors is a vital process underlying persistence. Furthermore, more highly institutionalized practices, being more objectified, are more easily transmitted than less institutionalized behavior (Tolbert and Zucker 1996).

Theorists taking a normative view emphasize the stabilizing influence of shared norms, which are both internalized and imposed by others. Kilduff (1993), for example, in his examination of "the reproduction of inertia" in a multinational corporation, stresses the role of social networks whose members draw "on shared normative frameworks, [and] continually monitor interpersonal behavior" and of accounts that provide "an interpretive and normative base" to support ongoing behavior. The ease of maintenance and transmission of institutional practices is affected by the extent to which new recruits share similar beliefs and interpretive frameworks of current personnel. The more different the new members, the more effort must be expended to transmit existing beliefs and practices. And, in her study of law firms, Tolbert (1988) found that firms employing recruits from more heterogeneous training backgrounds were more likely to use special training programs, mentoring systems, more frequent evaluations, and other socialization mechanisms than firms employing recruits from the same law school.

Other theorists focus on the central role of the environment, not only in fostering the acceptance of innovations (see below) but also in supporting and sustaining changes once they have occurred. In a study of public school districts in California, Rowan (1982) demonstrates that districts were more likely to adopt and retain innovations—new programs and personnel—when they were supported by "key members of the institutional environments of local systems," specifically, by state and federal legislatures, state educational agencies, state-level professional associations, and teacher-training institutions (p. 261). If support was lacking from one or more of these external constituencies, districts were less likely to adopt and more likely to drop the innovation, when viewed over a 40-year period.

Regulatory theorists are more likely to stress conscious control efforts, involving interests, agency and power, and the deployment of sanctions. Actors employ power not just to create institutions but also to preserve and maintain them over time (see Stinchcombe 1968; DiMaggio 1988). Neoinstitutional economists, including both transaction-cost and agency theorists, emphasize how important it is to devise appropriate governance structures and develop incentives and controls suited to the situation (see Pratt and Zeckhauser 1985). But if regulation is institutionalized, the rewarding and sanctioning take place within a framework of rules. Power is stabilized and legitimized, that is, institutionalized, by the development of rules.[9]

Some studies attend to the full range of forces supporting persistence: cultural-cognitive, normative, and regulative. In Miller's (1994) examination of a Pietist mission organization that has survived for almost two centuries, all of the institutional elements appear to be at work. The Basel Mission was founded in the early nineteenth century to educate missionaries and establish evangelical outposts in various parts of the world. Miller examined the records of this organization, focusing on the period 1815 to 1915, to ascertain the basis for its longevity. He argues that participants were recruited from a relatively homogeneous social base; were given intensive socialization, so that participants came to share similar beliefs and values; were placed in a strong authority structure combining aspects of charismatic, traditional, and bureaucratic control elements, together with formalized procedures of mutual surveillance; and were encouraged to develop a sense of "specialness and separation" that insulated them from being corrupted by the secular world.

In their study of the evolution over a 35-year period of a new industry devoted to the cochlear implant, a device to restore hearing to the deaf, Van de Ven and Garud (1994) analyze a series of events coded as creating variation (novel technical events), selection (rule-making events), and retention (rule-following events). The latter events, retention, are indicators of institutional persistence, because they refer to an event that "was programmed or governed by existing institutional rules and routines" (Van de Ven and Garud 1994:429)[10] Viewed over the period of study, their data show how novel technical events dominated during the developmental period from 1956 to 1983, rule-making and rule-following events grew in an oscillatory fashion during the middle period from 1983 to 1986, and then, by 1989, "no more institutional rule-making events occurred while rule-following events continued to occur" (p. 430). Van de Ven and Garud also describe how institutional rules operate to suppress innovation and to "constrain the flexibility of private firms to adapt to changing circumstances" as existing technologies were locked in to specific technological paths.

Institutional Diffusion

The diffusion of an institutional form across space or time has a triple significance in institutional analysis. First, diffusion of a set of rules or structural forms is often taken as an indicator of the extent or the strength of an institutional structure. In this sense, studies of institutional diffusion may be regarded as studies of increasing institutionalization. Second, because the diffusing elements are being adopted by and incorporated into organizations, studies of diffusion are also properly treated as studies of institutional effects. In such studies, early or later adoption is often argued to follow different principles because of the changing strength of the institutions and also because of the varying characteristics of the adopting organizations. Studies of factors affecting the adoption behavior of individual organizations are discussed in Chapter 7. Third, the spread of a new form or practice is also an instance of institutional change, but change of a particular kind. It is *convergent change,* change that reinforces and diffuses existing patterns (see Greenwood and Hinings 1996). Most institutional theory and research emphasize these processes. Only recently has attention turned to disruptive and divergent change, a topic I consider in Chapter 8.

Several distinctions are helpful in understanding the various ways in which institutions are diffused. DiMaggio and Powell's (1983) useful typology focuses attention on three contrasting mechanisms—coercive, normative, and mimetic—that identify varying forces or motives for adopting new structures and behaviors. As noted in Chapter 3, these mechanisms map well onto the three types of institutional elements I identify. Strang and Meyer (1993) distinguish between relational and cultural carriers of institutions. They point out that designs emphasizing relational carriers are based on social realist models, which assume that social actors are relatively independent entities who must be connected by specific networks or communication if diffusion is to occur.

By contrast, if cultural carriers are privileged, "diffusion processes often look more like complex exercises in the social construction of identity than like the mechanistic spread of information" (p. 489). Other analysts, such as Brown (1981), distinguish between demand- and supply-side explanations of diffusion. For many types of diffusion processes, it is equally or more useful to examine the character of the diffusion agent or the propagator than the attributes of the target or recipient units. These distinctions are employed to frame a brief review of diffusion studies.

Regulative Processes

To be effective, regulation requires relatively clear demands, effective surveillance, and significant sanctions. Beyond this, it also matters whether the mechanisms employed are primarily those of power, involving imposition of authority, where the coercive agent is viewed as a legitimate agent of control or whether they rely on the use of inducements (see Scott 1987). We would expect institutional effects—the depth or shallowness of institutionalization—to vary by these mechanisms, higher penetration being associated with authority. Numerous institutional forms are diffused by some combination of these mechanisms in the world of public and private organizations. Nation-states with statist or corporatist traditions are more likely to successfully employ coercive, regulative power in introducing innovations and reforms than pluralist or individualist systems (Jepperson and Meyer 1991). And private organizations routinely use their legitimate authority as well as carrots and sticks to introduce new forms and practices. Coercive mechanisms emphasize supply-side processes, directing attention to the characteristics of the diffusion agent and to relational carriers, noting the adequacy of information, inspection, and control systems.

Three empirical studies are described to illustrate the study of diffusion supported by regulatory authority. In their well-known study of the diffusion of civil service reforms, Tolbert and Zucker (1983) examine the diffusion of municipal civil service reform in the United States at the turn of the century, from 1885 to 1935. They contrast two types of diffusion process: the situation in which particular states adopted the reform and mandated that cities under their jurisdiction embrace it and the situation in which a state allowed individual cities to choose whether to adopt the reform. States mandating the reform employed legal procedures and official sanctions to enforce compliance; the institutional arrangement was that of a hierarchically structured authority system. By contrast, cities in states lacking mandates were responding to a social movement, a decentralized model of reform relying on normative and cultural-cognitive influences (see Chapter 7). Cities in states mandating the reform were much more likely to adopt civil service provisions than those in states lacking such mandates. They did so much earlier and more completely: Mandated reforms were adopted by 60% of the municipalities within a 10-year period (all did so within 37 years), whereas it took 50 years for unmandated reforms to approach the 60% level (see Tolbert and Zucker 1983:28-29).

In her study of profound social change in Japan in the late nineteenth century during the Meiji period, Westney (1987) provides a historical account of the conscious selection by Japanese officials of selected Western models regarded as successful for organizing particular organizational fields, such as police systems and postal services. These models, or organizational archetypes, were then imposed on the relevant sectors, employed as a basis for restructuring existing organizational arrangements. The diffusion of these models exhibited differing patterns, affected by the variable authority of the propagating officials, the presence of compatible pre-existing cognitive models supplied by indigenous organizations (e.g., the army for the police), and the availability of a supportive organizational infrastructure in the immediate environment. Westney emphasizes that although the original intent of the reformers had been to simply imitate and import successful practices from other societies, much inventiveness was required to fit these models into their new circumstances.

Cole (1989) examines differences among firms in Japan, Sweden, and the United States in the adoption and retention of innovative small-group activities such as quality circles. His analysis emphasizes the role played by varying national infrastructures—governmental agencies, trade associations, union organizations—in legitimating, informing, and supporting the innovations. Japan more than Sweden, and Sweden more than the United States, possessed such supportive structures, with the result that the innovations spread more widely and were more stable in the former than the latter societies. Although these three countries vary in the relative strength of regulatory statist authority, Cole's analysis also points to important differences in the extent to which trade associations and unions were mobilized to provide normative support for these innovations.

Normative Processes

Analysts focusing on normative processes stress the importance of network ties: relational structures as carriers. Many of the studies emphasizing normative processes focus on professional or collegial networks, on interlocking directorates (individuals who serve on multiple director boards), or on the support provided by informal ties.

Recent neoinstitutionalist scholars argue that regulatory activities thought to embody coercive pressures often depend more on normative and cognitive elements. Examining the effects of U.S. state influence on employers, Dobbin and Sutton (1998) call attention to the "strength of a weak state," as the state's inability to craft clear unambiguous legislation on employment gives rise to processes by which managers "recast policy-induced structures in the mold of efficiency" (p. 443). The state's role in eliciting change is obscured by managers' interests in collectively crafting a normative justification that creates a market rationale for their conformity. In a related discussion, Edelman, Uggen, and Erlanger (1999) suggest that it is not accurate to view legal actions by the state, such as the U.S. regulation of employment practices, as operating independently and from on high. Rather, when law is contested, "organizations actively participate in the meaning of compliance" in ways that "render law endogenous: the content and meaning of law is determined within the social field that it was designed to regulate" (p. 407). The meaning of laws mandating equal opportunity or affirmative action was negotiated and socially constructed by the actions and reactions of personnel managers, legislators, and the judiciary. And the diffusion of new forms and procedures was more responsive to norms carried by professional networks—for example, a firm's membership in personnel associations—than to changes in regulatory policies—for example, the weakening of regulation during the Reagan years (see also Baron, Dobbin, and Jennings 1986, discussed in Chapter 6).

Often, there is competition among those who promulgate normative models. For example, DiMaggio (1991) has described the contests occurring among professional camps holding competing visions for developing art museums during the early twentieth century in the United

States. Following Bourdieu, DiMaggio views professionalization as "the collective struggle of members of an occupation to define the conditions and methods of their work" (DiMaggio and Powell 1983: 147). We need more studies of the contested construction of normative models to guide organizing processes.

Normative standards may be explicitly established by self-appointed arbiters employing more or less representative bodies and deliberative procedures. Professional and trade associations present clear modern instances of such groups and processes. For example, after considerable struggle and compromise extending over many years, various medical associations joined forces with a managerial association, the American Hospital Association, to form the Joint Commission on Accreditation of Healthcare Organizations. Whereas licensure is a governmental, regulatory process, accreditation is a "nongovernmental, professional-sponsored process" aimed at promulgating high standards for the industry (Somers 1969:101). Although accreditation is not legally mandated, in professionally dominated arenas such as health care, organizations lacking accreditation are suspect and may not be eligible for reimbursement from certain funding sources. Empirical studies show for example that organizations such as hospitals, when accredited by appropriate professional bodies, were considerably more likely to survive than those lacking such normative support (see Ruef and Scott 1998).

In other cases, the norms governing organizations may arise more incrementally and informally. Westphal and Zajac (1994) examine the emergence in business circles, during the period 1970 through 1990, of an informal norm that the compensation of chief executive officers (CEOs) should be linked to the financial performance of their companies. Based on theoretical arguments by economists and supported by some empirical data showing the effects of such incentive plans on short-term stock prices, the argument took on moral weight as more and more boards of Fortune 500 companies adopted them. Corporate boards not taking such actions were regarded as negligent in their protection of stockholder interests. The practice spread rapidly among these companies.

Most empirical work focuses on factors affecting the diffusion of a successful normative model. Representative empirical studies of institutional diffusion of organizational forms and practices, perhaps the most widely studied aspect of institutional processes, are discussed in Chapter 7.

Cultural-Cognitive Processes

Following Berger and Luckmann, Strang and Meyer (1993) stress the centrality of cultural-cognitive elements in institutional diffusion processes. They argue that diffusion is greatly affected by various theorization processes. For diffusion to occur, the actors involved need to regard themselves as similar in some important respect (the creation of categories such as the generic *organizations* or particular subtypes such as *hospitals* facilitates this process). Theorization also provides causal accounts, explanations for why some kinds of actors need to add specific components or practices. Theorization contributes to objectification, a growing "consensus among organizational decision-makers concerning the value of a structure, and the increasing adoption by organizations on the basis of that consensus" (Tolbert and Zucker 1996:182).

Organizational ecologists have embraced the cultural-cognitive conception of institutions by recognizing that the density of organizations exhibiting a given organizational form—the simple number of organizations of a given type—can be interpreted as a measure of the legitimacy of that form: the extent to which it is institutionalized. For some years, ecologists documented the importance of *density dependence*: the observation that the number of organizations of a given type was positively correlated with the founding of additional organizations of the same type. Research on numerous, diverse populations of organizations revealed that as a new form emerged, numbers increased slowly at first, then more rapidly, finally tailing off or declining (for a review of these studies, see Hannan and Freeman 1989; Baum 1996: 84-89). Carroll and Hannan (1989) were the first to provide a theoretical interpretation of this empirical finding, arguing that organizational density serves as an indicator of the cognitive status of the form: its cognitive legitimacy. They propose that an organizational form is legitimate to the extent that relevant actors regard it as the natural way to organize for some purpose. From this perspective, rarity of a form poses serious problems of legitimacy. When few instances of a form exist, it can hardly be the natural way to achieve some collective end. On the other hand, once a form becomes prevalent, further proliferation is unlikely to have much effect on its taken-for-grantedness. Legitimacy, thus, grows in tandem with density but at a decreasing rate (pp. 525-26). In addition, as numbers increase in a given environment, legitimation processes give way to competitive processes.

This interpretation has proved to be controversial. Zucker (1989) argues that Carroll and Hannan provide no direct measure of legitimacy, simply assuming the connection between prevalence and legitimacy (see also Baum and Powell 1995). And Baum and Oliver (1992) suggest that prevalence may be only a proxy for other related effects such as embeddedness. Their study of day care centers in Toronto found that when measures of the latter, such as the number of relations between centers and governmental institutions, are included, density effects disappear. Carroll and Hannan (1989; Hannan et al. 1995) respond by noting the widespread use of indirect indicators in the sciences, the support for the association between prevalence and legitimacy provided by historical accounts related to the early experience of the populations studied, and the advantage offered by its applicability to any type of population.

Many other institutional scholars have studied the diffusion of ideologies or belief systems, forms, or archetypes—conceptions about how to organize—and processes or procedures. Nothing is as portable as ideas. They travel primarily by cultural carriers, although they also are conveyed by relations and artifacts. And although they may circulate via specific social networks, they also ride on more generalized media.

Mauro Guillén (1994) carried out detailed historical analyses comparing the diffusion of managerial ideologies in this century in the United States, Germany, Great Britain, and Spain. He differentiates between management theory—transmitted among intellectuals and indexed by the flow of books, articles, and professional discourse—and management practice, the use of techniques by practitioners as indicated by surveys and case studies. Scientific management, one of the major, early managerial ideologies, was discovered to be much more highly diffused among practitioners than among intellectuals and to have penetrated the United States and Germany much earlier than Great Britain and Spain. Guillén argues that differences among the four societies in international pressure, labor unrest, state involvement, and professional groups, among other factors, help to account for the differences in diffusion patterns observed.

Shocked out of their complacency by the fierce competition provided by Japanese automobile and electronics manufacturers in the mid-1970s, American firms began to explore and experiment with a range of practices that came to be labeled *total quality management* (TQM) (see Cole and Scott 2000). As described by Cole (1999), American businessmen were not quick to respond, unsure of the nature of the challenge they faced or what to do about it. A period of sense making ensued as communities of actors crafted and sifted interpretations (see Weick 1995, 2000). Although expert gurus offered insights, consulting companies proffered advice, professional associations (such as the American Society for Quality) offered normative justification, and award programs (for example, the Baldrige National Quality Award) offered prestige and financial incentives, little consensus developed regarding the core ingredients of TQM. The movement was not sufficiently theorized, nor was it supported by adequate normative and regulative structures, to diffuse widely or to have deep effects in this country. Some practices, such as quality circles, were widely discussed, but they tended to receive more lip service than use. Companies felt the need to change, but the directions and recipes they were offered did not provide clear guidelines. Perhaps the most important change associated with TQM was the cognitive framing of quality, shifting attention from the concerns of internal engineers to external customers and from a "detect and repair" to a "prevent and improve" mentality. And, although the quality fad seems to have run its course, it provided the basis for some useful organizational learning (see Cole 1999). All attempts at institutional diffusion do not succeed.

Concluding Comment

Students of organizations have paid more attention to how institutional forces affect organizational forms and processes than to how institutions themselves arise, persist, and diffuse. These latter questions, however, are attracting increased interest. In reviewing arguments and evidence on the development, persistence, and diffusion of institutions, we have put to work the distinctions developed in Chapters 3 and 4. In asking how institutions arise and persist, it matters whether they are conceived to be regulative, normative, or cultural-cognitive systems. The media that carry them and the level at which they operate also matter.

Another distinction is introduced that pertains more to how questions are posed by the analysts. Some, employing a variance approach, attempt to examine which factors best account for the characteristics or behavior of institutions. Others, employing a process approach, attempt to determine the way in which the factors came together—the sequence, the timing, the relative power and attentiveness of the actors—to produce the observed result. Both views shed light on how institutions are constructed and how they work.

How institutions persist, once created, is an understudied phenomenon. Our current understanding of social structures is that their persistence is not to be taken for granted. It requires continuing effort—both "talking the talk" and "walking the walk"—if structures are not to erode or dissolve. The conventional term for persistence, *inertia*, seems on reflection to be too passive and nonproblematic to be an accurate aid to guide studies of this topic.

By contrast, the diffusion of institutional forms over space and time has attracted considerable attention. Diffusion is of interest to the more theoretically oriented as a palpable indicator of institutional strength; to those of a more practical bent, and in a culture emphasizing modernity, such change is viewed as a sign of progress, and the adoption of new forms is seen as innovation. Most of the attention to diffusion has emphasized an adoption or demand-side approach. However, a supply-side perspective appears well suited to expanding our understanding of institutional processes, particularly those involving regulative mechanisms. It deserves more consideration.

A number of studies examining institutional diffusion processes were described, as I emphasized differences in the spread of regulative, normative, and cultural-cognitive forms. Additional research on diffusion, which emphasizes the interplay between institutional agents and organizational targets, is reviewed in Chapter 7.

Notes

1. Emirbayer (1997) examines the implications that follow from conceiving of the social world as consisting of substances or entities versus processes. I have pursued this topic with special reference to studying organizations versus organizing (see Scott forthcoming).

2. Alford (1998) proposes a similar distinction, differentiating between multivariant and historical approaches to the gathering of evidence. He also proposes a third, interpretive approach, and although many institutional theorists use these types of arguments, I do not pursue this here as a distinctive approach.

3. A possible limitation of this study is that it does not attend to potential sources of influence in field construction stemming from outside the United States. It is generally recognized that Americans looked to Europe for their models of high culture.

4. In addition to these macro approaches, a growing number of researchers are examining the cognitive dimension of the cultural-cognitive dyad, seeking to explore ways in which more

micro processes underlie macro structures. These studies focus on the perceptions and interpretations of managers as they consider what business they are in and which firms constitute their competitors and reference groups (see Chapter 6).

5. Note that whereas some types of organizational populations are defined in terms of their production technologies, service organizations tend to be defined in terms of their resource niche, including types of clientele served and funding sources (see McPherson 1983; Galaskiewicz and Bielefeld 1998).

6. Suchman (forthcoming) also identifies and illustrates a second reproductive process, *filiation,* in which single ancestor organizations reproduce themselves by spinning off new firms similar to themselves, often staffed by their own former managers and technical personnel.

7. More recent research suggests that this specific prediction may no longer hold in certain industries, including automobile manufacture. To protect and develop specific assets, partnering relations with suppliers are now more likely to be used than vertically integrated structures (Helper, MacDuffie, and Sabel 2000).

8. In his empirical work on the TVA, Selznick emphasizes the cressive, unplanned, and unintended nature of institutional processes. Valued commitments were generated over time as unplanned structures having unintended consequences. However, in his later, more prescriptive writing on leadership, Selznick (1957) argues for a more intentional model: Effective leaders are those who can define social values and obtain the support of others in preserving them.

9. Some have suggested that the new version of the golden rule is that he or she who holds the gold makes the rules! Still, rules can operate to constrain the arbitrary exercise of power (see Dornbusch and Scott 1975).

10. This is not meant to imply that institutional processes are only relevant to the retention phase. They also play a significant role in the variation phase (e.g., affecting the cognitive frames determining which models are devised) as well as the selection phase (where concerns for attaining legitimacy often determine which models are retained).

6

Institutional Processes
Affecting Societal Systems,
Organizational Fields,
and Organizational Populations

S ince the intellectual revolution that introduced open systems conceptions into the study of organizations during the 1960s, the importance of context or environment has come to be widely accepted
(see Katz and Kahn 1966; Scott 1998). But it was not until the late 1970s
that institutional facets of the environment were recognized and began
to be conceptualized and empirically examined. In this chapter and the
next, we trace the development of these ideas and describe and discuss
notable studies conducted to evaluate the various ways in which institutional forms and processes affect organizations. A substantial literature, both theoretical and empirical, exists on this topic (see Meyer and
Scott [1983b] 1992; Zucker 1988a; Powell and DiMaggio 1991; Scott
and Meyer 1994; Scott and Christensen 1995a; Brinton and Nee 1998).
Our review is organized primarily in terms of level of analysis, moving

from the more macro to the more micro. Although research has been conducted at all levels of analysis (see Table 4.2), we restrict attention to the four levels that have received the most attention from institutional analysts. In this chapter, effects on societal systems, organizational fields, and organizational populations are discussed. Effects on organizational structures and subunits are reviewed in Chapter 7.

To view organizations and organizational systems as being shaped by their environments without attending to the reverse effects—the ways in which organizations affect environments—is to oversimplify institutional processes to the point of distortion. Similarly, to attend too rigidly to the distinction between levels of analysis is to ignore the ways in which social phenomena operate as nested, interdependent systems, one level affecting the others. I consider these processes in Chapter 8 in connection with an examination of institutional change. The issue of change has come to the forefront in recent years, as organizational theorists recognize that institutions themselves are a moving target.

Institutional Agents and Processes

Before examining institutional effects at various levels, I begin by discussing four broad types of institutional influences that exercise strong effects at every level. DiMaggio and Powell (1983) astutely observe that the nation-state and the professions "have become the great rationalizers of the second half of the twentieth century" (p. 147). Other scholars point out the increasing importance of a wide array of international actors—professional and scientific associations, nongovernmental organizations, and multilateral agencies—that operate at a level above individual societies. Finally, cultural frameworks provide an important, newly recognized source of institutional influence. I briefly describe each source.

The Nation-State

From some perspectives, the state is simply another organizational actor: a bureaucratically organized administrative structure empowered to govern a geographically delimited territory. But such a view is limited and misleading. In our own time, and since the dawn of the modern era, the state has been allocated special powers and prerogatives and is consituted in such a way as to exercise them. As Streeck and Schmitter (1985a) point out, the state is not simply another actor in the environment of an organization: Its "ability to rely on legitimate coercion" (p. 20) makes it a quite distinctive type of actor. All organizations are correctly viewed as governance structures, but the state is set apart. Lindblom (1977) notes, "the special character of government as an organization is simply . . . that governments exercise authority over other organizations" (p. 21).

Campbell and Lindberg (1990) point out that the state exercises its effects in two distinct ways. On the one hand, the state is correctly viewed as a *collective actor,* or, more accurately in the case of liberal states, as a set of semi-autonomous actors. Among themselves and over time, state structures vary greatly in their overall strength or capacity, in the extent of their unification or fragmentation, and in their degree of federalization: the relative power and autonomy of local, regional, and national bodies (see Scott and Meyer [1983] 1991; Thomas and Meyer 1984; Abzug and Mezias 1993). They also vary in the extent to which public action and authority are concentrated in state agencies (the "strong" state) or distributed more widely throughout the society (the "weak state, strong polity") (see Jepperson and Meyer 1991).

As collective actors, agencies of the state can take a variety of actions, including granting special charters; allocating key resources, such as finance capital or tax-free loans; imposing taxes; and exercising regulatory controls. Political scientists and economists have examined the effects of such political controls on industries and firms (see Wilson 1980; Fromm 1981; Noll 1985). The state as a collective actor is associated particularly with the use of regulatory mechanisms of control. However, as discussed in Chapter 5, weak states, such as the United States, often exert their influence by stimulating normative pressures that induce change among targeted organizations (Dobbin and Sutton 1998; Edelman, Uggen, and Erlanger 1999).

Baron, Dobbin, and Jennings (1986) provide a descriptive historical account of the powers of the state to shape industry (field) and organizational features in their study of the evolution of modern personnel systems in the United States. The strongest evidence of state influence occurred in connection with the mobilization for World War II, when the federal government intervened to stabilize employment. Agencies such as the War Production Board, the War Labor Board, and the War Manpower Commission

> engaged in unprecedented government manipulation of labor markets, union activities, and personnel practices. These interventions . . . fueled the development of bureaucratic controls by creating models of employment and incentives to formalize and expand personnel functions. (Baron, Dobbin, and Jennings 1986:369)

In short, the pressures created were cultural-cognitive and normative, inducing conformity among professional managers, as well as coercive.

The second way in which the state can affect organizational systems at various levels is as an *institutional structure*. Campbell and Lindberg (1990) identify three modes of institutional effects. First, the state provides a "distinctive configuration of organizations" (p. 637), the structure of which itself exerts effects on the organizational systems at all levels. For example, Meyer and I (Scott and Meyer 1983) have examined the effects of state fragmentation—multiple, semi-autonomous centers of authority—on organizational fields and structures. Second, as institutional structures, states provide different arenas or forums within which conflicts between organized interests can be adjudicated (Campbell and Lindberg 1990). Political scientists Hult and Walcott (1990) provide a useful classification and analysis of a variety of such forums, ranging from hierarchical to adjudicative and from adversarial to collegial in their structure and modes of actions. Such arenas vary, for example, in where expertise resides, what decision rules are employed, and what forms of participation are permitted. These process differences, in turn, produce different outcomes. Hierarchies, for example, permit easier access and afford more rapid decisions but often ignore relevant differences among those presenting their cases. By contrast, courts pay close attention to the facts and circumstances surrounding particular cases but operate much more deliberately (see Jowell 1975; Melnick 1983).

Third, and arguably most important, states have the capacity to "define and enforce property rights, [that is], the rules that determine the conditions of ownership and control of the means of production" (Campbell and Lindberg 1990:635; see also Campbell, Hollingsworth, and Lindberg 1991). Labor laws, for example, affect what rights workers have to take collective action, and antitrust laws limit concentration of ownership and activities that constrain competition. The capacity to create and transform property rights is, of course, just a special case of the power vested in institutions to constitute actors, both individual and collective (see Chapter 3). For economic actors, property rights are among the most fateful and significant rights to be conveyed. Equally important are the rules established by nation-states to define the political rights accorded to citizens and interest groups. As institutional structures, arenas, and definers of property and political rights, states exert primarily cultural-cognitive effects on organizations and organizational systems (see Scott 1994d; Suchman and Edelman 1997).

Professions

In different times and places, varying groups lay claim to formal knowledge: In some situations, they are soothsayers; in others, they are priests; in still others, they are intellectuals; but in our own secularized and rationalized times, they are likely to be professionals.

Professionals exercise their control via cultural-cognitive and normative processes. More than other groups, "the professions rule by controlling belief systems. Their primary weapons are ideas. They exercise control by defining reality—by devising ontological frameworks, proposing distinctions, creating typifications, and fabricating principles or guidelines for action" (Scott and Backman 1990:290). The professions construct cognitive frameworks that define arenas within which they claim juridiction and seek to exercise control. Having knowledge in and of itself does not guarantee dominance, as Freidson (1986) and Abbott (1988) have been at pains to demonstrate. Governance structures must be created and jurisdictional claims defended—often with the aid of the state—if professional power is to be realized.

The interrelations between professional and political actors show exceeding variety and complexity over time and place, but such connections are in evidence for all successful professions. In some instances, the professional associations and practitioners have been so effective in staking out and defending their jurisdictional claims against competitors that they have been invited to assist the state in exercising control over all providers of designated services, both individual and corporate. Such has been the strong position of the medical profession in the United States, which is authorized both to exercise controls over a domain in lieu of state power and to share the powers of the state in governing the medical arena (see Freidson 1970; Scott 1982; Starr 1982). In other cases, the state has been in the forefront of creating a structure of rules, which have then been taken over and extended by professionals. This is the situation described by Baron, Dobbin, and Jennings (1986), when employment systems created by state coercion during the crisis of World War II were retained and diffused by a rapidly growing cadre of managerial and personnel professionals.

International Organizations and Associations

Joining nation-states and professions as important institutional actors exercising normative and regulative authority is an increasingly diverse array of organizations and associations operating at the international level. The dominant global actors in the contemporary world, in addition to nation-states, include transnational corporations and international nongovernmental organizations (INGOs). Although much attention has recently been devoted to globalization, the trend toward increased interdependence and the development of associations and movements with transnational agendas has been under way for many decades (see Boli and Thomas 1997, 1999). Still, a great upsurge in the development of both corporations and INGOs occurred in the period after World War II and continues up to the present. For example, whereas in 1900 about 200 INGOs were active, by 1980, over 4,000 were in existence.

How do INGOs obtain and exercise their influence? Boli and Thomas (1997) point out that, at the present time, they do not presume to displace or replace nation-states and, unlike states, they cannot make or enforce law. Unlike global corporations, they are not able to exercise coercive power and lack economic resources. Rather, "INGOs are more or less authoritative transnational bodies employing limited resources to make rules, set standards, propagate principles, and broadly represent 'humanity' vis-à-vis states and other actors" (p. 172). To account for the influence of INGOs (but also that of other forms such as professional associations and nation-states), Meyer, Boli, and Thomas (1987) prefer to see them primarily as carriers of more general cultural rules, as discussed below.

Cultural Frameworks

All of the institutional agents just discussed—nation-states, professions, international associations—are usefully regarded as important agents of normative and coercive influence on social life in many spheres. The perspective, however, draws heavily on a social realist ontology, which views such units as natural and purposive, as products of their own history and inherent needs. The picture is one of autonomous, albeit interdependent, collective social actors engaged in transactions and linked through dense networks of exchange and influence.

John Meyer and colleagues have developed and systematically pursued an alternative framework, labeled *macrophenomenological*, that embraces a social constructionist perspective and emphasizes cognitive-cultural processes (see Meyer, Boli, and Thomas 1987; Meyer 1994; Meyer et al. 1997; Boli and Thomas 1997). They argue that all of the collective actors we have described—nation-states, professions, and INGOs—are themselves a product and serve as carriers of broader, worldwide cultural frameworks supporting rationalization activities of many types. They function less as independent agents and more as enactors of social scripts.

Cultural arguments can, of course, be formulated at any and all levels of analysis. However, Meyer and colleagues develop their arguments at the world-system level, attempting to show that some of the ostensibly most powerful and autonomous actors, such as nation-states, are constituted by cultural forces. They argue that nation-states follow blueprints developed and promulgated at the level of the world system. How else can the isomorphism of nation-states be explained, the extent to which national societies claim the same prerogatives and exhibit similar structures despite widely varying histories, economic circumstances, geography, and demographic composition? Numerous studies by Meyer and colleagues show that nation-states that have more ties to the world system (for example, more connections to INGOs) are more likely to exhibit structures and processes associated with modernity (Meyer et al. 1997).

Similarly, although the global environment is increasingly traversed by a complex mix of transnational actors—businessmen, financiers, scientists, and activists, as well as a growing number of INGOs—these individual and collective actors can be viewed as carriers of global cognitive-cultural elements. As Meyer (1994) asserts, "this environment functions less as a coherent rational superactor (e.g., a tightly integrated state or a highly coordinated invisible hand) than as an evolving set of rationalized patterns, models, or cultural schemes" (p. 33). These organizations do not command and control but rather inspire and inform. The same general argument can be applied to the professions. "Such institutionalized patterns affect the rise and evolution of organizations through their dominance as cognitive models" (Meyer 1994:33).

Tolbert and Zucker (1996) insist that "a focus on the role of cultural understandings" is the argument that gives institutionalism its "theoretical distinctiveness" (p. 180). They suggest that arguments involving regulative and normative processes, because they emphasize sanctions and instrumental behavior, are conflated with those associated with resource-dependence theory, as developed by Pfeffer and Salancik (1978). However, this appears to me to be largely a "family quarrel" among different types of institutionalists, some embracing a more cultural and others a more regulative or normative perspective. Institutional arguments emphasize rules, norms, and cognitive frameworks, but it does not follow that other mechanisms of control are excluded, only that they occur in combination with rule-based elements, such as legitimate power (authority) or morally governed expectations.

Institutional Processes and Societal Systems

Three studies are reviewed to illustrate empirical work examining institutional processes at the societal level, focusing particularly on those having consequences for organizations. The studies compare institutional systems across two or more societies and examine their effects on economic policies and industrial structure. The studies reviewed are Whitley's examination of differences in how firms and markets are socially constructed in China, Japan, and Korea; Dobbin's study of the effects of industrial policy in England, France, and the United States on the development of railroads; and Biggart and Guillén's study of the rise of auto industries in South Korea, Taiwan, Spain, and Argentina. All of the studies emphasize the importance of history, attending to when and how developments occurred, and they use primarily a process approach.

Whitley (1992a) focuses on institutional arrangements shaping economic activities: the structure of markets and firms. He takes a relatively broad view in his conception of institutions. He differentiates between more basic or "background" institutions "that structure general patterns of trust, cooperation, identity, and subordination in a society" and those "proximate" institutions that are more directly involved in the economic system, including arrangements for obtaining financial resources and labor power, together with the "overall political and legal system which institutionalizes property rights [and] provides security and stability . . . for business activities" (Whitley 1992c:19, 25). The latter are often created as a by-product of the industrialization process itself and frequently develop in association with the formation of the state.

The key dimensions of business systems that Whitley (1992b) seeks to account for are (a) the nature of firms as economic actors, including the extent to which firms dominate the economy and how they share risks; (b) the nature of authoritative coordination and control systems within firms, including the types of authority exercised and extent of differentiation and decentralization; and (c) the nature of market organization, including the extent of interdependence among firms and the role of competitive versus cooperative ties (pp. 129-30).

In particular, Whitley (1992b) proposes to analyze and explain the

> emergence of distinctive "business recipes" in various institutional environments. . . . These business recipes, or systems, are particular ways of organizing, controlling, and directing business enterprises that become established as the dominant forms of business organization in different societies. They reflect successful patterns of business behaviour and understandings of how to achieve economic success that are reproduced and reinforced by crucial institutions. (p. 125)

Whitley argues that no single economic logic exists; rather, the rules of markets and the recipes for succeeding in them are socially constructed, varying over time and place. As supporting evidence for his argument, Whitley provides a detailed analysis of the quite substantial differences in the types of firms—their rights, composition, extent and modes of interdependence—and in the nature of what is defined as successful and legitimate business practice in contemporary China, Japan, and Korea (see Whitley 1992a).[1]

Dobbin (1994b) examines the effects of diverse political cultures at the societal level on industrial policy strategies and the resulting industrial structure for promoting the growth of railroads during the late nineteenth century. He contrasts the underlying cultural frames operating in Britain, France, and the United States to support and guide railroad development. American political culture gave early priority to community control over planning and finance but subsequently located authority in the market rather than the town meeting, with the central state acting as referee. "French political culture constructed state sovereignty as the key to political order, and rail policies made state control over planning, finance, coordination, and competition the key to economic order and efficiency" (p. 214). British political culture symbolized the sovereignty of the individual and accorded legitimacy to entrepreneurs to control planning, finance, and coordination (pp. 214-15). These varying conceptions as to where to locate agency and how to construct governance structures led to very different approaches to finance (mixes of public and private funds) planning (central versus local) and coordination (market versus state) and, hence, to the development of different railway systems. For example, the French system was publicly funded and regulated and highly centralized: All rail lines converged on Paris. By contrast, the U.S. system was privately financed (albeit with state subsidies, particularly land grants), planning was in the hands of individual states and local communities, and coordination was through market forces. The initial result was a gerrymandered nonsystem of discrete rail systems, ill-coordinated until a late period of market consolidation.

Biggart and Guillén (1999) contrast paths of economic development in four countries: South Korea, Taiwan, Spain, and Argentina, focusing on the automobile assembly and components industries. They propose that these divergent paths of economic development can be explained by taking account of a society's distinctive institutional pattern of organizing and the opportunities made available by global markets. Each society acquires, as a result of its distinctive historical development, a set of organizing logics: beliefs, norms, routine practices. These logics—like Whitley's recipes—are systems of internally coherent ideas that (a) inhibit the development of alternative models, even if they are "more efficient"; and (b) provide "repositories of distinctive capabilities that allow firms and other economic actors to pursue some activities in the global economy more successfully than others" (p. 726).

All four countries recognized the importance of auto manufacturing as a strategy for development, but they pursued different paths and experienced varying degrees of success. South Korea and Spain currently rank among the top auto-assembly exporters; Spain also exports components. Taiwan exports components, whereas Argentina has not been able to compete successfully in international markets. Biggart and Guillén argue that pre-existing organizational patterns account for the relative success of each strategy. For example, South Korea's *chaebol* (large family-dominated business groups) enabled them to be effective at assembly, but the structure of these groups prevented suppliers from establishing effective, independent export ties for components.

Whitley, Dobbin, and Biggart and Guillén all employ a comparative approach, contrasting differing societies. Their studies are historical, following the course of events in each society over time. Dobbin gives particular attention to agency, noting which actors are active and effective and whose interests are advanced. So also do Biggart and Guillén, who examine the role of local business enterprises, multinational companies, and the state. All the analysts take a social constructionist perspective: Actors may be pursuing their interests, but the actors, their social location, and modes of action are socially constituted. Whitley embraces a relatively broad conception of institutions, and Biggart and Guillén emphasize institutional logics (normative and cultural-cognitive elements), whereas Dobbin gives primacy to cultural-cognitive elements. Of most interest, all of these analysts expand the scope of institutional analysis by insisting that "instrumental practices are at the same time cultural" (Dobbin 1994a:127). Culture is not restricted simply to the study of norms but also encompasses the social rules by which we create value and craft "intersubjective understandings of cause and effect" (Dobbin 1994b:18). Institutional studies are not restricted to churches, schools, and museums that are self-consciously cultural in purpose but encompass all organizations, including instrumental, market-oriented, for-profit forms.

Note how far these studies have taken us from the earlier, restricted (and flawed) conception associated with the founding statements of sociological neoinstitutional theory by Meyer and Rowan (1977) and DiMaggio and Powell (1983). Rather than viewing institutional processes as working in opposition to efficiency concerns, or as operating orthogonally to them, as Meyer and I proposed (Scott and Meyer 1983), these later arguments see institutional processes as shaping and interacting with interest-based efforts. Institutional structures do not frustrate but frame rational decision making.

Holm (1995) hammers this point home:

> The more institutionalized forms will easily escape our attention because they remain taken for granted, but they are no less a part of the subject area of institutionalist analysis. The social practices that show themselves as technical, natural, and self-evident are the most heavily institutionalized and should therefore take center stage in institutional analysis. (p. 417)

Note, however, that to detect broad institutional effects on instrumental structures and practices, some type of comparative analysis is essential, examining differences in organizational systems over time—perhaps long periods—or space.

Institutional Processes and Organizational Fields

Most studies of institutional effects have examined social structures specialized around a subset of activities within a single society, either specific types of organizations (an organizational form or population) or an organizational field. As discussed in Chapter 4, the emergence of the concept of organizational field, which isolates for analysis sets of differentiated, interdependent organizations that "constitute a recognized area of institutional life" (DiMaggio and Powell 1983:143), has provided a valuable new level of analysis for students of organizations. Organizational fields are most often treated as independent variables, as a collection of contextual factors or conditions affecting organization structures or processes (see Chapter 7). Here, however, we consider theory and research that seek to determine how to identify field-level characteristics and what factors affect their definition and attributes. Concepts such as organizational field challenge and supersede earlier concepts, such as environment, which favor a passive construction. The notion of field reminds us that environments of organizations are not random collections of resources and schemas, nor are they constructs defined by disembodied dimensions, such as complexity and munificence; rather, they are themselves organized. Also, although organizations may operate in the "same" environment, their specific location in the relational/cultural system matters greatly for their survival prospects (see DiMaggio 1986; Scott 1994a).

How are organizational fields shaped? We have already touched on this question in Chapter 5, where we considered the construction of institutions at various levels, including fields. Clearly, both exogenous and endogenous forces are at play and must be considered. To illustrate approaches to field-level structures and processes, I consider four topics: boundaries, logics, governance, and structuration.

Field Boundaries

Most analysts adopt a commonsense definition of field: a set of diverse organizations engaged in a similar function. Investigators may employ conventional definitions, such as SIC industry codes, to identify core producer forms, but they also can be highly imaginative in identifying organizational fields. For example, McCarthy and Zald (1977) delineated a cluster of "social movement industries," organizations engaged in similar protest and reform activities within specialized arenas such as civil rights or feminist concerns.

Most analysts embrace a "top down" approach, emphasizing the role of global institutions, nation-states, or professional groups in shaping field definitions. Meyer (1977), for example, argues that widely held cultural beliefs operating at the world-system level provide much structure and support to educational systems in specific societies and account for much of the uniformity and coherence observed within this field. When cultural rules are strong, administrative frameworks may be unnecessary or an afterthought (Scott 1987). Nation-states often play a strong role in field delineation, employing mechanisms such as antitrust and regulatory policies. For example, banks, insurance companies, and investment firms operated in relatively insulated fields in the United States until the 1970s, because of controls exercised under the Glass-Steagall Act of 1933. And there are many accounts of the field-building and boundary-policing function exercised by successful professional bodies, such as the American Medical Association (see Starr 1982). Weaker professional bodies, such as those formed by psychiatrists and mental health specialists, are less successful in defining and defending field boundaries, with the result that in the United States, estimates are that only one in five people with a mental disorder receives treatment from a mental health professional (Regier, Goldberg, and Taub 1978; Scott 1985).

Commercial fields are often shaped by the existence of various types of information-gathering systems in business, which provide objective information to all field participants about field activities: for example, sales, mergers, or market growth. Anand and Peterson (2000) refer to such sources as the Nielsen television ratings and the Educational Testing Service as providing "market information regimes." The researchers report an instructive example of the role played by *Billboard* in structuring the commercial music field. A change in the way this trade publication collected information—shifting from a reliance on information provided by a panel of 200 sales outlets to the use of scanning equipment in a much wider array of stores—resulted in a redefinition of field structure. Record companies were obliged to redefine their conception of consumer tastes, giving a much more central position to the country music genre, the popularity of which had been underestimated by the earlier information sources.

Recently, some scholars have asked what role microprocesses play in creating macro-level phenomena, such as field boundaries. These analysts are exploring a cultural-cognitive approach to determining the boundaries of fields by asking how organizational participants determine what business they are in, who their competitors are, or from whom they can profitably learn. Porac and Thomas (1990) argue that the structure of a field not only influences managers' cognitions but also is shaped by them (see also Abrahamson and Fombrun 1994). Researchers have examined the development and role of managers' conceptions of their field in such diverse areas as iron and steel manufacturing (Stubbart and Ramaprasad 1988), Scottish knitwear (Porac, Thomas, and Badden-Fuller 1989), and New York hotels (Lant and Baum 1995). Lant and Baum, for example, examine the ways in which hotel managers categorized other firms as within or outside their competitive set and selected a set of firms they defined as relevant to their strategic choices. This collection of firms operated as a set of cognitive communities exhibiting increasing convergence in the perceptions and beliefs of managers. Although such processes are an important aspect of the boundary-setting process within a field, this approach emphasizes the salience of organizations viewed as similar and may overlook the role played by different organizations, such as exchange partners or regulators.

For some types of organizations, sector or industry definitions of field may be inappropriate. Fligstein (1990:19), for example, points out that the largest corporations in the United States are highly diversified, operating in many markets and across different industries. For these firms, the relevant field consists of other similar, large corporations, whose actions managers monitor and take into account. Similarly, students of multinational corporations suggest that rather than assuming that these companies straddle several fields, it may be more helpful to conclude that "global industries *in toto* constitute a single organizational field" (Westney 1993:63).

Field Logics

Institutional logics refer to the belief systems and related practices that predominate in an organizational field. As Friedland and Alford (1991) suggest, institutional logics provide the "organizing principles" (p. 248) that furnish guidelines to field participants as to how they are to carry out the work. The importance of logics for field definition and structure has been stressed by Biggart and Guillèn and by Whitley (in his related concept of recipes), as discussed above.

Systems of logics within fields vary along a number of dimensions, including content, penetration, linkage, and exclusiveness (see Scott 1994a). Institutional analysts, to be true to their calling, must pay close attention to *content*, examining the specific belief systems as they are understood and interpreted by field members. As Friedland and Alford (1991) point out,

> Without content—that is, the distinctive categories, beliefs, and motives created by a specific institutional logic—it will be impossible to explain what kinds of social relations have what kind of effect on the behavior of organizations and individuals. (p. 252)

Institutional logics also vary in their *penetration* or, in Krasner's (1988) term, "vertical depth." DiMaggio's (1991) research, identifying which particular social purposes and techniques became the basis around which the museum field was constructed (described in Chapter 5), provides an illustration of how deeper logics can be identified. *Linkage* refers to the extent to which the logics are connected horizontally to other belief systems (see Krasner 1988). Studies by Snow and colleagues (1986) point to the importance of "frame alignment" processes by which groups seeking social change succeed to the extent that they are able to connect (align) their arguments to existing logics, eliciting support and legitimacy.

Organizational fields differ in the extent of *exclusiveness* enjoyed by their dominant logics. Some fields are characterized by one central, relatively coherent set of beliefs, whereas other fields contain either secondary logics that compete for adherents or multiple conflicting belief systems. More pluralistic political systems tend, in general, to produce more contentious organizational fields. As Berman (1983) points out, "Perhaps the most distinctive characteristic of the Western legal tradition is the coexistence and competition within the same community of diverse jurisdictions and diverse legal systems" (p. 10). In addition, the strength and unity of dominant field participants, such as professional and trade associations, affect the diversity of field logics. My colleagues and I (Scott et al. 2000) note, for example, that the fragmentation in the unity of organized medicine occurring during the 1960s in the United States, as indicated by the decline in American Medical Association membership and the rise of specialty associations, was associated with the rise of alternative medicine and managed care.

Governance Structures

Abbott (1988) has observed that "jurisdiction has not only a culture, but also a social structure" (p. 59). Applied to the organizational field,

> Governance structures refer to all those arrangements by which field-level power and authority are exercised involving, variously, formal and informal systems, public and private auspices, regulative and normative mechanisms. (Scott et al. 2000:172-73)

It is obvious that governance systems for the society as a whole will influence governance systems for sectors in that society. What is perhaps less obvious is the great variety of mechanisms and arrangements employed to govern different sectors or fields in the same society. This diversity has come to be recognized, somewhat to their surprise and, perhaps, dismay, by political scientists conducting comparative research on national political organization. For example, a collection of political scientists, sociologists, historians, and economists studying "the institutional structure of capitalism" under the auspices of the Social Science Research Council discovered that

Despite the apparently homogenizing effect of a burgeoning "world capi-talist system" (and, perhaps, even because of it), the practices of capitalism are becoming more, not less, diverse within national economies, at the same time that they are becoming more similar across national economies. (Schmitter 1990:12)

Sectors have been found to vary greatly in their governance structures, ranging from the more spontaneously equilibrating operation of markets to various types of self-enforcing mechanisms, such as alliances or net-works, to externally enforced hierarchies and regulatory structures (see Cawson 1985; Kitschelt 1991; Peters 1988; Wilks and Wright 1987). Such arrangements may arise and be sustained by the actions of mem-bers of the field or they may be imposed by rule and sanction by au-thorities from above; most often, some combination of both will be at work. For example, in their study of the evolution of governance re-gimes in industrial sectors, Campbell and Lindberg (1991) argue that actors within the sector engage in a process of "constrained selection" (p. 328) involving negotiations between producer organizations, other organizations (suppliers, labor, financial institutions, consumers), and state agencies. Together with their colleagues, they examine these pro-cesses in detail for selected U.S. industries, such as telecommunica-tions, the steel industry, and the nuclear energy sector (see Campbell, Hollingsworth, and Lindberg 1991).

In his study of the governance structures constructed by the largest U.S. firms (see above), Fligstein (1990) examines the changing patterns of what he terms *conceptions of control*: views of "how firms ought to solve their competitive problems" (p. 12), which are collectively held by organizations in the field. In my terms, these conceptions encom-pass both institutional logics and governance structures. Fligstein ex-amines a variety of historical data from 1880 to 1980 to conclude that governance structures shifted during this period from an emphasis on direct control of one's competitors to a manufacturing conception (emphasizing the vertical and horizontal integration of production), to a sales and marketing conception (as firms focused on finding and keeping markets), to a finance conception (as firms increasingly re-garded themselves as "collections of assets earning differing rates of re-turn, not as producers of given goods"; p. 15). Fligstein argues that the conceptions of control "are best viewed as a result of the strategic inter-action between actors in the state and actors in firms" (p. 19). Within a given field, central players work out their competitive strategies, but always within a wider framework negotiated with agencies of the state.

Regulative activities undertaken by the state differ greatly in their scope. Wholey and Sanchez (1991) point out that economic policies are more likely to be field- or sector-specific, whereas social policies, such as equal employment opportunity or occupational safety controls, tend to be applied more broadly across sectors. Among policies aimed at a specific sector, Barnett and Carroll (1993b) distinguish between particularistic regulations, targeted to some subset of organizations in the field, and universalistic policies, aimed at all organizations in the field. They argue that the former are more likely to produce unintended effects, as, for example, was the case when particularistic efforts to reduce the power of American Telephone & Telegraph triggered unexpected competition between large and small independent telephone companies (Barnett and Carroll 1993a). However, perhaps the unintended effects of universalistic policies may be more apparent in changing the relations among fields rather than within them.

Political scientists have also viewed regulatory policy from the other side of the fence, emphasizing the great differences in policy setting and political processes, politicization, administrative arrangements and capacity, and regulatory mechanisms that apply in agencies that oversee the many societal sectors (see Noll 1985; Wilson 1980, 1989). In addition to variations in administrating regulatory policies, the "state may manipulate property rights in different ways in different sectors of the economy, and this will influence governance regimes in these sectors accordingly" (Campbell and Lindberg 1990:635). For example, substantial differences are observed between sectors in the interpretation and enforcement of antitrust and labor laws.

Field Structuration

Giddens (1979) defines *structuration* quite broadly to refer to the recursive interdependence of social activities and structures (see Chapter 4). The verb form is intended to remind us that structures only exist to the extent that ongoing activities reproduce them. DiMaggio and Powell (1983) employ the same term but define it more narrowly to refer to the degree of interaction and the nature of the interorganizational structure that arises at the level of the organization field. Among the indicators they propose to assess structuration are the extent to which organizations in a field interact and are confronted with larger amounts of information to process; the emergence of "interorganizational structures of domination and patterns of coalition"; and the development of "mutual awareness among participants in a set of organizations that they are involved in a common enterprise" (DiMaggio and Powell 1983:148). To these indicators, others can be added, including extent of agreement on the institutional logics guiding activities within the field, increased isomorphism of structural forms within populations in the field, increased structural equivalence of organizational sets within the field, and increased clarity of field boundaries (see Scott 1994a; Scott et al. 2000; see also Chapter 8). Three studies examining field structuration are reviewed.[2]

In his analysis of an organizational field defined by organizations devoted to the arts (e.g., theaters, orchestras, and museums), DiMaggio follows Bourdieu (1977) in viewing the field as signifying both common "purpose and an arena of strategy and conflict" (DiMaggio 1983:149). He evaluates the proposition that the more centralized the resources on which organizations in the field depend, the greater the structuration of the field. His empirical study examines the effect on the arts field of a new pot of centralized resources created by the establishment in the United States in 1965 of the National Endowment for the Arts (NEA). DiMaggio describes how interaction among the various arts organizations increased, in part because of the NEA's efforts to solidify its constituency, but also because diverse types of organizations were now competing for the same resources. New layers of public bodies were created at the individual state level to process the block grants, and new trade associations were created and dormant ones restored to life. Coercive, mimetic, and normative (as well as competitive) pressures led to increased isomorphism among state structures and arts organizations in their internal structure. Receipt of federal funding by some but not all applicants tended to increase the legitimacy of successful enterprises and the dominance and centrality of their managers. Although DiMaggio provides little systematic data to support his arguments, he does illustrate the types of evidence relevant to examining structuration processes.

A study by Meyer and colleagues (Meyer et al. 1988) examines changes in the field of public elementary and secondary education in the United States during the period 1940 to 1980. Employing data collected from the universe of school and district organizations, the authors provide considerable evidence of increasing structuration, as schools and districts are shown to become more similar over time in size and internal staffing characteristics. However, unlike DiMaggio's study, which emphasizes the effect of centralization of funding, based on both cross-sectional and longitudinal analyses of state-level data, Meyer and colleagues found no consistent effects of centralized state or federal funding on structuration. Rather than signifying the impact of the power of centralized state control systems, the authors suggest that increased structuration of public education reflected a process of societal rationalization. They find no evidence for a unified organizational center but rather the "classic" U.S. pattern of "a profusion of professional standards, court decisions, special-purpose legislative interests, and a huge network of interest groups" (p. 165)—a strong polity and lively civic culture. The structuration of education "reflects a growing national institutional structure, but not one controlled by the central bureaucratic state" (p. 166).

Laumann and Knoke (1987) conducted an ambitious study comparing the relative organization and operation of the field of organizations involved in the setting of U.S. national policy in two arenas, health and energy, at the end of the 1970s. In an imaginative approach, Laumann and Knoke employ network techniques to examine the interrelation of organizations, both private and public, of issues, and of organizations activated by issues. They argue,

> Because a specific policy event is embedded in the context of other antecedent, concurrent, and impending events, we must systematically consider the unfolding structure of organizational participation as it is embedded in a structure of events that are tightly or loosely coupled because of institutional, substantive, and historical considerations. (p. 39)

Organizational location in a policy arena is mapped in terms of core/periphery (relational ties) and interest differentiation (issue involvement). Of principal interest here is the comparison between the degree of structuration of the two fields. Laumann and Knoke argue that at the time of their study, the health policy arena was much more highly structured, with well-established scientific and professional organizations operating from the beginning of the twentieth century. By contrast, for most of that century, policies on energy were fuel-specific; only relatively recently had a unitary arena for energy policy emerged. Their systematic data confirm this conclusion:

In contrast to the health policy domain during the late 1970s, activity related to energy issues was marked by fragmented participation, enduring conflicts, and a lack of consensus concerning the distribution of influence within the domain. (Laumann and Knoke 1987:72)

Field structure was found to influence policy processes and outcomes.[2]

Institutional Processes and Organizational Populations

A promising development in organization theory is the growing convergence between ecological and institutional approaches to organizations (see Hannan and Freeman 1989; Singh and Lumsden 1990; Baum 1996; Aldrich 1999). Although these efforts originated as quite independent approaches, since the mid-1980s there has been fruitful interchange and overlap in theoretical frameworks. Because ecological theorists deal primarily with factors affecting the growth and decline of populations of organizations,[3] it was not long before they became aware of the influence of institutional processes on these phenomena. Note that in this section, I review only theory and research relating to organizational populations and population processes; effects on individual organizations are described in the following chapter.

In Chapter 5, I described the treatment by ecologists of organizational density as an indicator of cultural-cognitive legitimacy, measuring the extent to which a form is taken for granted. The approach treats this aspect of institutions as an effect of ecological processes: Taken-for-grantedness is viewed as a consequence of density or increasing prevalence. As the number of organizations of a given type increases, the form becomes accepted as natural, and new instances enjoy improved survival rates. Moreover, such beliefs may diffuse widely. In research on automobile manufacturers in selected European countries between 1886 and 1981, Hannan and colleagues (1995) report that the legitimacy effects associated with increasing density tended to have broader, cross-societal effects, density in one country being positively associated with entry rates in other countries.[4]

Other ecologists have argued that the positive effect of increasing population density on founding rates may reflect not only cognitive supports but also vicarious learning effects and the assistance received from an increasingly elaborated infrastructure of associated organizations (see Delacroix and Rao 1994). To test the latter argument, Baum and Oliver (1992) examined the effect of "institutional embeddedness" or "relational density" on the founding and failure rates of day care centers in Toronto. Relational density referred to the "number of linkages between the [day care center] population and the dominant institutions in the environment that confer resources and legitimacy" (p. 547). Both population and relational density measures, considered independently, increased foundings and reduced failures. However, when considered simultaneously, relational density continued to show these legitimating effects, whereas "the relationship between population density and founding and failures became competitive [reduced foundings and increased failures] over the entire range of population density" (p. 556).

Baum and Oliver's operationalization of relational density includes measures not only of numbers of ties to other community organizations (e.g., site-sharing arrangements) but also of purchasing agreements between the day care centers and the Children's Services Division, a measure tapping both resource flows and normative endorsement. Thus, relational density shifts emphasis from the cultural-cognitive aspects of institutions, emphasized by population density, to the normative and regulative components of institutions.

Hybels and Ryan (1996) offer another approach to assessing changes in normative support for a novel and somewhat controversial organizational population, commercial biotechnology firms. They conducted a content analysis of abstracts from the U.S. business press from 1970—a date just prior to the appearance of these organizations—to 1989. Articles were counted and coded as positive, negative, mixed, or neutral in their evaluation of the new form. A measure of "cumulative legitimacy"—the sum of negative articles subtracted from the sum of positive articles published up to and including each month during the period—was positively associated with founding rate. And, as with relational dependence, when normative (cumulative) legitimacy was taken into account, the positive effects of population density on foundings became negative (competitive).

As a final example of normative legitimacy, Rao (1994) proposes the useful concept of "certification contests": social tests of organizations that help to enhance the reputation of the form and to serve as a diffusion mechanism increasing knowledge of the product. He examined the effect on the growth of early automobile manufacturers of road races, which served to establish the reliability and safety of cars and, thus indirectly, of car companies. His analysis shows that not only did winning such races enhance the survival chances of individual automobile companies, an organizational level effect, but the cumulative prevalence of contests lowered the aggregate failure rate in the industry.

In addition to examining cognitive and normative effects of institutions on organizations, researchers have also examined the effects of regulative processes: legitimacy that stems from being legally mandated or sanctioned. Regulatory facets of institutions are conventionally assumed to affect the behavior of targeted organizations, but recent studies by ecologists indicate they can also affect their life chances. For example, Hannan and Freeman (1989) report that the founding rate for labor unions increased significantly during the New Deal period, 1923 to 1947, when the Norris-LaGuardia and the Wagner Acts gave increased legal protection to unions and union-organizing campaigns. Similarly, a study of Manhattan banks and U.S. insurance companies found the onset of state and federal regulation to be strongly and positively related to increases in the growth of the two populations (Ranger-Moore, Banaszak-Holl, and Hannan 1991).[5] Wholey and Sanchez (1991) have offered a series of interesting hypotheses detailing the range of potential regulatory effects on populations, including their impact on ease of entry of firms into markets, the diversity of firms within a market, effects on population growth dynamics (the rate of growth or decline of populations), the carrying capacity of the environment, and the level of competition between populations.

Other researchers have examined the effects of the broader ideological and normative political climate on population dynamics. For example, in a series of studies, Carroll and colleagues (Carroll and Delacroix 1982; Carroll and Huo 1986; Carroll 1987) found that political turbulence (political events evoking intense reactions) was positively associated with the founding of newspapers in Argentina, in Ireland, and in the San Francisco Bay Area. They also report that newspapers founded during these periods were more likely to fail. Dacin (1997) demonstrated the impact of normative pressures associated with the nationalist movement in Finland on Finnish language newspapers. Such papers were more likely to be founded, even in predominantly Swedish-speaking locales, during periods of intense nationalist fervor.

Carroll, together with Barnett (Barnett and Carroll 1993a), has also examined the effects of fragmentation in state authority—the existence of many semi-autonomous units exercising authority—on the number

of telephone companies operating in the United States during the early
years of the twentieth century. At that time, telephone companies were
subject to local community control. Barnett and Carroll found that the
larger the number of political units issuing charters, the larger the number of telephone companies in existence in these areas. More generally,
Carroll, Delacroix, and Goodstein (1988) offer a wide-ranging collection of propositions linking characteristics of political environments—
including political turmoil, revolution, war, regulation, and institutional
structure—to various aspects of organizational populations. Many of
these arguments have yet to be empirically evaluated.

Concluding Comment

Much attention by institutional theorists has been devoted to examining the effects of institutions on social life at the macro, societal level.
Such studies have long been the stock-in-trade of historical institutionalists, as they have examined the effects of varying rules, beliefs,
and legal requirements on social structures and practices. In particular,
much effort has correctly been directed to documenting the role of the
nation-state, the professions, and international associations in promulgating and enforcing institutional requirements. In addition, theorists have called attention to the independent role of cultural beliefs on
social arrangements. Surprisingly, however, it is only relatively recently
that much attention has been explicitly directed to examining such institutional effects on the organizational realm.

Supplementing the longer-term efforts to examine societal-level effects, more recent work has concentrated on examining institutional
effects on organizational fields and on organizational populations. As
DiMaggio (1986) asserts, "the organization field has emerged as a critical unit bridging the organizational and the societal levels in the study
of social and community change" (p. 337). Wider societal forces operate to structure organizational fields, which develop their own distinctive institutional logics and governance systems, and these systems, in
turn, influence the structure and activities of individual organizations.

Institutional processes are also being examined at the level of the organizational population. Population forms and boundaries between
populations are themselves the product of ongoing constitutive processes, which act to blend and segregate varying organizational forms

over time. Recent research has examined the effect of legitimacy processes—defined in the cognitive sense, as prevalence of a form; in the normative sense, as moral endorsement or certification; and in the regulative sense, as legal sanction—on organizational vital statistics, foundings and failures. Although effects have been observed for all three modes of legitimacy, it remains to be determined how these forces interact and for which types of populations each mode is most salient.

Virtually all of the more recent theoretical and empirical work views institutional processes as operating in conjunction with, rather than in opposition to, rational purposive action. Institutions provide the framework—regulative, normative, and cultural-cognitive—within which actors define and pursue their interests.

Notes

1. In related work, Biggart, Hamilton, and colleagues have closely studied the institutional underpinnings of three East Asian economies—those of Japan, South Korea, and Taiwan—examining how the various network forms constituted in these settings differ from each other as well as from Western models of corporate organization. (See Hamilton and Biggart 1988; Biggart and Hamilton 1992; Orrù, Biggart, and Hamilton 1997.)

2. The studies by DiMaggio (1991), Dezalay and Garth (1996), and Suchman (1995a, forthcoming), described in Chapter 5, provide additional illustrations of field-level studies of structuration processes.

3. As Carroll (1984) has noted, ecological arguments can be applied at the level of the individual organization, the organizational population, or the organizational community (multiple interacting populations). We restrict attention here to the population level.

4. On the other hand, the competitive processes generated by increasing density were more localized to a specific country.

5. However, when density dependence was taken into account, these effects were substantially reduced. The researchers propose that rising density may "drive the process of initial government regulation, not the reverse" and that growth in numbers may also signify strength of the industry, allowing it to "influence authorities to take actions that favor the interests of those organizations and their elites" (Ranger-Moore, Banaszak-Holl, and Hannan 1991:63).

7 Institutional Processes
Affecting Organizational
Structure and Performance

M ost research on institutional processes by organizational scholars
has focused on their effects on individual organizations. In this
chapter, I review representative arguments and associated evidence.
Earlier studies emphasized the effects of institutional context on all organizations within the relevant environment. The institutional environment was viewed as unitary and as imposing structures or practices
on individual organizations, which were obliged to conform either because it was taken for granted that this was the proper way to organize,
because to do so would result in normative approbation, or because it
was required by legal or other rule-like frameworks. Later studies began to emphasize differences among organizations, recognizing that
whether, when, and how organizations respond depends on their individual characteristics or connections. Recent theorists and researchers
have stressed the varied nature of organizational responses to institutional demands. In some situations, individual organizations respond

strategically, either by decoupling their structures from their operations or by seeking to defend themselves in some manner from the pressures experienced. In others, the demands themselves are negotiated, as organizations collectively attempt to shape institutional requirements and redefine environments. I review examples of studies that address these issues.

Legitimacy and Isomorphism

Weber was among the first social theorists to call attention to the central importance of legitimacy in social life. In his theoretical and historical work, he gave particular attention to those forms of action that were guided by a belief in the existence of a legitimate order, a set of "determinable maxims" providing models viewed by the actor as "in some way obligatory or exemplary for him" (Weber [1924] 1968:31). In his analysis of administrative systems, both public and private, Weber examined the changing sources of legitimation, as traditional values or a belief in the charismatic nature of the leader increasingly gave way to a reliance on rational/legal underpinnings. Organizations were regarded as legitimate to the extent that they were in conformity with rational (e.g., scientific) prescriptions and legal or law-like frameworks.

Parsons ([1956] 1960a) applied the concept of legitimacy to the assessment of organizational goals. As specialized subsystems of larger societal structures, organizations are under normative pressure to ensure that their goals are congruent with wider societal values. The focus of the organization's value system "must be the legitimation of this goal in terms of the functional significance of its attainment for the superordinate system" (p. 21). This conception of legitimacy, emphasizing the consistency of organizational goals with societal functions, was later embraced by Pfeffer and colleagues (Dowling and Pfeffer 1975; Pfeffer and Salancik 1978).

Meyer and Rowan (1977) shifted the focus from organizational goals to the structural and procedural aspects of organizations. The *structural vocabulary* of modern organizations—their emphasis on formality, offices, specialized functions, rules, records, routines—was seen to be guided by and to reflect prescriptions conveyed by wider rationalized institutional environments. These structures signal rationality, irrespective of their effects on outcomes. The master proposition Meyer and Rowan advanced was that "independent of their productive efficiency, organizations which exist in highly elaborated institutional environments and succeed in becoming isomorphic with these environments gain the legitimacy and resources needed to survive" (p. 352). The principle of isomorphism was first applied to organizations by human ecologist Amos Hawley (1968), who argued that units that are subjected to the same environmental conditions and that interact frequently acquire a similar form of organization (see also Hawley 1950). However, whereas ecologists proposed that isomorphism resulted from competitive processes, as organizations were pressured to assume the form best adapted to survival in a particular environment (see Hannan and Freeman 1989), neoinstitutionalists emphasized the importance of *social fitness*: the acquisition of a form regarded as legitimate in a given institutional environment. DiMaggio and Powell (1983) reinforced this emphasis on institutional isomorphism, focusing attention on coercive, normative, and mimetic mechanisms that "make organizations more similar without necessarily making them more efficient" (p. 147). And more than Meyer and Rowan, DiMaggio and Powell recognized that the models developed and the mechanisms inducing isomorphism among structural features operate most strongly within delimited organizational fields rather than at more diffuse societal levels.

These arguments help to account for two notable features of all contemporary organizations. First, there exists a remarkable similarity in the structural features of organizational forms operating within the same organizational field. One university tends to resemble closely another university, and one hospital is much like other hospitals. The recognition that organizations not only must be viable in terms of whatever competitive processes are at work but must also exhibit structural features that make them both recognizable and in conformity with normative and regulative requirements goes a long way to explain observed similarities among organizations in the same arena. Second, students of organizations, at least since Barnard (1938), have long observed the presence of both a formal and an informal structure, the former reflecting officially sanctioned offices and ways of conducting business, the latter, actual patterns of behavior and work routines. An uneasy tension exists between these structures. What was not clear until the work of the neoinstitutionalists is why such tensions exist; more

fundamentally, if they are disconnected from the work being performed, why do the formal structures exist at all? By positing an environment consisting not only of production pressures and technical demands but also of regulative, normative, and cultural-cognitive
elements, the relatively independent sources of informal versus formal
structures are revealed.

Hence, there are good theoretical reasons for attending to isomorphism
among organizational models and formal structures, and in the following sections, I review additional research examining isomorphic pressures. However, to treat the existence of structural isomorphism as the
litmus test for detecting institutional processes oversimplifies the complexity and subtlety of social systems. Varying, competing institutions
and multiple institutional elements are often at work, and although
they constitute new forms, they also interact with a variety of previously existing forms with varying characteristics and in differing locations. Conformity is one response to isomorphic pressures but not the
only one, as institutional processes combine with other forces to shape
structure and action.

Varying Elements and Mechanisms

The meaning of legitimacy and the mechanisms associated with its
transmission vary somewhat with the three institutional elements, as
previewed in Chapter 3. General effects of institutional processes on
organizational structures are readily apparent but often overlooked.
They become most visible when a longer time period is considered. A
clear instance of the effects of regulatory forces, combined with cultural-cognitive constitutive processes, on for-profit organizations is
represented by the structuring influence of incorporation statutes.
These social arrangements, allowing for the pooling of capital from
many sources and setting limitations on liability for those who managed these assets, were created at the end of the eighteenth and beginning of the nineteenth centuries. In its early development, the corporate form was restricted to enterprises pursuing broadly public
purposes, such as turnpikes and canals, but gradually, it was appropriated for use by private firms, as detailed by social historians Seavoy
(1982) and Roy (1997). Individually crafted charters granted by state
legislatures were replaced by statutes providing a template for incorporation that was available to a wide range of organizations. These legal

(and cultural) changes were associated with the rapid expansion of business enterprise in the United States during the second half of the nineteenth century.

The effect on organizational structure of normative influences is illustrated by the distinctive features of the American community hospital. During the late nineteenth and early twentieth centuries, American physicians consolidated their social and cultural authority, upgraded their training systems, and exercised increasingly strong jurisdictional controls over the medical domain (Starr 1982). Although they became dependent on hospitals, which provided the technical equipment, laboratory facilities, and nursing services required for effective acute care, physicians were able to remain independent of administrative controls, organizing themselves into an autonomous staff to oversee clinical activities. This dual control structure—one administrative, the other professional or collegial, embodying professional norms—provided the organizing principle for community hospitals throughout the twentieth century (White 1982). Only during the last decade have managerial interests begun to exert more direct controls over rank-and-file physicians in hospitals (see Scott et al. 2000).

The power of shared cultural models as a basis for organizing is highlighted in the study by Certina (1999) of high-energy physics and molecular biology laboratories. She argues that more than most types of organizations, these knowledge societies use a structural blueprint that is object- rather than person-centered. The work takes place in the context of shared scientific knowledge, "distributed cognition, which then also functions as a management mechanism: Through this discourse, work becomes coordinated and self-organization is made possible" (pp. 242-43). Many of the distinctive features of professional organizations are possible because of the unobtrusive controls exercised by shared symbolic systems linking actors to the objects of their work.

We can supplement these more historical and process-oriented accounts with studies employing variance-based quantitative evidence. Fligstein's (1985, 1990) study of the diffusion of the multidivisional (M-form) structure among the largest U.S. corporations during the twentieth century, which is discussed in more detail below, provides an example not only of how firms instrumentally adapt their structure to their strategy, as Chandler (1962) proposed, but also of how organizations seek cultural-cognitive legitimacy. Corporations in arenas containing higher numbers of similar corporations that had adopted the M-form at an earlier period were themselves more likely to adopt it by the end of the decade, irrespective of the extent or type of their diversification. Fligstein (1985) concludes, "These large organizations operate in similar environments and hence watch one another and come to resemble one another independent of considerations of strategy" (p. 388; see also Rumelt 1974). In a study of the same phenomena, focusing on the period since 1960, Palmer, Jennings, and Zhou (1993) report similar findings but also observe evidence of normative forces at work. They found that companies headed by chief executive officers (CEOs) with degrees from elite business schools and companies with more interlocking ties to other M-form companies were more likely to adopt the M-form structure. Ideas concerning what business forms are appropriate are promulgated by elite professional schools and circulate through elite interbusiness board relations.[1]

The value placed on a commercial organization depends not only on its economic performance but also on its conformity to cultural-cognitive categories. This generalization is tested by Zuckerman (1999) in an ingenious study of the effects on stock prices of the ratings made by security analysts, a set of intermediary actors who provide information useful to buyers of stocks. He finds that to earn high ratings from such analysts, firms need to attract the attention of those who specialize in the industry category in which its products are marketed. Those firms whose portfolio of products could not be readily classified, reflecting some confusion over the firm's identity, suffered poorer ratings than would be predicted on the basis of performance indicators, resulting in reduced stock prices. Because they did not conform to the analysts' model of a proper firm in the industry, they were accorded, in Zuckerman's terms, an "illegitimacy discount."

The sustaining effects of regulative and normative processes are illustrated by findings from a study of social service organizations in Canada by Singh, Tucker, and House (1986). They report that organizations acquiring a charitable registration number from Revenue Canada, signifying that they have met state standards and are eligible for tax-deductible contributions, were more likely to survive during the first years of their existence, the period during which they are most vulnerable to "the liability of newness." Social service organizations acquiring normative support—listing in a community agency directory— were also much more likely to survive through their early years.

Varying Sources and Salience

Who—which agencies or publics—has the right to confer legitimacy on organizations of a given type may not be a simple question in fields characterized by complexity or conflict. It is a truism of modern organization studies that organizations are highly differentiated, loosely coupled systems in part because they must relate to many and different environments. Universities, for example, relate not only to educational accreditation agencies and professional disciplinary associations but also to federal agencies overseeing research grants and contracts and student loans, to the National Collegiate Athletic Association for sports activities, and to local planning and regulatory bodies for buildings and roads, among many other oversight bodies (see Wiley and Zald 1968; Stern 1979).

In his study of commercial banks operating in the Minneapolis-St. Paul metropolitan area, Deephouse (1996) examines the effects of two different sources of legitimation; state regulatory agencies, which made on-site assessments of the safety and soundness of a bank's assets, and metropolitan newspapers, which reported information to the public about banking activities. Both sources were found to be positively associated with isomorphism in the asset strategies pursued by banks. Banks that experienced fewer enforcement actions from regulatory agencies and banks that received a higher proportion of positive reports in the public media were more likely to exhibit conformity to the industry average in their strategies for distributing assets across various categories of borrowers, such as commercial loans, real estate loans, and loans to individuals. This finding held up after differences in their age, size, and performance (return on assets) were taken into account. Both of the legitimation sources were significantly associated with strategic isomorphism, although there was only a modest association of .34 between measures of regulatory and public endorsement. This result suggests that legitimation sources vary in the attributes to which they attend in conferring legitimacy.

The salience of such legitimation agents can vary among organizational subunits or programs and also over time. In our study of hospitals in the San Francisco Bay Area, for example, Ruef and I (Ruef and Scott 1998) found that accreditation by an assortment of medical bodies, such as the American College of Surgeons, was independent of (and in some cases negatively associated with) accreditation by various managerial bodies, such as the American Hospital Association. Although the endorsement of both types of accreditation agencies was positively associated with hospital survival throughout the period 1945 to 1995, the strength of this relation was found to vary over time. During the period before 1980, when professional medical associations exercised greater influence in the field, medical association accreditations were more strongly associated with hospital survival than were managerial endorsements, whereas after 1980, managerial accreditations were a stronger predictor of survival than medical endorsements. We argue that market and managerial logics have become more prevalent in the health care field since 1980, challenging and, to some degree, supplanting the logics of the medical establishment. Thus, it appears that the influence of various regulatory and normative bodies varies depending on the institutional logics dominant within the wider institutional environments.

In sum, individual organizations exhibiting culturally approved forms and activities (including strategies), receiving support from normative authorities, and having approval from legal bodies are more likely to survive than organizations lacking these evaluations. Legitimacy exerts an influence on organizational viability independent of its performance or other attributes or connections.

In the following section, I review arguments and related research concerning the effects of the institutional context on organizational structures. In much of this work, the underlying rationale implied is that the effects are due to legitimacy processes. However, other causal processes may also be at work.

Institutional Context and Organizational Structure

Stinchcombe (1965) was the first theorist to recognize the strong influences of social (including institutional) conditions on organizational structure at the time of the founding of the organization, but his focus was on organizational forms or populations, not on individual organizations (see Chapter 5). However, his concept of imprinting has also been applied to the level of individual organizations, accompanied by the same assumption: Such imprinting processes are important because they tend to persist, to become institutionalized. Kimberly (1975) evaluated the imprinting argument by studying a collection of 123 rehabilitation organizations (sheltered workshops) established in the New York region during the period 1866 to 1966. During the latter part of this period, beliefs and norms supporting these workshops shifted from a commercial emphasis on the production of goods and services to a therapeutic emphasis on the psychological rehabilitation of the clients. Whereas only 18% of the workshops founded before 1946 were rehabilitation-oriented, 64% of those founded after that date exhibited this orientation. Moreover, the later in the period that a workshop was founded, the more likely it would embrace a rehabilitation orientation. Although this study did not systematically assess changes in the normative and cultural-cognitive models and norms governing these organizations, it is clear that the more recently founded organizations differed substantially from earlier forms in their institutional logics and internal characteristics.

Boeker (1989) studied factors affecting the institutionalization of power differences present at the time of founding in a sample of 53 semiconductor companies. Boeker contrasts the impact of entrepreneurial and environmental effects present at the time of the firm's founding on current firm strategy. He found that the previous functional background of the entrepreneur influenced the selection of the firm's strategy, but this decision was independently influenced by the industry's stage of development at the time the firm was founded. Firm strategies were significantly affected by industry stage in three of the four stages examined. For example, firms founded during the earliest era were more likely to embrace and to continue to pursue first-mover strategies, whereas firms founded during the most recent period studied were more likely to develop and to pursue a niche strategy.

Cultural models of organizing precede the creation of organizations. Most organizational fields present not a single but a (limited) number of organizational models or archetypes. Research by Baron, Hannan, and Burton (1999) attempted to assess the types of models or blueprints governing employment practices adopted by the founding CEOs in a sample of start-up firms involved in computer hardware, software, and semiconductors in Silicon Valley. Examining the characteristics of these firms after their first few years of operation revealed that companies whose CEOs held a more bureaucratic conception of employment practices were more likely to exhibit higher managerial intensity (proportion of managers to full-time employees) than companies whose CEOs held a more egalitarian commitment model.

Gradually, both theorists and researchers have come to realize that although organizations confront and are shaped by institutions, these institutional systems are not necessarily unified or coherent. A variety of scholars have explored the effects on organizations of environmental complexity and inconsistency (see Brunsson 1989; Meyer and Scott [1983b] 1992; Zucker 1988a).

Several researchers have examined the effect of institutional complexity on organization structure. For example, Meyer and I proposed that organizations confronting more complex, fragmented environments, such as multiple authorities and/or funding sources, would develop more complex and elaborated internal administrative structures, holding constant the complexity of their work processes (Scott and Meyer 1983). Powell (1988) found evidence consistent with this prediction in his study comparing a scholarly book-publishing house and a public television station. He concluded that "organizations, such as [the public television station] WNET, that are located in environments in which conflicting demands are made upon them will be especially likely to generate complex organizational structures with disproportionately large administrative components and boundary-spanning units" (p. 126).

Meyer, Scott, and Strang (1987) employ data on the administrative structure of districts and elementary and secondary schools to demonstrate that schools and districts depending more on federal funding, which involves many independent programs and budgetary categories, had disproportionately large administrative structures compared to schools relying primarily on state funding, which tended to be more integrated.[2]

D'Aunno, Sutton, and Price (1991) examined effects on community mental health organizations exposed to two conflicting models for staffing and service provision in drug abuse programs. The conventional mental health approach prescribed a psychosocial model of treatment administered by mental health professionals, whereas the competing model, more common in the drug abuse treatment sector, endorsed the Alcoholics Anonymous model, relying on ex-addicts and client-centered approaches. As some mental health centers, termed hybrids, elected to treat drug abuse cases, they were confronted with the two conflicting institutionalized models of treatment. These organizations reflected the conflicts in their environments by attempting to incorporate some features consistent with both the mental health and the drug abuse institutional practices. These organizations "responded by combining hiring practices" from the two sectors; "hybrid units also adopted conflicting goals for client treatment and somewhat inconsistent treatment practices" (pp. 655-56). Conflicts in the environment were mapped into the structure and practices of these organizations.

In a historical analysis spanning more than 200 years, Mouritsen and Skærbæk (1995) recount the never-ending attempt to reconcile the claims of two logics—art and accounting—that shape the life of the Royal Danish Theater. Each logic has its representatives in the wider environment and is built into the structure of the organization, each points to different standards and criteria in measuring success, and each was ascendant during different periods of the theater's stormy history. "The analysis portrays art and accounting as dialectically related in the production of civilization. Both art and accounting, it is argued, are integral to civilization inasmuch as they legitimate two different spheres of modern life" (p. 110).

As a final example, Stark (1996) describes the hybrid structures that characterize postsocialist Hungary, as individual companies attempt to adapt to a developing and highly uncertain mixed economy by forming complex network structures. In these arrangements, boundaries between firms, between public agencies and private organizations, and between legitimating principles become blurred. When it is not clear what logic or selection criterion is at work—the market, political connections, state sponsorship—then firms engage in "organizational hedging that crosses and combines disparate evaluative principles" (p. 1014).

Interactive Processes

Although all organizations within a given institutional field or sector are subject to the effects of institutional processes within the context, all do not experience them in the same way or respond in the same manner. Just as social psychologists call attention to differences among individuals in their definition of and response to the same situation, students of organization have increasingly attended to differences among organizations in their response to the "same" environment. I review here studies examining how adoption responses vary because of differences among organizations in the amount of pressure they experience, in their characteristics, or in their location within the field. In a later section of this chapter, I consider a broader array of responses by organizations to their institutional environments.

The general question addressed is why some structures or practices are adopted by some organizations but not by others in similar situations. This question is of interest not only to institutionalists but also to students of the diffusion of innovation (see Abrahamson 1991; Rogers 1995; Strang and Soule 1998) and of organizational learning (see Levitt and March 1988; Haunschild and Miner 1997). The latter ask in this connection how organizations learn both from their own experience and from the experience of others. Institutional arguments, emphasizing the effects of rules or norms or constitutive beliefs, shade off into stratification and instrumental arguments, for example, that organizations imitate others whom they perceive to be successful or prestigious (see, e.g., Haveman 1993; Burns and Wholey 1993). Many motives conduce toward conformity: fads, fashion, status enhancement, vicarious learning. All mimetic behavior does not involve institutional processes.

Variable Institutional Pressures

All organizations in the same field are not equally subject to the institutional processes at work there. Organizations vary in the extent to which they are under the jurisdictional authority of oversight agencies. Regulative requirements regarding employee protections, such as health and safety rules, often apply only to organizations of a given size. Equal opportunity laws apply more clearly to public sector organizations and to organizations receiving federal grants and contracts than to all rank-and-file employers (see Dobbin et al. 1988; Edelman 1992). As another example, Mezias (1990) examined the adopting of new procedures for reporting income tax credits by the 200 largest nonfinancial firms in the United States during the period 1962 to 1984. He discovered a number of organization-level factors that influenced adoption, including whether the firm was under the jurisdiction of the Interstate Commerce Commission.

Variation in institutional pressures also comes from differences over space and time in the strength of cognitive beliefs or normative controls. As described in Chapter 5, both ecologists and institutional scholars view the increasing prevalence of a form or practice as an indicator of increasing legitimation. This temporal variation has given rise to an interesting line of research that contrasts the characteristics of early versus late adopters. Two studies were particularly influential in shaping the arguments.

The first, conducted by Tolbert and Zucker (1983), was the study of the diffusion of civil service reforms among municipalities at the turn of the century, portions of which were discussed in Chapter 5. Turning their attention to those states in which civil service was not mandated, Tolbert and Zucker show that its adoption by cities during the initial period varied according to their characteristics: Larger cities, those with higher proportions of immigrants and a higher proportion of white-collar to blue-collar inhabitants, were more likely to adopt the reform. The authors argue that these cities were rationally pursuing their interests: Some local governments confronted more severe governance problems, encouraging them to adopt changes that would buffer them from "undesirable elements." Although such city characteristics were strongly predictive of adoption during the earliest period (1885-1904), in each subsequent period, the association became weaker, so that by 1935, these variables no longer had any predictive power. The authors interpret these weakening correlations as evidence of the development of widespread and powerful cultural norms supporting civil service reform, so that all cities were under increasing pressure to adopt the reform, regardless of their local needs or circumstances.[3]

The second study, by Fligstein (1985), was briefly discussed above but merits more detailed examination. Fligstein tested a number of alternative arguments for why large firms adopted the multidivisional (M-form) structure. His data, collected to reflect five decades between 1929 to 1939 and 1969 to 1979, included information on the 100 largest U.S. industrial corporations for each period.[4] During the earlier decades, firms that were older, pursuing product-related strategies in their growth patterns, and headed by managers from sales or finance departments were more likely to adopt the M-form than firms lacking these characteristics. During the 1939 to 1949 period, these same factors continued to operate, but another variable also became relevant. If firms were in industries in which other similar firms had adopted the M-form, they were more likely to adopt this structure themselves. All of the factors, with the exception of age, continued to be significantly correlated with M-form adoption during the last two decades included in the study.

Fligstein's study provides empirical support for two different versions of institutional arguments. The findings linking structural forms to strategies support Williamson's (1975) arguments that organizational managers attempt to devise governance structures that will economize on transactions costs. The findings relating M-form adoption to a number of other similar firms employing the structure are consistent with DiMaggio and Powell's (1983) views of mimetic, and perhaps normative, processes operating in uncertain environments.

These findings have been replicated in a number of later studies, some of which are described below. They suggest the following general pattern. In the early stages of an institutionalization process, adoption of the practice by organizations represents a choice on their part, which can reflect their varying specific needs or interests. As the institutionalization process proceeds, normative and cultural pressures mount to the point where adoption becomes less of a choice and more of a requirement. Differences among individual organizations are of less consequence when confronted by stronger institutional imperatives. Although, in one sense, the logic of action has shifted from one of instrumentality to appropriateness, in another sense, the situation confronting each organization has changed so that it is increasingly in the interest of all to adopt the practice. Not to do so is to be regarded as deviant or inattentive or behind the times. Not to do so can result in loss of legitimacy and, perhaps, attendant material resources.

The question of what types of benefits are associated with early and late adoption is further explored in a study of over 2,700 U.S. hospitals encouraged to adopt total quality management (TQM) procedures in response to increased normative pressures from the Joint Commission on Accreditation of Healthcare Organizations. Westphal, Gulati, and Shortell (1997) found that hospitals slower in adopting these practices conformed more highly to the pattern of practices implemented by other hospitals to which they were connected or to a particular standardized approach, compared to early adopters. That is, hospitals adopting early were more likely to customize their TQM practices to their specific situation; those adopting later exhibited a more ritualistic pattern, mechanically following standard TQM models or imitating the practices of other hospitals with whom they were connected in alliances or systems. The adoption of TQM improved hospital legitimacy (overall ratings by the Joint Commission) for both early and late adopters, but only early adopters of TQM also improved their productivity and efficiency, as measured by a number of objective and subjective indicators. We see, again, that although early and late adoption had different effects, all hospitals adopting TQM improved their professional legitimacy, and some improved their performance.

To examine further studies of differential organization response to their institutional environments, I briefly review findings from selected studies employing a variance approach and then review studies that emphasize a process view.

Variables Associated With Adoption

A generation of recent studies has attempted to identify what organizational features are associated with early adoption. Of course, these features vary greatly depending on the nature of the innovation. Most of the studies reviewed examine the adoption of some type of administrative innovation, for example, new managerial structures or employment systems. A number of general characteristics appear to be associated with adoptive behavior. Without attempting to be comprehensive, I identify three classes of variables that have received attention from recent scholars.

Attributes

Organizations vary in many ways, but only a few of these differences have been found regularly to be associated with early adoption. Numerous studies have found that organization *size* is important, larger organizations being prone to early adoption. Size effects have varying interpretations, each of which is conducive to earlier response. Larger organizations tend to be more resource rich; larger organizations are more differentiated and hence more sensitive to environmental changes; and larger organizations are more visible to external publics, including governance bodies (see Dobbin et al. 1988; Edelman 1992; Greening and Gray 1994). Organizations that operate within or are more closely aligned with the *public sector* are more likely to be responsive to institutional pressures, particularly legal and regulatory requirements (see Dobbin et al. 1988; Edelman 1992). Organizations possessing differentiated *personnel offices* are more likely to be receptive to innovations, particularly those pertaining to employment matters, for example, the adoption of hiring, training, and due-process procedures (see Baron, Dobbin, and Jennings 1986; Baron, Jennings, and Dobbin 1988;

Dobbin et al. 1988; Edelman 1992; Kalleberg et al. 1996). *Unionization* has been shown to affect selected types of adoption, in particular, grievance procedures and internal labor market practices (Pfeffer and Cohen 1984; Sutton et al. 1994; Kalleberg et al. 1996). In private sector organizations, the characteristics of CEOs have been found to affect adoptive behavior. *CEO background*—for example, whether the CEO's experience comes from production, marketing, or finance (Fligstein 1985, 1990)—and *CEO power* vis-à-vis the corporate board (Westphal and Zajac 1994) are associated with the adoption of new structural forms and with CEO compensation protections and incentive systems. Firms experiencing *turnover* in their top management teams are more likely to adopt new accounting procedures (Mezias 1990). Finally, *organizational performance* has been found to influence the adoption of CEO income protection and incentive plans (Westphal and Zajac 1994).

Linkages

Organizations also differ in the number and kinds of linkages they have with other actors in their environment. The effects of such ties on the adoption of two types of innovations are examined in a study by Davis and Greve (1997). They compared the diffusion patterns of two recent governance innovations, "golden parachutes" and "poison pills," which were adopted by many U.S. corporations in response to the takeover waves of the 1980s.[5] Parachutes, perceived to principally advantage incumbent executives of takeover targets, were found to diffuse among Fortune 500 firms slowly during the 1980 to 1989 period. Their adoption was primarily related to geographic proximity: "firms adopted to the extent that other firms in the same metropolitan area had done so" (p. 29). By contrast, pills, perceived as protecting the integrity of the firm against hostile takeover attempts, diffused very rapidly after they were introduced in 1985, their spread being strongly related to the pattern of board interlocks among firms. Thus, the spread of parachutes was associated with firm ties to local (regional) companies, whereas the spread of pills was associated with links to national elite networks. Also, Davis and Greve propose that the two innovations were associated with different carriers and exhibited different diffusion patterns because they involved different institutional elements. Pills acquired "substantial normative legitimation in the eyes of the directors adopting them" (p. 33) and diffused via formally constituted national networks, whereas the spread of parachutes was based more on their cognitive legitimacy—the information available locally to managers that others occupying the same role had secured such protections.

The distinction between being connected and being similar to another social unit is an important one to network theorists. The former, referred to as *cohesion*, pertains to the presence of exchange relations or communication between two or more parties. The latter, termed *structural equivalence*, refers to social units that "occupy the same position in the social structure"; they "are proximate to the extent that they have the same pattern of relations with occupants of other positions" (Burt 1987:1291). In situations where information is widely available, for example, via the mass media, social contagion—the diffusion of some practice or structure—may be more influenced by the behavior of those we regard as similar to ourselves than by those with whom we are in contact (recall the similar arguments made by Strang and Meyer 1993, discussed in Chapter 5).

The relative importance of cohesion versus structural equivalence is evaluated in a study by Galaskiewicz and Burt (1991), who examined factors affecting diffusion of norms and standards among contributions officers in corporate firms pertaining to the evaluation of nonprofit organizations seeking donations. The study examines how a normative system develops within an organizational field, affecting how individual officials come to view their social environment, share standards, and arrive at similar evaluations. Results were based on evaluations made by 61 contributions officers of 326 local nonprofit organizations eligible to receive donations from corporations. Judgments by officers (as to whether they recognized the nonprofits and, if so, regarded them as worthy prospects) were correlated with the evaluations of other officers, who were either (a) in contact or (b) in equivalent structural positions. "The results show weak evidence of contagion by cohesion and strong evidence of contagion by structural equivalence" (p. 94). Differences in judgment were also influenced by differences in the personal characteristics of officers, such as gender and prominence, but these did not eliminate the structural effects.

Reference Groups

These and related studies raise the general question, If organizations imitate the behavior of other organizations, how do they determine which organizations to emulate? Clearly, organizations must choose among their many network connections, and they must decide what criteria to employ to assess similarity. A number of recent scholars explore these questions, using network approaches. Notably, much of this research focuses on the adoption by market-based organizations of various competitive strategies, including acquisition behavior, entry into new markets, choice of an investment banker, or construction of a comparison set (for example, for justifying CEO compensation). Illustrative findings are that organizations are prone to imitate the behavior of organizations that are *geographically proximate* (Davis and Greve 1997; Greve 1998); that are perceived to be *similar* to themselves (for example, operating in the same industry) (Palmer, Jennings, and Zhou 1993; Haunschild and Beckman 1998; Porac, Wade, and Pollock 1999); that are closely connected by ties, including resource, information, and board interlocks (Haunschild 1993; Uzzi 1996; Kraatz 1998; Galaskiewicz and Bielefeld 1998); that have high *status* or prestige (Burns and Wholey 1993); and that are more (visibly) *successful* (Haveman 1993; Haunschild and Miner 1997; Kraatz 1998). On the other hand, firms may select less successful others as a comparison set to justify or place their own actions in a favorable light (Porac, Wade, and Pollock 1999). The arguments associated with these variables range from strictly institutional ones to vicarious learning to political maneuvering. More important, however, these studies begin to show the ways in which institutional processes interact with interest-based motivations to guide organizational choices and behaviors (see also Baum and Dutton 1996; Dacin, Ventresca, and Beal 1999).

Institutional and Organizational Processes

The public policy literature contains numerous studies providing examples of the ways in which organizations both engage in regulatory activities and respond to attempts to control their behavior. Some of these accounts take a top-down perspective (for example, Wilson 1980), focusing on the structure and tactics of the enforcement agency, whereas others take a bottom-up view, examining how the policies are interpreted and carried out at local sites (for example, Lipsky 1980). Organizations operate at every level in these accounts: as policy makers, as units of the implementation machinery, and as targets of policy reform. Although these studies have received scant attention from mainstream organizational scholars, they contain important insights concerning how organizations participate in and respond to regulatory efforts. (See, e.g., McLaughlin 1975; Peterson, Rabe, and Wong 1986; Landy, Roberts, and Thomas 1990.)

A more general process-oriented perspective is provided by organizational scholars who focus attention on organizations as information systems: as symbol-processing, sense-making, and interpretation systems. Pfeffer and Salancik (1978) stress the importance of the information system developed by the organization, the specialized units and routines that determine the variety and types of information routinely collected by the organization. Information is more likely to be salient and used, simply because it is available. The availability of information, thus, influences the attention structure of decision makers. Because "time and capabilities for attention are limited," as March (1994) notes, "theories of decision making are often better described as theories of attention or search than as theories of choice" (p. 10). Rather than assuming a straightforward, unified, demand-response model, a more ambiguous, complex, and nuanced portrait is painted of organizations staffed by multiple actors with conflicting agendas and interests confronting diverse and imperfect information. Demands or requirements trigger not automatic conformity but multiple questions: Does this apply to us? Who says so? Is this something to which we should respond? What might we do about it? Who else may be in the same situation? What are they doing? These demands become occasions for interpretation and initiate sense-making processes (Barley 1986; Daft and Weick 1984; Whetten and Godfrey 1999). Weick (1995) provides a penetrating and provocative analysis, reminiscent of Suchman's (1995a) discussion of theorization, of these processes that occur within and across organizations.

Related efforts to foster the development of more interactive and subtle models of the ways in which organizations relate to institutional environments have been carried out by law and society scholars, who complain that institutionalists too often embrace a legal formalism stressing the external, objective, rational nature of law. Rather, as Suchman and Edelman (1997; see also Edelman and Suchman 1997) propose, laws and regulations are socially interpreted and find their force and meaning in interactions between regulators and the regulated. This approach is well illustrated in a series of studies examining the response of a diverse sample of U.S. organizations to equal opportunity/affirmative action laws passed in the early 1960s (see Dobbin et al. 1988; Edelman 1992; Dobbin et al. 1993; Sutton et al. 1994; Edelman, Uggen, and Erlanger 1999). All laws are subject to variable interpretation, but these statutes—in part reflecting underlying, unresolved political conflicts—were particularly ambiguous, to the point where even cooperative organizational managers could not determine what it meant to be in compliance. The passage of the legislation set in motion an elaborate sense-making process in which personnel managers engaged in discourse with their counterparts—within their organizations, in their professional journals, at conventions—attempting to discern what measures would be found acceptable. Proposals were floated, prototype programs were developed, and over time, these responses were evaluated by the federal courts (yet another collection of state-based, professional actors), who served as the final arbiters of adequate compliance. Personnel managers were much more willing to initiate procedural rather than substantive solutions (that focused on the consequences of employer actions) (Edelman 1992), and their proposals were often couched in language emphasizing their contributions to organizational efficiency (Dobbin and Sutton 1998). When the programs eventually selected were declared to meet the requirements of the law, they diffused rapidly through the field. The overall process that occurred was one in which legal changes could best be understood as an endogenous process engaging various actors and working through sense-making and problem-solving activities within the organizational field, guided more by normative constructions among professional actors than by coercive mechanisms emanating from the state and better understood as a structuration process changing rules and behaviors across the entire field rather than as a simple process by which individual organizations were confronted by and conformed to centralized directives.

Strategic Responses

The process approaches described above begin to suggest that organizations may not be quite so powerless or passive as depicted in earlier institutional accounts. Noting the oversocialized conception of organizations and the limited response repertoire proffered by early formulations—in effect, Conform, either now or later!—Oliver (1991) called for an expansion of the choice set (see also Perrow 1986; DiMaggio 1988). Drawing on resource dependence arguments, she outlined a broad range of potential responses, emphasizing throughout more self-interested, strategic alternatives. I begin by reviewing her arguments and typology, but because they focus on responses by individual organizations, I conclude by pointing to the possibility of more collective strategic actions.

Individual Organizational Responses

Although it is useful to recognize that organizations can react to institutional pressures in a number of ways, it is also important to observe the extent to which institutional environments influence and delimit what strategies organizations can employ. Just as institutions constitute organizations, they also define and set limits on their appropriate ways of acting, including actions taken in response to institutional pressures. Strategies that may be appropriate in one kind of industry or field may be prohibited in another. For example, public agencies are frequently enjoined to coordinate services, whereas private organizations are expected to refrain from becoming overly cozy. Tactics that can be successfully pursued in one setting may be inconceivable in another. Not only structures but, as we have noted in studies previously reviewed, strategies are institutionally shaped.

Oliver (1991:152) delineates five general strategies available to individual organizations confronting institutional pressures: acquiescence, compromise, avoidance, defiance, and manipulation. The first, *acquiescence* or conformity, is the response that has received the lion's share of attention from institutional theorists. As we have seen, it may entail either imitation of other organizations selected as models or compliance to the perceived demands of cultural, normative, or regulative authorities. It may be motivated by anticipation of enhanced legitimacy, fear of negative sanctions, or hope of additional resources.

Compromise incorporates a family of responses that include balancing, placating, and negotiating institutional demands. It is particularly likely to occur in environments containing conflicting authorities. We have described research by D'Aunno, Sutton, and Price (1991) on the compromises effected by mental health agencies incorporating drug abuse programs. Although this seems to be a special case, as we have noted in Chapter 6, in liberal, pluralist societies like the United States, inconsistent and contesting institutional frameworks are common-place (Friedland and Alford 1991). This implies that organizations will frequently find themselves in situations in which they have consider-able room to maneuver, to interpret, to bargain, and to compromise. For example, Abzug and Mezias (1993) detail the range of strategies pursued by organizations responding to court decisions regarding comparable worth claims under Title VII of the Civil Rights Act of 1972. The federalized structure of the court systems, allowing for quasi-inde-pendent rulings by federal, state, and local courts, allowed a greater va-riety of appeals and also provided avenues for reform efforts to con-tinue at one level when they had been blocked at another.

Alexander (1996) describes a combination of compromise strategies pursued by curators of fine arts museums in the United States, whose organizations increasingly rely on diverse funding streams—wealthy individuals, corporations, government, and foundations—each of which holds different goals in providing support. Alexander finds that cura-tors, whose prestige "rests on the scholarliness and quality of their work, including the exhibitions they mount" (p. 803), tend to alter the format of exhibitions to please their funders—for example, creating block-buster and traveling exhibitions to please corporate and government sponsors—but to compromise less on the content of exhibitions. Other specific strategies employed included resource shifting, multivocality—sponsoring exhibitions with many facets that appeal to a variety of stakeholders—and creative enactment—inventing linkages between particular types of art and the specific interests of a potential sponsor.

The strategy of *avoidance*, as defined by Oliver, includes concealment efforts and attempts to buffer some parts of the organization from the necessity of conforming to the requirement. This is a strategy that, from the outset of neoinstitutional theory, has received considerable attention. In their seminal essay on institutional environments, Meyer and Rowan (1977) argued that organizations confronting demands fre-quently respond by "decoupling" their structural features from their tech-nical activities. This is assuredly a possible response. Loose coupling among differentiated units is a characteristic feature of all organiza-tions, indeed, of all open systems (see Glassman 1973; Weick 1976; Orton and Weick 1990). Organizations, in particular, are known to deal with external demands by developing specialized administrative units map-ping on to these external sources (Buckley 1967; Thompson 1967). Or-ganizations under pressure to adopt particular structures or procedures may opt to respond in a ceremonial manner, making changes in their formal structures to signal conformity but then buffering internal units, allowing them to operate independent of these pressures. This is certainly a possible response, and Meyer and Rowan imply that it is widespread: Indeed, decoupling is treated as a hallmark of institutional conformity. I believe this implication and interpretation to be incorrect.

To begin, these decoupled responses are often seen to be merely symbolic, the organizational equivalent of "smoke and mirrors" (see Perrow 1985). However, to an institutionalist, the adjective *merely* does not fit comfortably with the noun *symbolic*. The use of symbols, a process by which the organization connects to the wider world of meaning, exerts great social power (see Brunsson 1989; March and Olsen 1989). Second, numerous studies suggest that although organizations may create boundary units for symbolic reasons, these structures have a life of their own. Personnel employed in these units often play a dual role: They both transmit and translate environment demands to organizations, but they also represent organizational concerns to institutional agents (see Taylor 1984; Hoffman 1997). In addition, the very existence of such units signals compliance. Edelman (1992) elaborates this argument in her discussion of organizational responses to equal employment opportunity/affirmative action (EEO/AA) requirements:

> Structural elaboration is merely the first step in the process of compliance. Once EEO/AA structures are in place, the personnel who work with or in those structures become prominent actors in the compliance process: They give meaning to law as they construct definitions of compliance within their organizations. . . . But while actors within organizations struggle to construct a definition of compliance, structural elaboration signals attention to law, thus helping to preserve legitimacy. (p. 1544)

Finally, rather than assuming that decoupling automatically occurs, we should treat this as an empirical question: When and under what conditions do organizations adopt requisite structures but then fail to carry out the associated activities? Again, what elements can be expected to affect the response? Organizations are more likely to practice avoidance when confronted with external regulatory requirements than with normative or cognitive-cultural demands. They also may decouple structure from practice when there are high symbolic gains from adoption but equally high costs associated with implementation. A situation of this type was studied by Westphal and Zajac (1994, 1998) in one of the few studies to date that empirically examines decoupling. They examined the behavior of 570 of the largest U.S. corporations over two decades when such firms were adopting long-term CEO compensation plans in an attempt to better align CEO incentives with stockholder interests. Although many companies adopted these plans, a substantial number failed to use them to restructure executive compensation within a subsequent two-year period. Adopting plans was found to enhance organizational legitimacy with stockholders and stock purchasers. Westphal and Zajac (1998) found that plan adoptions, whether or not the plans were used, resulted in improved market prices; and they found adoption to be associated with greater CEO influence over the board. At the same time, use of these plans could negatively affect CEO compensation, and the researchers found, accordingly, that nonimplementation was also associated with greater CEO influence. In addition, Westphal and Zajac (1994) observed the familiar pattern involving late versus early adoption: Late adopters were less likely to implement the plan than early adopters, suggesting that decoupling is more likely to occur among reluctant adopters responding to strong normative pressures.

A fourth strategy identified by Oliver (1991) is *defiance*. Defiant organizations not only resist institutional pressures to conform but do so in a highly public manner. Defiance is likely to occur when the norms and interests of the focal organizations diverge substantially from those attempting to impose requirements on them. Covaleski and Dirsmith (1988) provide a process description of an organization's attempt to defy the state's efforts to impose a new budgetary system on them. The University of Wisconsin system attempted to devise and obtain public support for an alternative budgetary system that would more clearly reflect its own interest in research and educational programs and retention of top-flight faculty. In the end, state power prevailed, and the university was forced to accept the state's enrollment-based approach.

Fifth, organizations may respond to institutional pressures by attempts at *manipulation*, "the purposeful and opportunistic attempt to co-opt, influence, or control" the environment (Oliver 1991:157). Numerous scholars, from Selznick (1949) to Pfeffer and Salancik (1978) to Alexander (1995), have examined the ways in which organizations attempt to defend themselves and improve their bargaining power by developing linkages to important sources of power. Of special interest to institutional theorists are the techniques used by organizations to directly manage views of their legitimacy. Elsbach and Sutton (1992) report a process study of impression management techniques employed by Earth First! and ACT UP, two militant reform organizations that employed "illegitimate actions to gain recognition and achieve goals" (p. 702). Their analysis suggests that such techniques were employed to gain media attention for the organization and its objectives. Once such attention was forthcoming, spokespeople for each organization stressed the more conventional aspects of the organization and attempted to distance their organization's program from the illegal activities of some members. They sometimes claimed innocence or justified their actions in light of the greater injustices against which they were contending. Endorsements and support received from other constituencies were emphasized. In these and related ways, organizations attempt to manage their impressions and improve their credibility. However, as Ashforth and Gibbs (1990) point out, organizations that "protest too much" run the risk of undermining their legitimacy.

A final caution. In recognizing the possibility of strategic action by organizations confronting institutional pressures, it is, at the same time, important that institutional theorists not lose sight of the distinctive properties of institutions, in particular, those associated with the cultural-cognitive forms. As Goodrick and Salancik (1996) point out,

> A problem with the direct incorporation of a strategic choice perspective into institutional theory is that it discounts the social-fact quality of institutions. Rather than being social facts that make up the fabric of social life, they assume the special and arbitrary positions of dominant social agents. . . . The notion that organizations act at times without choice or forethought is lost. . . . The institutional context [then becomes] . . . of no special importance for understanding organizational action. It is simply a constraint to be managed like any other constraint, a choice among many choices. (p. 3)

Goodrick and Salancik (1996) examined the behavior of various types of California hospitals in adopting cesarean operations during the period 1965 to 1995, a time when the rates for these procedures increased greatly. Professional practice norms encourage the use of these procedures for high- but not low-risk births. Comparing cesarean-section rates among for-profit and nonprofit hospitals, the researchers observed differences among them only for births of intermediate risk. For-profit hospitals were more likely than nonprofit hospitals to carry out these relatively profitable procedures under these conditions. But this self-interested, strategic behavior only occurred for those types of patient conditions for which professional norms did not provide clear guidelines. Institutional rules set the limits within which strategic behavior occurs.

Collective Responses

More than the actions of single organizations, concerted responses by multiple organizations have the potential to shape the nature of the demands and even to redefine the rules and logics operating within the field. We review several studies that have dealt with these collective responses to institutional environments but reserve for Chapter 8 a discussion of more general field-level changes.

Earlier in this chapter, we have discussed a number of empirical studies depicting the ways in which organizations subject to some type of normative or regulative pressure respond in ways that reshape or redefine these institutional demands. Recall the behavior of personnel officers confronted by equal opportunity legislation. We suspect that such processes—in which rules or normative controls are proposed or legislated, interpretations and collective sense-making activities take place among participants in the field to which they are directed, and then the requirements are redefined and clarified—are more often the rule than the exception.

A study by Kaplan and Harrison (1993) examines the reactions by organizations to changes in the legal environment that exposed board members to a greater risk of liability suits. Corporations pursued both acquiescent strategies, adapting to conform to environmental requirements, and reactive strategies, attempting to alter environmental demands. Both involved collective as well as individual efforts. The Business Roundtable, a voluntary governance association, "took the lead in coordinating the conformity strategy by making recommendations on board composition and committee structure" (p. 423), consistent with the concerns raised by such regulatory bodies as the Securities and Exchange Commission. Reactive collective strategies included lobbying efforts directed at states to broaden the indemnification protection for outside directors as well as the creation of insurance consortia to underwrite the costs of providing director and officer liability insurance to companies. The strategies pursued were judged to be highly successful:

"New legislation and the insurance consortia enabled most corporations to substantially improve director liability protection. As a result, most board members are less at risk of personal liability now than they were a decade ago" (pp. 426-27).

A somewhat more contentious process of negotiation and compromise is detailed by Hoffman (1997) in his historical account of reactions by the U.S. chemical and petroleum firms and industries during the period 1960 to 1995 to increasing regulatory pressures intended to reduce threats to the natural environment. Trade journals were examined to assess industry response to these challenges. During the 1960s, relatively little attention was devoted to environmental concerns; most accusations and concerns were dismissed as groundless. However, with the formation of the Environmental Protection Agency in 1970, in response to a number of highly visible environmental accidents, governmental scrutiny of both industries increased dramatically, as did the mobilization of environmental activists. The Chemical Manufacturers Association and the American Petroleum Institute initially pursued primarily confrontational strategies in an attempt to influence regulatory behavior—in particular, standard-setting—but by the late 1980s, a more cooperative framework had evolved as the industries and related corporations began to embrace a policy of corporate environmentalism. Public agencies and corporate actors accommodated one another's interests, erecting new types of understandings, norms, and hybrid public/private governance arrangements.

But more conflict-laden collective reactions have occurred in which resolution proved more difficult. Miles (1982) examined the interesting case of the response by the "Big Six" tobacco companies in the United States to the Surgeon General's report linking smoking and cancer. Each of these companies reacted individually, some developing their foreign markets, and others diversifying their products. But they also engaged in collective action, creating the Tobacco Industry Research Committee to conduct their own scientific studies and cooperating to hire lobbyists and create political action committees to guide legislation and resist the passage of punitive laws. Collective efforts to shape the regulative and other governance structures to which they are subject continue up to the present day in response to heightened activities on the part of federal and state officials.

A different kind of negotiation process and redefinition of the organization field is described by Halliday, Powell, and Gransfors (1993) in their study of state bar associations in the United States. These associations were first formed at the beginning of the twentieth century as market-based organizations, competing for the support of lawyer members. However, during the early decades, failure rates were high. A different model of organizing was developed in the early 1920s, which relied on state support: Membership in the association was mandated as a condition for practicing in the state, and annual fees were imposed on all members. This new form, which required either legislative action or a ruling by the state supreme court, rapidly diffused through a number of states, although it did not supplant the market-based form in all states. Event-history analysis revealed that the state-based mode was more likely to be adopted in rural states and in those states where the market-based form had attracted only a small proportion of lawyers or states that were favorably disposed to licensing professions. The state-based form was also promoted by a centralized propagator association, the American Judicature Society, created to advance legal reform and diffuse the new structure. Collective action in this case resulted in the transformation of an organizational form, moving it out of the competitive marketplace and under the protective wing of the state.

Concluding Comment

Although organization analysts early embraced an open systems conception of organizations, it has taken a long time for us to begin to comprehend the extent to which organizations are creatures of their distinctive times and places, reflecting not only the technical knowledge but also the cultural rules and social beliefs in their environments. As Schrödinger (1945) observed in his treatise on open systems: "The device by which an organism [or organization] maintains itself stationary at a fairly high level of orderliness . . . really consists in continually sucking orderliness from its environment" (p. 75).

Much of the important work by institutional theorists over the past two decades has been in documenting the influence of social and symbolic forces on organizational structure and behavior. Empirical research has examined how institutional systems shape organizations variably, as a function of their location in the environment, their size and visibility, their nearness to the public sphere, their structural position, and their relational contacts.

and visibility, their nearness to the public sphere, their structural position, and their relational contacts.

Organizations are affected, even penetrated, by their environments; but they are also capable of responding to these influence attempts creatively and strategically. By acting in concert with other organizations facing similar pressures, organizations can sometimes counter, curb, circumvent, or redefine these demands. And collective action does not preclude individual attempts to reinterpret, manipulate, challenge, or defy the authoritative claims made on them. Organizations are creatures of their institutional environments; but most modern organizations are constituted as active players, not passive pawns.

In this chapter, I have tried to reflect the gradual but significant shift in scholarly treatments of institution-organization relations. Turning from a concern with one-way, determinant institutional "effects," most contemporary researchers are instead crafting research designs to examine the complex recursive processes by which institutional forces both shape and are shaped by organizational actions.

Notes

1. For a review of other recent studies that report evidence of such mimetic isomorphism among organizations within the same field, see Mizruchi and Fein (1999). These authors argue that many American researchers, more than their European colleagues, ignore or downplay the role of coercion in institutional analysis. They suggest that the bias of U.S. researchers favors a more individualistic view of firm behavior and the operation of more market-like processes. In adopting this view, Mizruchi and Fein suggest that the researchers are themselves the object of normative isomorphism induced by an overly managerial orientation among American students of organization.

2. These findings were not replicated in a study of agricultural cooperatives in Hungary by Carroll, Goodstein, and Gyenes (1988), but this may be because more of the administrative work of these cooperatives was absorbed by agencies in the then-socialist state.

3. Tolbert and Zucker here use density or prevalence of adoption of reforms as an indicator of their increasing legitimacy, although, later, Zucker (1989) criticized Hannan and Carroll for employing a similar "indirect" indicator.

4. Note that this sample design is unusual in that each of the decades represents a different set of firms. In subsequent analyses, Fligstein did examine the strategic behavior of both firms that had entered and left the category of 100 largest corporations, so that the characteristics of "stayers" and "leavers" could be compared. (See Fligstein 1990, 1991.)

5. "Golden parachutes" provide severance benefits to top executives unemployed after a successful takeover. "Poison pills" give shareholders the right to buy shares at a two-for-one rate in the event of a hostile takeover attempt (Davis and Greve 1997:10).

8 Institutional Change

On the one hand, change poses a problem for institutional theorists, most of whom view institutions as the source of stability and
order. If the nature of actors and their modes of acting are constituted
and constrained by institutions, how can these actors change the very
institutions in which they are embedded? On the other hand, much
theory and research on institutions focuses on change: the creation of
new institutional forms and associated changes in organizational fields,
populations, and individual organizations as these entities respond to
pressures to adopt new structures or practices. Much of this attention
to change, however, tends to privilege two moments: the formation of
new elements and their diffusion across host forms. Emphasis has been
on institutional construction and on convergent change processes.
This focus assumes that institutions are put in place and then exert
their effects but are not themselves subject to further change. Only in
the last decade have theorists and researchers begun to examine arguments and situations involving institutional change that witness the
deinstitutionalization of existing forms and their replacement by new
arrangements, which, in time, undergo institutionalization. Using language proposed by Giddens, institutionalists have focused attention

on structuration processes but have neglected processes leading to destructuration or restructuration.

This chapter begins by reviewing ideas and evidence concerning deinstitutional (destructuration) processes, then considers the ways in which institutions are reconstructed. I review studies that reflect these processes at field, population, and organizational levels. And, equally important, I examine the ways in which actors at these various levels interact to construct and reconstruct institutions.

Deinstitutionalization Processes

As noted in Chapter 5, persistence of institutional beliefs and practices cannot be presumed. Deinstitutionalization refers to the processes by which institutions weaken and disappear. As expected, some analysts emphasize primarily the regulative systems, noting enfeebled laws, diluted sanctions, and increasing noncompliance. Others stress eroding norms and evidence of the diminished force of obligatory expectations. And still others point to the erosion of cultural beliefs and the increasing questioning of what was once taken for granted.

Regardless of which elements are emphasized—of course, all or various combinations may be involved and examined—analysts should attend to both beliefs and behaviors: to schemas and resources. Beliefs and behaviors are loosely coupled, as generations of sociologists have emphasized, but changes in our ideas and expectations put pressure on related activities, and vice versa.

The possible causes of deinstitutionalization are multiple. As noted, Zucker (1988b) emphasizes the general phenomenon of entropy associated with "imperfect transmission" and modification of rules under the pressure of varying circumstances and the erosion of roles by the personal characteristics of occupants. Oliver (1992) describes three general types of pressures toward deinstitutionalization: functional, political, and social. *Functional* pressures are those that arise from perceived problems in performance levels associated with institutionalized practices. For example, public schools in the United States have clearly suffered some loss of legitimacy in recent years due to lower scores on standardized educational tests compared to children in comparable societies (see National Commission on Excellence in Education 1983). Reduced legitimacy allows increased consideration of alternative programs, such as vouchers. There is an ecology of institutions as well as of organizations and actions. When institutional structures are found by some important constituency to be inadequate in the guidelines they provide, these structures are candidates for reform or replacement as problems accumulate.

Political pressures result from shifts in interests or underlying power distributions that provided support for existing institutional arrangements. Scott et al. (2000) show how the long-term reduction in membership in the American Medical Association, associated with the rise of specialty associations, resulted in the weakening and fragmentation of physician power and, as a consequence, a reduction in professional control over the health care field. *Social* pressures are associated with differentiation of groups and the existence of heterogeneous divergent or discordant beliefs and practices. The presence of multiple competing and overlapping institutional frameworks undermines the stability of each. We have, for example, "the numerous studies from Eastern Europe documenting parallel and contradictory logics in which ordinary citizens were already experiencing, for a decade prior to 1989, a social world in which various domains were not integrated coherently" (Stark 1996:994).

Empirical studies of deinstitutionalization are relatively rare. As might be expected, the indicators employed to assess the extent of deinstitutionalization range from weakening beliefs to abandonment of a set of practices. Geertz (1971) describes a subtle and barely discernable pattern of deinstitutionalization under way in two Islam societies, as fundamentalist belief systems gradually loosen their hold on believers:

> What is believed to be true has not changed for these people, or not changed very much. What has changed is the way in which it is believed. Where there once was faith, there now are reasons, and not very convincing ones; what once were deliverances are now hypotheses, and rather strained ones. There is not much outright skepticism around, or even much conscious hypocrisy, but there is a good deal of solemn self-deception. (p. 17)

Tolbert and Sine (1999) describe an intermediate stage of deinstitutionalization based on changing practices. They examine a decline in the use of tenure systems in American institutions of higher education during the period 1965 to 1995. Although only a very few colleges and

universities abandoned the tenure system, "many higher education institutions have, in the last three decades, steadily increased the number
and proportion of non-tenure-track faculty positions" (p. 7). The tenure
institution, strongly supported by the normative structures of the teaching profession, persists, but its scope is narrowing, so that the protections
apply to ever smaller numbers of faculty members. Using data from the
period 1989 to 1995, Tolbert and Sine show that whereas some costs, primarily labor costs, are associated with compliance to the tenure system,
other costs, primarily legitimacy costs, attend reduced compliance.

Outright abandonment of an institutionalized practice represents
the extreme case of deinstitutionization. Greve (1995) examines the
decision by a sample of radio stations to discontinue use of a broadcasting format, a strategic decision regarding choice of the targeted au-
dience. Although this is not a strong instance of an institution, such
strategy decisions once made tend to be held in place by sunk costs,
cognitive conceptions, commitments to "what kind of station we are,"
and routinized patterns of activity. Greve (1998) finds that the same
kinds of factors that help to predict the adoption of a new format also
explain abandonment. Stations were more apt to abandon a format if
their social reference groups—other stations in the corporation, market contacts both within and outside the focal market—had done so.
Such findings suggest that it is useful to place studies of deinstitutionalization in a broader context of institutional change, because the weakening and disappearance of one set of beliefs and practices is likely to be
associated with the arrival of new beliefs and practices.

Change Processes

Three Studies of Institutional Change

I begin the more general discussion of processes involved in institutional change by briefly reviewing three studies, one conducted at the
subsystem (micro) level, one at the organizational form (meso) level,
and one at the organizational field (macro) level.

In a much-praised study, Barley (1986) examined changes occurring
over a one-year period in the social structure of radiology departments
of two community hospitals in Massachusetts. The impetus for
change was the introduction of new diagnostic technology, computed

tomography (CT) scanners, in each department, leading to alterations in the routine scripts and associated activities governing interactions of radiologists and technicians. By carefully analyzing the content of interaction scripts between occupants of the two roles, Barley shows that the same technology was associated with different change processes in the two settings, although in both cases, decision making became more decentralized. The study uses content analysis of interactions between organizational actors to describe the process by which established institutional arrangements governing behavior of key actors in radiology departments were disrupted by the new technology and then replaced by new scripts and routines.

Greenwood and Hinings (1993) examine changes over time in the models or archetypes governing the structural features of a given type of organization. They studied a sample of 24 municipal governments in England and Wales as they evolved during the period 1969 to 1982. These units had discretion to organize as they wished, but they were asked by oversight authorities to submit reorganization plans in 1974, a process that stimulated increased awareness and discussion of governance structures. The thesis examined by Greenwood and Hinings is that organizations tend to exhibit coherent patterns or configurations of features, in the sense that core values and beliefs will be reflected in practice patterns. "We are positing that archetypal coherence comes from the consistent relationship between an interpretive scheme and an organization's structures and systems" (p. 1056). The two interpretive schemas identified among municipal governments were a "corporate" and a "heteronomous professional" model.[1] The former was associated with higher centralization, less autonomy of functional departments, and generally higher levels of administrative control; the latter, with lower centralization and more autonomy for professional departments. The researchers observed a trend over the period of study for governments to change archetypes, shifting from the professional to the corporate model. They also observed tendencies for municipalities exhibiting "discordant" patterns—inconsistency between schemas and system components—to become more coherent over time.

Working at the level of the organizational field, my colleagues and I (Scott et al. 2000) examined changes occurring over a 50-year period among five populations of organizations providing health care services in the San Francisco Bay Area. Although the focal populations—hospitals, integrated health care systems, health maintenance organizations (HMOs), home health agencies, and kidney disease centers—were confined to the geographically delimited Bay Area, forces affecting these populations were assessed at the national and state as well as local levels. We demonstrate how changes in the institutional environment, including changes in governance structures and institutional logics, were associated with changes over time in the density (relative numbers) of organizations in the five populations. During an early period of professional dominance, marked by the hegemony of the medical establishment with its central emphasis on quality of care, care was provided primarily by independent physicians and nonprofit community hospitals. The era of federal involvement was ushered in by the passage in 1965 of the Medicare/Medicaid legislation. Public actors joined professional associations in exercising governance, and a focus on equity of access to treatment joined quality of care as a central institutional logic. Increased (public) resources encouraged the growth of hospitals, as well as the emergence of a number of more specialized forms, including kidney treatment centers and home health agencies. Largely in response to increasing health care costs, a third era of managerial controls and market mechanisms commenced in the early 1980s and continues to the present time. A new logic was introduced, the logic of efficiency, which was associated with the introduction of new types of incentives and new types of governance structures, including purchasing coalitions and for-profit health services firms. Independent hospitals began to decline in numbers and centrality, as HMOs, combining financial oversight and delivery functions, rose to prominence. Changes in institutional logics, as well as associated changes in governance systems, are shown to affect the types and relative numbers of health care provider organizations. In Greenwood and Hinings's terms, different institutional logics are associated with varying organizational archetypes.

Although conducted at varying levels of analysis, the three studies share important similarities. All focus on changes over time as one stable institutional pattern is shown to give way to another, different pattern. Each distinguishes between ideas (scripts, schemas, logics) and ordered activities (organizational routines, systems, forms). All employ a combination of process and variance approaches. And, although it may be obscured by my cursory review, all emphasize Giddens's structuration model, in which rules/schemas and activities/resources interact to produce structures which, over time, are reproduced but are always subject to change. Institutional structures are medium and outcome: They shape and are themselves shaped by subsequent inter-pretations and activities.

Accounting for Institutional Change

Theorists and researchers have been active, particularly during the most recent decade, in attempting to better understand institutional change processes as they interact with organizational change (see Baum and Singh 1994; Powell and Jones forthcoming). As a first step, it is useful to distinguish between processes or factors exogenous to the institutional system under study that trigger change versus forces internal to the system. Of course, the smaller the scope of the system studied, the more likely external factors will be involved. Change in the social structure of the radiology departments studied by Barley (1986) was triggered by the external event of introducing new technology from outside. The changes examined by Greenwood and Hinings (1993, 1996) apparently involved primarily endogenous forces, although the corporate archetype itself clearly was developed in sectors external to that of the municipal government. The health care study involved forces both internal (decline in the power of organized medicine) and external (the rise of a conservative, market-oriented political ideology) to the field.[2]

Among the external factors that have been identified by scholars as initiating institutional change are introduction of new technologies, in particular, "competence-destroying" (versus "competence enhancing") technologies (Tushman and Anderson 1986); management innovations, such as total quality management (e.g., Cole 1999); major changes in political policies, including industrial regulation (e.g., Fligstein 1990) and employment rules (e.g., Baron, Dobbin, and Jennings 1986); major political upheavals, such as wars and revolutions (e.g., Carroll, Delacroix, and Goodstein 1988); social reform movements, such as civil rights (e.g., McAdam 1982) or womens' liberation (e.g., Clemens 1993); economic crises or dislocations (e.g., Stark 1996); and shifts in cultural beliefs and practices, such as changing conceptions of the natural environment (e.g., Frank et al. 1999)

In highly institutional systems, endogenous change seems almost to contradict the meaning of institution. However, two general features of social systems render change possible, if not inevitable. First, there is

> the ever present gap or "mismatch" between the micro and macro levels.... This mismatch is explained by the distance between the experiences, thoughts, and actions of the many single individuals on the micro level on the one hand, and by the content and regulations embedded in the socially constructed institutions on the macro level, reflecting more general perspectives in society, on the other. (Sjöstrand 1995:20)

Adjustments, refinements, amendments, shortcuts, modifications, departures at the micro level—all take their toll on the macro frameworks. Second, if we recognize that virtually all social structures, particularly in the modern world, contain multiple institutional systems that intersect, overlap, compete for attention and adherents, and constrain some actors and actions but enable others, then endogenous change is easier to contemplate. At the societal level, Friedland and Alford (1991) remind us that kinship systems and work arrangements significantly overlap and interact but are defined by quite different institutional logics. Heimer (1999) describes the complex ways in which legal, medical, and family system norms and logics overlap and interact to influence decisions and actions in neonatal intensive care organizations. And Selznick (1969) has examined the ways in which political ideologies, espousing citizenship models, have been introduced into private firms affording due process rights and procedural safeguards for employees within these "private governments." Although a logic may arise in one arena, it may often be applied to another, providing a rationale for acting differently. Labeling this the "transposability of schemas," Sewell (1992) observes that "the schemas to which actors have access can be applied across a wide range of circumstances" (p. 17). Similarly, resources are often usable across institutional borders: Material resources or prestige earned in one system may be employed to alter one's situation in another.[3]

Just as the locations where sea water meets fresh water are particularly supportive of varied marine life, so the areas of overlap and confluence between institutional spheres generate rich possibilities for new forms. Morrill (forthcoming) depicts the emergence of a new organizational field staffed by new actors at the boundary where conventional legal structures overlap with social welfare forms. The field of alternative dispute resolution (ADR) emerged between 1965 and 1995 in response to a growing number of minor disputes that were clogging the law courts. A community-mediation model, championed by the social work community, and a multidoor-courthouse model, supported by lawyers, competed for the jurisdiction of this interstitial arena. Morrill details the processes by which new roles and practices were created (innovation), legitimation and resources were acquired from key players in existing organizational fields (mobilization), and a stable, uncontested, institutional settlement achieved (structuration). Morrill concludes,

> In the interstices created by overlapping resource networks across organizational fields, rules, identities, and conventional practices are loosened from their taken-for-granted moorings and alternative practices can emerge, particularly in the face of perceived institutional failure.

Conflicting norms and cultural models can occur not only between institutional frameworks but also within them. A given field may contain competing frameworks that prescribe varying forms and activities for participants, with the winners and losers to be sorted out over time. Haveman and Rao (1997) describe the co-evolution of institutions and organizational forms in their historical study of the California thrift industry between 1890 and 1928. In the early period, the industry was dominated by the terminating plan, based on conceptions and norms of mutual self-help. Members were shareholders, not depositors, and plans were dissolved when all participants had saved sufficient funds to build or buy their own homes. A competing model, the Dayton/guarantee-stock plan, made a sharp distinction between members and managers and depositors and borrowers, minimizing mutuality and shared fate. Bureaucratic impersonality and expertise were celebrated over voluntaristic mutual assistance. A variety of hybrid forms also appeared (Haveman and Rao forthcoming) but, over time, the Dayton plan became dominant.[4] Haveman and Rao argue that whereas the terminating plan was consistent with the informal patterns of rural communities, the Dayton plan was more congruent with the institutional logics of the Progressive era, "appealing to well-understood rational-bureaucratic procedures and arguing in efficiency terms" (p. 1641).

Change can be associated with features of particular institutional components or with tensions between components. Institutional schemas vary in their mutability, the extent to which they mandate specific beliefs and actions or allow for alternative formulations and behaviors (Clemens and Cook 1999:448). In addition, schemas may relate to specific resources, such as social networks, that can become fragmented or "cross important social cleavages" (p. 451), inducing change. Ideas, including institutional beliefs, require social carriers, and human actors are highly mobile. As Campbell (1997) argues, "changes in interaction may precipitate changes in interpretation" (p. 17).

Individual organizations within organizational fields differ in their social location, for example, their connection to existing networks and centrality. Such differences are typically associated with varying levels of commitment to extant logics. In their study of institutional practices in the U.S. radio broadcasting industry, Leblebici and colleagues (1991) describe changes occurring between 1920 and 1965. Three stages are identified, differing in terms of who the dominant players were, what served as the medium of exchange, and which institutionalized practices governed these exchanges. The problem posed by the investigators is, "Why do those who occupy the positions of power in the existing institutions willingly change its practices?" (p. 337). Their analysis suggests that, at least in this industry and during the period under study, change was primarily endogenous, involving innovations introduced by marginal participants that were later adopted by leading members, driven to do so by increased competition. These new practices became conventions when used recurrently and subsequently became "institutional practices by acquiring a normative character, when sustained through some form of legitimacy" (p. 342).

Changes in practice co-evolve with changes in legitimating logics. Hirsch (1986) examined the diffusion of an innovation initially regarding as deviant by dominant field participants: the "hostile takeover." Originating at the periphery of big business during the late 1950s, the practice of buying controlling shares in a corporation against the opposition of its executives soon spread to threaten mainstream firms. Changes in the legal environment in 1968 were accompanied by the creation of new financial instruments ("junk bonds") and together triggered increases in hostile takeover attempts, which continued through the 1980s. But in addition to new regulations and new practices, changes in "linguistic framing" were instrumental in transforming what had been considered a marginal, deviant practice to a mainstream business technique. The business press condemned the tactics of "corporate raiders" but increasingly employed metaphors more tolerant of takeover attempts. One-way stigmatization, employing epithets such as *pirate* and *raider*, gave way to more balanced language, takeovers being described as "contests" or as "corporate cockfights" between status equals (Hirsch 1986:818-19).

Davis, Diekmann, and Tinsley (1994) augment Hirsch's argument about the importance of framing metaphors in legitimating new behaviors. They propose that changes leading to the breakup of the conglomerate firm during the 1980s were associated with a more general change in the "authoritative analogies" legitimating ways of organizing. They argue that the long-used organic metaphor of the "firm as body" was replaced during the 1960s through the 1980s by the metaphor "firm as portfolio" (see also Fligstein 1991). "The firm-as-portfolio model was promoted through a range of institutional processes over a period of three decades, including the actions of the state, organizational imitation, the advice of business consultants, and the efficiency rationales of organization theorists" (Davis, Diekmann, and Tinsley 1994:552). This view fueled the deconglomeration movement by undermining "the notion of organizations as primordial social units in favor of a radical individualist view in which corporations were simply 'financial tinker toys' which could be arranged at whim, without regard for organizational boundaries" (p. 549). During the more recent decade, however, the portfolio model appears to be fading in favor of models emphasizing "core competence" and network forms.

Changing cognitive frames act to shift the dynamics of organizational fields. Such changes can empower some actors—individuals, organizations, professions—and constrain or disadvantage others. Pursuing their work on changing organizational archetypes, Greenwood and Hinings (1996) propose that an important mechanism of change is to be found within organizations, in the coalitions of participants with varying interests. A change in logics at the field level acts to advance the cause and promote the interests of some actors while disadvantaging others. In their study of accounting organizations, increasing competition and an emphasis on market growth strategies have increasingly benefited managerial and marketing interests over those of traditional accountants (see Greenwood and Hinings 1996; Cooper et al. 1996). These changed internal political dynamics provided the mechanisms driving the substitution of one organizational archetype (the managerial/professional) for another (the professional/partnership model).

Recall in this connection, Fligstein's (1987, 1991) similar arguments about the linkages between the strategies pursued by firms and the background of chief executive officers (CEOs).

Related kinds of political processes operate at the wider, inter-organizational field level, as some types of organizations gain advantage over others by changing institutional logics. Economists brought their ideas of cost-benefit analysis and market controls into the health care sector in the early 1970s and, with the aid of conservative politicians, challenged the dominant normative models of medical professionals and coexisting models of public regulation. These changes in institutional logics were, in turn, associated with the appearance and rapid growth of new actors and activities, both individual (for example, physician executives) and collective (for example, HMOs) (see Montgomery 1990; Scott et al. 2000). As Stryker (2000) observes,

> Contemporary societies provide many opportunities for institutional politics, defined as the strategic mobilization and counter-mobilization of diverse institutional logics as resources for interpretive understanding-based, instrumental interest-based and internalized value-based conflicts.... Legitimacy processes . . . are the heart of institutional politics. (p. 190)

Many of the "new" institutional forms arising from such politicized intergroup processes are not completely new but rather novel combinations of earlier institutional components. Existing institutions do not just pose constraints; they "are also enabling to the extent that they provide a repertoire of already existing institutional principles (e.g., models, analogies, conventions, concepts) that actors use to create new solutions in ways that lead to evolutionary change" (Campbell 1997:22). Fragments of pre-existing institutions are cobbled together by coalitions of actors in an innovative process labeled *bricolage* (Douglas 1986). Principles are amended and compromises reached to form new settlements; models are reconfigured or combined into various hybrid forms; and routines are reassembled to serve modified goals. New institutions borrow aspects of order, meaning, and legitimacy from earlier institutions. This conception of institutional change seems particularly apt as a model for understanding change processes under way in Eastern Europe at the end of the twentieth century (see Stark 1996; Campbell and Pedersen 1996). As Stark (1996) observes,

Change, even fundamental change, of the social world is not the passage from one order to another but rearrangements in the patterns of how multiple orders are interwoven. Organizational innovation in this view is not re-placement but recombination.

Thus, we examine how actors in the postsocialist context are rebuilding organizations and institutions not *on the ruins* but *with the ruins* of commu-nism as they redeploy available resources in response to their immediate practical dilemmas. Such a conception of path dependence does not con-demn actors to repetition or retrogression, for it is through adjusting to new uncertainties by improvising on practice routines that new organizational forms emerge. (p. 995, emphasis in original)

Agency, Power, and Institutional Change

Many of the arguments and studies just reviewed suggest increased attention to the play of power and the role of agency in institutional analysis. Early versions of neoinstitutional theory seemed to allow little room for variety of response, for resistance, for efforts to change commonly held beliefs and established rules. Critics (both within and outside the camp), weary of reading about convergence, conformity, and isomorphism, have become increasingly critical of a developing orthodoxy that takes the focus off conflicting interests and power. Perrow (1985) expressed concern about "this infatuation with cultural myths and symbols to the neglect of power and group interest" (p. 154); DiMaggio (1988) pointed to the "chronic use of passive constructions" in institutional arguments, which "systematically deemphasize human agency" (p. 10); Oliver (1991) stressed the "lack of attention to the role of organizational self-interests and active agency" (p. 145); Hall (1992) lamented the "distressing tendency to turn everything into myth and legend" (p. 77), ignoring the realities that lie behind these construc-tions; Barley and Tolbert (1997) complained that "more often than not . . . institutionalists have concentrated on an institutions' capacity to constrain" (p. 95) actors and actions; Hirsch (1997) charged that neoinstitutionalists, in their attention to ideas and rules, neglected "social structure," in particular, "the capacity for individual and col-lective actors to act, and pursue independent goals" (p. 1714); and Stinchcombe (1997) expressed the fear that neoinstitutionalists were in danger of leaving out the "guts" of institutional analysis by ignoring commitments to values backed by resources and sanctions.

Given recent developments, however, these accusations seem a bit outdated, and the dangers to which they point now appear more remote. First, the concept of agency itself has undergone clarification. Rather than presuming that agency is the ability of an actor to take actions independent of structural constraints, theorists argue that:

> All social action is a concrete synthesis, shaped and conditioned, on the one hand, by the temporal-relational contexts of action and, on the other, by the dynamic element of agency itself. The latter guarantees that empirical social action will never be completely determined or structured. On the other hand, there is no hypothetical moment in which agency actually gets "free" of structure. (Emirbayer and Mische 1998:1004)

Second, and more important, researchers during the past decade have skillfully blended arguments and data concerning ideas and interests, normative frameworks and power processes, rule systems and strategic action. A number of these efforts have already been described in earlier chapters, but notable examples include DiMaggio's (1991) historical study of the contested construction of the art museum field; Brint and Karabel's (1991) analysis of the transformation of American community colleges, as they increasingly converted from a liberal arts transfer to a vocational focus during the 1970s; Fligstein's (1990, 1991) examination of the evolution of organizational forms in the organizational field comprising the largest U.S. industrial corporations; Holm's (1995) study of the cooperative actions of Norwegian fishermen in creating mandated sales organizations governing fish sales, until they were swept away by the new regulations promulgated by the European Free Trade Association; Dezalay and Garth's (1996) description of the emergence and maturation of the field of international commercial arbitration; Biggart and Guillén's (1999) comparative study of the diverse paths of economic development in the auto industries of four societies; and our (Scott et al. 2000) study of the profound changes occurring in the U.S. health care sector during the past half century.

All of these studies view power as vested in institutions but also allow for conflicting logics and interests giving rise to challenges leading to institutional change.

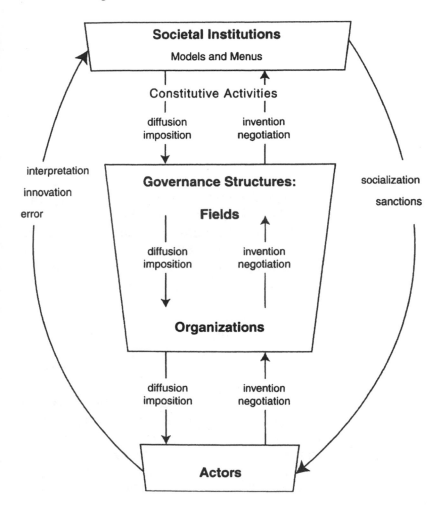

Figure 8.1. Top-Down and Bottom-Up Processes in Institutional Creation and Diffusion

SOURCE: Adapted from Scott 1994c (Figure 3.1, p. 37).

Multiple Levels

A common feature of all of these studies of various institutional processes—building, extending, maintaining, revising, and dismantling—is that the analysts consider multiple levels—individuals, organizations,

fields, nation-states, international associations—in tracing the interweaving of actions, processes, and structures. Although no single study
can hope to definitively analyze all of the causal connections across levels for a complex institutional arrangement, the most informative
studies are those that identify and trace the effects of salient and influential processes across two or more levels. Figure 8.1 depicts a generalized multilevel model of institutional forms and flows. World-system,
trans-societal, or societal institutions provide a context within which
more specific institutional fields and forms exist and operate, and
these, in turn, provide contexts for particular organizations and other
types of collective actors, which themselves supply contexts for sub-
groups and for individual actors and actions. Various "top-down" processes—constitutive activities, diffusion, socialization, imposition, authorization, inducement, imprinting (see Scott 1987)—allow higher-level
(more encompassing) structures to shape, both to constrain and empower, the structure and actions of lower-level actors. But simultaneously, counterprocesses are at work by which lower-level actors and
structures shape the contexts within which they operate. These "bottom-up" processes include, variously, selective attention, interpretation and sense making, identity construction, error, invention, conformity and reproduction of patterns, compromise, avoidance, defiance,
and manipulation (see Oliver 1991).

Earlier neoinstitutional sociologists emphasized top-down processes, focusing on the ways in which models, menus, and rules constrained organization-level structures and processes. Neoinstitutional
economists and rational choice political scientists have emphasized
bottom-up processes, as actors pursue their interests by designing institutional frameworks that solve collective action problems or improve
the efficiency of economic exchanges. Thelen (1999) proposes that although the time may not have arrived for a synthesis of economic and
rational choice with more historical and sociological views of institutions, we might "strive for creative combinations that recognize and attempt to harness the strengths of each approach" (p. 380).

Recent and interesting work has begun to surface that emphasizes
the interweaving of top-down and bottom-up processes as they combine to influence institutional phenomena. We have previously discussed the studies by Edelman and associates (Edelman 1992; Edelman,
Uggen, and Erlanger 1999) and Dobbin and associates (1993), who explore how top-down regulative processes initiated by federal agents

trigger collective sense-making processes among personnel managers, who construct new structures and procedures, which are reviewed and eventually authorized by the federal courts. Regulative (federal laws), normative (professional managerial codes), and cognitive (sense-making) processes are connected in complex and changing mixtures. Rules, ideas, and interests play independent, but interdependent roles. Either-or dichotomies are usefully ignored; fruitless theoretical debates are resolved by empirical research.

In formulating a recursive, iterative model of institutional change, Holm (1995) proposes that it is helpful in examining the processes connecting adjacent levels to distinguish between two nested types of processes: practical versus political actions. The former are actions taken within a given framework of understandings, norms, and rules, serving to reproduce the institutional structure or, at most, stimulate incremental changes. The latter political processes are actions taken whose purpose is to change the rules or frameworks governing actions. For example, explicit rules govern the activities of professional sports teams, but, from time to time, team representatives and officials meet to review and make alterations in the rules based on accumulated experiences or specific problems encountered. Although, in some cases, changes in rules are based on collective mobilization and conflict, in many organized systems, formal structures are in place to support routine reviews of and revisions in rule systems. The creation of such formalized decision-making and governance systems serves to institutionalize the process of institutional change.

Widening Theoretical Frameworks

In addition to employing more multilevel and recursive models in institutional studies, institutional scholars have begun to widen their theoretical frames, taking advantage of ideas and approaches developed in related areas. I have already discussed, in Chapters 3 and 7, the constructive connections being developed between students of the legal environment and institutionalists. Edelman and Suchman (1997) distinguish three dimensions of legal environments relevant to organizational studies. Legal systems offer a facilitative environment, supplying tools, procedures, and forums that actors can employ to pursue goals, resolve disputes, and control deviant and criminal behavior within and by organizations (see Sitkin and Bies 1994; Vaughn 1999).

They provide a regulatory environment consisting of a set of "substantive edicts, invoking societal authority over various aspects of organizational life" (Edelman and Suchman 1997:483; see also Noll 1985). And, most fatefully, they offer a constitutive environment that "constructs and empowers various classes of organizational actors and delineates the relationships among them" (Edelman and Suchman 1997:483; see also Scott 1994d). Edelman and Suchman suggest that we need much more research on the ways in which constitutive legal processes function to construct interorganizational relations (e.g., tort law, bankruptcy law), construct distinctive forms of organization structure (e.g., corporate law), and contribute to an underlying cultural logic of legal-rationality.

Another rapidly developing productive intersection is that between social movement theory and institutional change. For many years, social movement theory has productively borrowed from organizational theory as Mayer Zald, John McCarthy, and others showed us how collective movements, if they were to be sustained, required the mobilization of resources and leadership to create social movement organizations (Zald and Garner 1966). And, as numerous movement organizations pursued similar types of reforms, they identified social movement industries or fields within which similar organizations competed, cooperated, and learned from each other (McCarthy and Zald 1977).

As institutionalists have become more interested in the subject of change, it is not surprising that they have begun to attend more closely to the work of social movement theorists. Among the younger researchers who are connecting movement arguments and insights to institutional and organizational change are Clemens (1993), with her work on the alternative organizational models adopted by the women's movement at the end of the twentieth century; Davis (1994), who used social movement perspectives in his analysis of the politics of corporate control; Rao (1998), who examined the construction of consumer watchdog organizations, some forms of which advocated radical political change; and Morrill (forthcoming), whose examination of the emergence of the interstitial field of alternative dispute resolution was discussed earlier in this chapter.

More than organizational institutionalists, social movement theorists call attention to the importance of mobilizing structures—"the forms of organization (informal as well as formal) available to insurgents"— and to political opportunities—the "structure of political opportunities and constraints confronting the movement" (McAdam, McCarthy, and Zald 1996:2). Clemens (1993), for example, makes insightful use of both of these concepts in her analysis of women's political groups at the turn of the last century in the United States. Lacking access to normal forms of political action (the franchise), they "adapted existing nonpolitical models of organization for political purposes" (p. 758). An "organizational repertoire" is the "set of organizational models that are culturally or experientially available" for women at this time and place: unions, clubs, and associations. Employing these conventional models in unconventional ways mobilized around new purposes led to profound institutional change.

> At the institutional level, women's groups were central to a broader reworking of the organizational framework of American politics: the decline of competitive political parties and electoral mass mobilization followed by the emergence of a governing system centered on administration, regulation, lobbying, and legislative politics. (p. 760)

Both social movement and institutional theorists attend to framing processes—the "collective processes of interpretation, attribution, and social construction that mediate between opportunity and action" (McAdam, McCarthy, and Zald 1996:2)—but movement theorists have emphasized frame alignment as a process of particular value to disadvantaged groups. When one is a suppressed or challenging movement, support depends on the extent to which it is possible to align one's ideas and interests with those of others, whether allies or authorities (see Snow et al. 1986).

As noted above, many institutional frameworks have built-in mechanisms to allow incremental change, but these frameworks invariably privilege some interests over others and exclude some parties entirely. Excluded groups must resort to collective action to have their voices heard, and social movement theory provides important insights into when and how such mobilization activities occur. Institutional change proceeds by mobilization efforts and revolutionary processes as well as by formalized procedures and incremental reform activities. Institutional theory must attend to the wide range of processes, structures, and mechanisms by which institutional change occurs.

Institutional theory will benefit greatly by continuing to cultivate connections with law and society scholars, social movements theorists, and other rapidly developing research communities, such as network theorists (Nohria and Eccles 1992), students of society and accounting (Hopwood and Miller 1994), economic sociology (Smelser and Swedberg 1994), and international and comparative management (Ghoshal and Westney 1993). All of these communities can bring theoretical insights and useful methodologies to our understanding of institutions and institutional change processes.

Structuration Processes

I introduced and defined Giddens's concept of structuration in Chapter 4 and described its application to organizational fields in Chapter 6. Here, I emphasize its utility as a framework for studying institutional change processes. Although some critics have suggested that Giddens's formulation tends to conflate structure and action, Barley and Tolbert (1997) argue that this need not be the case. Structures can be understood as "historical accretions of past practices and understandings that set conditions on action" (p. 99), existing prior to action but then, in turn, being affected by that action. Analysis of this relation requires longitudinal data and separate indicators of structure (spanning settings and time) and of action (localized to a given setting).

Although structuration processes occur at all levels, from micro (recall Barley's 1986 study of structuration with radiology departments in response to the introduction of new technology) to macro (recall Boli and Thomas's 1997 examination of the rapid growth of international nongovernmental organizations at the world-system level), I focus here on the intermediate level of the organization field.

Most empirical research has focused on the construction of fields and on processes promoting increasing levels of structuration. In addition to the studies reviewed in Chapter 6 by DiMaggio, Meyer and colleagues, and Lauman and Knoke, other studies focusing on structuration processes include those by Stern (1979), of the development of the National Collegiate Athletic Association; by Leblebici and Salancik (1982), of rule-making processes in the Chicago Board of Trade, by DiMaggio (1991), of the museum field; by Suchman (1995a), of the semiconductor firms in the Silicon Valley; by Dezalay and Garth (1996), of the field of transnational commercial arbitration; and by Powell (1999), of the biotechnology field. Complementary discussions, employing somewhat different assumptions and language, appear in accounts by organizational ecologists and strategic management scholars of "interorganizational community building" and "industry formation" processes (see Van de Ven and Garud 1989; Aldrich and Fiol 1994; Garud and Rappa 1994; Hannan and Carroll 1995; Aldrich 1999). The latter discussions give more attention to the creation of a distinctive environmental niche and the securing and consolidation of resource flows, but they also attend to increased stability of interaction patterns and the securing of legitimacy from critical governance units.

More recent research by institutionalists has begun to include the examination of destructuration and restructuration processes. Davis, Diekmann, and Tinsley (1994) examined the decline and fall of the conglomerate firm during the 1980s; Thornton (1995), the displacement of editorial by marketing logics in the book-publishing industry; and Holm (1995), the rise and fall of the mandated sales organization governing Norwegian fisheries. Organizational fields can move toward decreased structuration, and their legitimacy can be challenged and undermined by the emergence of new logics and forms.

In a historical study of the effects of the U.S. environmental movement on the chemical and oil industries from 1960 to 1990, Hoffman (1997) argues that during this period, one cognitive frame or institutional logic displaced another. During the 1960s, firms embraced an "industrial" environmentalism, based on "technological self-confidence," viewing pollution as a "problem it could handle itself." Thirty years later, an entirely new cognitive frame, "strategic environmentalism," had emerged, which took a fieldwide view of the problem, included governmental agencies and activists as legitimate players, and elevated environmental managers into high-level corporate positions (pp. 12-13). Yesterday's heresy has become today's dogma. Hoffman argues that deficiencies with the initial cognitive frame preventing the industries from dealing adequately with significant problems first resulted in new regulative requirements. These, in turn, evoked new normative responses from managers and engineers, which over time created new conceptions of the nature of the problems and appropriate solutions: new cognitive frames (p. 157). Cognitive, regulative, and normative elements were all involved but were dominant during different periods of the institutional transformation.

In an attempt to better specify empirical indicators for assessing field structuration, my colleagues and I (Scott et al. 2000:358-60) propose a number of dimensions along which the structuration of fields can vary. Eight dimensions are identified:

- Funding centralization—the extent to which financial resources employed by actors in the field are concentrated
- Unity of governance—the extent to which governance structures are congruent in jurisdiction and consistent in the rule systems enunciated and enforced
- Public-private mode of governance—the extent to which public versus private authorities exercise control over the field
- Structural isomorphism—the extent to which organizational actors in the field conform to a single archetype or structural model
- Coherence of organizational boundaries—the extent to which organizational forms in the field exhibit clear, well-demarcated boundaries
- Consensus on institutional logics—the extent to which actors in the field embrace and adhere to the same general beliefs and recipes of action in carrying out field activities
- Organizational linkages—the extent to which there is a relatively large number of formal or informal connections between organizational actors in the field
- Clarity of field boundaries—the extent to which there exists relatively high insulation and separation of field actors and structures from neighboring fields

Empirical measures for each are suggested, based on our study of the health care field (see p. 361).

More succinctly, my colleagues and I (Scott et al. 2000) propose that change processes within organizational fields can be charted by attending to changes over time in (a) the numbers and types of social *actors*, both individual and collective; (b) the nature of institutional *logics*; and (c) the characteristics of *governance systems*. Actors, reflecting changing archetypes, tap into significant changes in cultural-cognitive, constitutive processes; logics, because they deal with the selection of appropriate ends and means, tap into a combination of cultural-cognitive and normative processes; and governance systems capture changes in both normative and regulative processes.

Our research (Scott et al. 2000) demonstrates that during the course of the past half century, the U.S. health care field has undergone dramatic destructuration processes, as governance structures have become less unitary, including complex mixtures of public and private oversight bodies; organizational forms for delivering health care have become more diverse and richly interconnected; the boundaries of these forms have become more blurred and indistinct; consensus on logics governing field behavior has been sharply reduced; and field boundaries have become less clearly defined and more highly penetrated.

Institutionalized systems rise and fall. Even highly stable and socially embedded fields supported by powerful constituencies can be dethroned and dismantled. Challenging logics carried by marginal actors or by mainstream actors invading from neighboring fields can undermine current truths and provide the foundation for the legitimation of new actors, practices, and governance systems.

Concluding Comment

Until recently, neoinstitutional researchers have concentrated their efforts on understanding the ways in which institutions arise and diffuse, studying construction and convergent change processes. During the past decade, however, they have accorded increased attention to how institutions decline, fail, and give way to new logics, actors, and forms.

The seeds of change are lodged both within and outside of institutions. Internal tensions are created as general rules are applied to specific situations; rules must be adapted and amended so that, over time, rules evolve and erode. Tensions arise within frameworks as regulative, normative, and cultural-cognitive elements move out of alignment. Various collections of actors within the jurisdiction of a given institution can interpret the rules in conflicting ways. External tensions are produced when multiple institutions overlap, providing diverse schemas and recipes for action. Wider environmental conditions—political, economic, technological—can shift, rendering current institutions vulnerable to precipitous change.

Change processes are best examined by designs that incorporate multiple levels of analysis. Social actions and structures exist in dualistic relation, each constraining and empowering the other. And social structures themselves are nested, groups within organizations or networks of organizations, organizations within fields, fields within broader societal and trans-societal systems. Although every study cannot attend to all levels, analysts should be aware of them and craft designs to include critical actors and structures engaged in maintaining and transforming institutions.

Notes

1. "Heteronomous professional organizations" are organizations staffed by professions who are subordinated to a managerial framework. They have discretion over technical or clinical tasks but are subject to routine supervision. (See Scott 1965.)

2. Note that, in the case of organizational fields, many factors are external to a specific organization or population of organizations but internal to the field. (See Scott, Mendel, and Pollack forthcoming.)

3. But note that status and prestige systems are designed to prevent easy transferability of resources. Derogatory terms such as "nouveau riche" and "social climber" illustrate the stickiness of status processes.

4. The researchers show that dominance of the Dayton plan was achieved primarily by selection rather than adaptation processes. That is, terminating plans could not readily be converted into Dayton plans; rather, their growth was primarily due to differential foundings over failure rates (Haveman and Rao 1997).

9   Looking Back,
Looking Forward

In this brief coda, I begin by describing some of the significant contributions that I believe are associated with the resurgence of institutional theory in the social sciences. Then, I collect some evidence that I take to signal progress in the development of neoinstitutional theory in its brief history since the mid-1970s. Finally, I call attention to unresolved issues and to areas where additional work is needed.

Accomplishments

Although all movements ebb and flow, the interest in institutions has, during the past three decades, swelled into a sizable flood of work, both theoretical and empirical. And there is no sign of diminishing interest. Even though any assessment may be premature, I believe the work produced to this point shows evidence of substantial positive fruits.

One of the signal accomplishments of institutional analysis is that it has refocused attention on knowledge and rule systems. These cultural frameworks attracted the attention of earlier generations of social scientists but were not the focus of later theorists, who concentrated on resources and exchange processes external to the organization and on participant behavior and attitudes within it. Resource-dependence and contingency theory emphasized the importance of the technical features of environments and their associated power-dependence effects. And, within organizations, analysts concentrated on examining leadership, morale, and productivity. Emerging in the late 1970s, neoinstitutional views called attention to cultural, normative, and legal frameworks in the environments of organizations and to formal governance structures within them. It was argued that organizational structures have importance apart from—and regardless of—their impact on participant behavior. The structures were viewed as signaling purposefulness and rationality internally but especially to external audiences, demonstrating the organization's connections to and congruence with wider belief and rule systems. Formal structures—constitutions, corporate forms, rule systems, charters, governance systems—once again became proper subjects of scientific study.

Another of the major continuing contributions of institutional theory is that it provides valuable bridges linking the work of scholars past and present and across the social sciences. Before the advent of institutional theory, scholars such as Veblen, Commons, Coase, Durkheim, Weber, and Parsons were either ignored or read as classical theorists. Their concerns and agenda seemed hopelessly outdated. Neoinstitutional scholars have given new life to the ideas of these brilliant scholars by connecting them to new developments in rational choice theory, cultural studies, and cognitive psychology. Thanks to institutional theory, contemporary readers consult the classics in more purposive ways.

Also, more than other intellectual movements, the interest in institutions transcends the disciplinary divisions of the social sciences. Institutional theory and research are flourishing in economics, political science, and sociology, and they are increasingly forging links to cognitive and social psychology. Within organizational and management studies, institutional analysis has captured the interest of both micro and macro students of organizations, of organizational economists, and, more recently, of students of strategy and international management.

It is largely because of the institutionalists that economists have become enlisted in the study of organizational structures. Rather than treating organizations only as "black boxes"—as places within which unanalyzed economic transactions take place—an increasing number of economists now accept the premise that "organization form matters" (Williamson 1985:274): The structural features of organizations, the specifics of their governance structures, affect economic processes and outcomes. Similarly, political scientists are again attending to the distinctive features of political structures and are examining how the particular characteristics of legislatures, agencies, and committees arose and how they affect political processes and outcomes. And sociologists, who in the decade of the 1960s had moved beyond informal networks to investigate variation in formal structures, have been emboldened to examine the connection of these structures to wider rule systems.

Another contribution of institutional analysis is its endorsement and exploitation of a new level of analysis. To an increasing extent, sociologists, political scientists, economists, and management scholars have come to recognize the importance of organizational fields. Whether the particular vocabulary invokes markets, industries, societal sectors, or organizational communities, scholars are increasingly investigating these meso-level systems that mediate between societal structures and individual organizations, and there appear to be promising signs of cross-fertilization and conjoint learning among these camps. The definition of field is, to a large extent, coterminous with the application of a distinctive complex of institutional rules. Because such rules define—constrain and empower—much of the activity within the field, analysts are wise to be cautious in generalizing across fields. But we need to understand and compare fields precisely because they constitute somewhat distinctive worlds that operate under different rules, with different logics and different kinds of players.

Increased awareness of the importance of institutional context has generated renewed interests in comparative studies. Rather than assuming that all organizations are alike or, when differences are found between organizations situated in varying social and cultural contexts, attempting to understate or explain them away, current work is more likely to celebrate diversity and seek to explain why different forms arise and persist.

Because of institutional arguments, the research community exhibits new awareness of the importance of history and of process. There is increasing recognition that time matters, in two senses (see Zald 1990). First, contexts change over time, and the particular context within which an organization, population, or field develops and operates affects what it does and how it does it. Thus, like comparative studies, historical studies help to make us aware of and inform us about the importance of institutional context. Social scientists have long been too provincial in their research designs, content to examine modest differences among organizations operating in the same time and place. The renewal of interest in institutional theory has stimulated more analysts to undertake historical research on organizations and has also encouraged scholars to pay more attention to the historical research already conducted, such as Chandler's (1962, 1977) magisterial history of corporate forms in America.[1]

Second, time matters in that each institution and organization has its own history, its own time-dependent line of development. How a social system develops and operates affects its structure and capacities for action. Institutionalization is a process occurring over time that affects what kinds of structures develop and persist. An interest in institutionalization has encouraged longitudinal studies of particular organizations and of organization fields.

Indicators of Progress

In a review article written nearly 15 years ago, I described institutional theory as passing through the troubled time of adolescence (Scott 1987), showing progress but confronting trying experiences and difficult choices. I believe that we have now passed safely through the purifying fires—that institutional theory can claim to have achieved a promising youthful adulthood. What are the signs of progress? Comparing the arguments and assumptions of the pioneer theorists of the 1970s with contemporary scholars, consider the following indicators.

Early theorists tended to assume that institutional frameworks were monolithic and unified. Today there is widespread recognition that, in most situations, multiple institutions exist, overlap, and offer competing alternative formulations and prescriptions. Legal frameworks and rule systems were earlier assumed to command compliance, to exercise efficient control. Now, it is more widely understood that regulative systems often exert only weak effects and may bring about change not by exerting coercion but by stimulating other institutional mechanisms such as normative and identity processes.

Early institutional students of organizations too often assumed that institutional contexts affected only superficial organizational components or processes. Organizations were thought to decouple their structures so that core units would be protected. Cosmetic changes could be made to surface systems; empty but visible changes could be displayed to pacify external publics. For some, superficial, ceremonial changes were regarded as evidence demonstrating that institutional processes were at work. Later analysts did not deny that some organizational responses to institutional stimuli may be shallow and cynical. Such behavior represents one, but only one, type of response available to organizations. But, just as institutional processes assume many forms and ride on varied carriers, so organizations exhibit a wide repertory of responses. Rather than focusing on a single type, analysts increasingly are open to the wide array of reactions, and, appropriately, they have begun to theorize the conditions under which one rather than another response occurs.

Early conceptions of institutions often treated institutional forces as being external to the organizational systems affected and as determining outcomes. Increasing structural isomorphism was taken as the hallmark of institutional effects. More recent formulations stress the nondeterminant, interactive nature of institutional processes. Actors, whether individual or collective, are recognized to exercise agency, varying in force among actors and across situations, but ever-present. Isomorphism is one possible indicator of institutional forces at work, but only one. Theoretical emphasis has shifted from an examination of institutional effects, which presumes the existence of an external, all-powerful agent confronting passive subjects, to the study of institutional processes, a view that makes the action endogenous and recognizes the wide distribution of agency across actors in most organizational fields.

Early conceptions tended to presume that institutional processes applied to some types of collective actors more (or rather) than others. Some organizations were presumed to operate in "more institutionalized" environments than others. Researchers concentrated on schools, mental health agencies, and voluntary associations to the exclusion of organizations more subject to market controls and efficiency pressures. Public organizations were more frequently studied than private organizations. In particular, economic firms were thought to be exempt from institutional forces, with the exception of regulative processes: to be "culture-free." More recent institutionalists recognize that all types of social actors, all types of organizations, operate in institutional contexts. Markets themselves are institutional frameworks that vary over time and place in the constitutive and regulative rules they establish. The mix of environmental controls varies, some organizations being more subject to procedural and some more subject to outcome controls, but the latter contain important institutional components—for example, selecting what properties are defined as salient and what standards are to be applied. Far from being culture-free, economic firms exemplify some of the most firmly held beliefs and are subject to some of the strongest norms at play in our secularized, rationalized, instrumental modern culture.

Early analysts sometimes employed cultural explanations rather casually and descriptively, providing accounts that were not susceptible to replication or verification. Scholars employing such arguments were sometimes dismissed as being "storytellers" or as engaging in "cheap talk." Recent work is characterized by more systematic analytic techniques and by considerable creativeness in the development of indicators to assess logics, discourse, and artifacts.

There is also evidence of progress in debates about the relation of institutions and rationality. Early formulations that tended to pit institutional against rational arguments have been replaced either by attempts of rational choice theorists to provide interest-based explanations for the origins and operation of institutions or by attempts of other, largely sociological theorists to subsume or embed rational choice explanations in institutional frameworks. Although differences and disagreements persist, both camps have broadened their arguments to take better account of the interplay of interests, information, ideas, and norms.

Finally, in its early stages, institutional theory emphasized the ways in which institutional processes produced stability, uniformity, and order, giving scant attention to the ways in which institutional frameworks stimulate diversity and themselves undergo change. However, in recent years, analysts have accorded increasing attention to the diversity of organizational involvement in institutional processes, examining the varied responses of organizations as they act both individually and collectively. And, numerous scholars have theorized the bases of institutional change and developed methods for empirically examining the complex interplay—the co-evolution—of organizations and their institutional environments. It is recognized that change may be initiated from above or below: Fields may react to developments in wider societal systems, with repercussions for constituent organizations; or individual participants or organizations may serve as the source of innovation, their actions causing waves that destabilize wider systems. Often, institutional agents propose while organizational actors negotiate and dispose innovations and reforms. Institutional change has today taken a central place in the agenda of organizational researchers.

The Challenge Continues

I do not intend the foregoing comments to suggest that no problems remain to be solved or that no useful work remains to be done. Indeed, all of the trends just described are only directions and tendencies at this point, not secure accomplishments. Important work remains as we:

- examine the relation—interaction, conjoint effects, conflicts—of regulative, normative, and cultural-cognitive processes.
- consider why some organizations react in more superficial or more in-depth ways to externally imposed rules and beliefs.
- understand the bases for the varying types of organizational responses—ranging from isomorphic adoption to hostile defiance—to institutional initiatives.
- reconcile the ancient freedom/control debate by better theorizing the ongoing interdependence of structure and agency.
- extend the institutional framework to encompass all manner of organizations, but in a way that illuminates rather than suppresses differences among types of organizations.
- improve the strength and variety of empirical indicators of institutional processes, particularly those involving cognitive-cultural elements, so that arguments can be better informed by empirical research.
- continue the ongoing dialogue between rational-choice and other institutional scholars in ways that reduce contentious controversy and support constructive discussion and debate, so that the important relation between interests and rules and ideas is better understood.
- extend theoretical and empirical efforts to better understand how stable structures become destabilized, how inertia gives way to innovation, how institutional change occurs.

Other issues to be examined include

- to better understand why some kinds of innovation become candidates for institutional processes, whereas other ideas never gain attention or become "also-rans" in the innovation marathon.

- to better integrate the supply versus demand—the push versus pull—views of institutional construction. In some cases, institutional arrangements arise as a response to localized problems, and in others, externally generated ideas are "marketed" in new contexts. But combinations also exist: Groups with problems search for previously crafted solutions.

- to better formulate the processes leading to organizational genesis: the creation of new organizational forms. Our notion of the vital process by which new organizational blueprints are created and disseminated remains primitive and underdeveloped.

- to explain why it is that some historical actions are terribly significant, generating path-dependent forms that become locked in, resisting subsequent improvements, whereas others remain open to modification.

- to improve our understanding of deinstitutional processes—the conditions under which established forms and processes decay and dissolve—and, as a consequence, gain better comprehension of the mechanisms working to maintain institutional arrangements.

- to account for the prominence and power of the state, professions, and international associations—the critical institutional agents of our time—and to identify alternatives in other eras and contexts. We also need to better understand why some of these agents are more persuasive and powerful than others of the same type.

- to better conceptualize structuration (including destructuration) processes as they operate at the level of the organizational field. This central topic has received surprisingly little sustained theoretical or empirical attention from the organizations community.

- to better connect the relation between institutional processes and organizational characteristics so as to understand why an organization responds as it does to institutional stimuli.

- to better understand the conditions under which strategic responses by organizations are more or less likely to be contemplated. We also know little about why organizations select one type of strategic response rather than another.

I conclude with three more general observations about the challenges still ahead. First, I urge that we try to avoid and, to the extent possible, eliminate theoretical arguments based on exclusivist (often, dichotomous) thinking. Too many contemporary scholars decide, for example, that if resource-dependence mechanisms are present, then institutional arguments cannot apply. We need to see that the two formulations may lead to identical predictions; or, more interestingly, that institutional considerations affect what solutions are sought and judged to be acceptable in power-dependency situations. Similar arguments used to swirl around discussions involving institutional and ecological theorists, and their abatement has benefitted students in both camps. The dialogue between institutionalists and ecologists has been generally productive, and scholars have found insightful ways of combining the approaches. But just as some warring camps move toward settlement, other battles break out. Initiated by a distinction suggested in the generally productive review of institutional theory by DiMaggio and Powell (1991), there has developed in recent years an overly competitive dichotomy between the "old" and the "new" institutionalism. These distinctions may have historical utility, but it is neither appropriate nor productive to pit one against the other in a competition for theoretical hegemony or explained variance. The regulative and normative emphases of the old institutionalists are essential to understanding institutional processes and are neither negated nor replaced by the cultural-cognitive emphases of the new institutionalists.

Second, I believe that for too long, social scientists have privileged an entity-based view of social systems to the exclusion of a relational or process-based view (see Emirbayer 1997). As I have emphasized in previous chapters, institutional theory embraces both conceptions—institutions as entities; institutions as processes—but, to date, the entity approach has received the lion's share of attention. Most of the research during the past 30 years has located institutional forces in the organizational environment and, rather than focusing on the ways in which new rules or conceptions arise, has featured variance-based studies to examine their diffusion as affected by organizational characteristics.[2]

The wisdom of substituting structurational for structural conceptions of organizations is rapidly becoming more apparent in today's world of dynamic organizing processes. Network and relational models are becoming more widespread, and the major differences among theorists concern the substance or content carried by these processes: Are they symbols, schemas, narratives? influence? information? resources? Do firms consist of a portfolio of assets? Are organizations a network of contracts? Whatever the answer, all such processes are potentially subject to institutionalization: becoming the object of cultural theorization, the subject of normative and regulative controls.

Processes, as well as structures, can be "infused with value." Institutional theory can accommodate—and we can hope it will enable—the development of a process concept of organization/organizing.

Finally, I have stressed that institutional frameworks are particularly supportive of historical and comparative studies. It remains true, however, that up to the present time, we have been overly timid and modest in our theoretical conceptions and research designs. The number of theoretically informed, systematic, comparative (cross-cultural) studies of organizations remains minuscule, as does the number of studies of organizations or fields that extend over significant periods of time. However, it is only across wider areas and periods that we can expect to observe significant variation in institutional regimes. Most investigators settle for designs examining modest institutional variations—tinkering at the margins—and then express surprise when modest differences are observed. Institutionalists need to "craft a wider lens" (Scott and Christensen 1995a) to advance the science.

Perhaps the golden age of institutional research is about to dawn. The eminent political scientist/historian Samuel P. Huntington (1996) argues in a recent provocative essay that we are moving into a global era in which numerous "civilizations" compete for loyalty and supremacy. The civilizations—each defined in terms of shared "ancestry, religion, language, history, values, customs, and institutions" (p. 21)—are expected to become more vocal and visibly conscious of their distinctive natures. Differences suppressed during the twentieth century by the horror of two world wars and a lengthy cold war that recognized only the Western versus all other civilizations are now being rediscovered, advanced, and celebrated. The Western claim of a single viable model of development and modernization—the "one best way"—is being challenged. Varied modes of capitalism are being recognized (Masten 1986). Multiple rationalities are being proposed.

Just as industrial societies contain more institutional diversity than primitive social structures, the developing postindustrial global community may foster more institutional variety than has our previous world order. Should this prove to be the case, it will mean even more work—and more interesting work—for institutional scholars in the years to come.

Notes

1. In addition to pressures stemming from institutionalists to pay more attention to history, ecologists have also made historical time and developmental processes more salient in the study of organizations.

2. Only the more recent and sophisticated studies have combined variance and process approaches to the analysis of these phenomena, using, for example, event-history models.

References

Abbott, Andrew. 1988. *The System of Professions: An Essay on the Division of Expert Labor.* Chicago: University of Chicago Press.

———. 1990. "A Primer on Sequence Methods." *Organization Science* 1:375-92.

———. 1992. "An Old Institutionalist Reads the New Institutionalism." *Contemporary Sociology* 21:754-56.

Abell, Peter. 1995. "The New Institutionalism and Rational Choice Theory." Pp. 3-14 in *The Institutional Construction of Organizations: International and Longitudinal Studies*, edited by W. Richard Scott and Søren Christensen. London: Sage.

Abrahamson, Eric. 1991. "Managerial Fads and Fashions: The Diffusion and Rejection of Innovations." *Academy of Management Review* 16:586-612.

Abrahamson, Eric and Charles J. Fombrun. 1994. "Macro-cultures: Determinants and Consequences." *Academy of Management Review* 19:728-55.

Abzug, Rikki and Stephen J. Mezias. 1993. "The Fragmented State and Due Process Protections in Organizations: The Case of Comparable Worth." *Organization Science* 4:433-53.

Albert, Stuart and David A. Whetten. 1985. "Organizational Identity." Pp. 263-95 in *Research in Organizational Behavior*, vol. 14, edited by L. L. Cummings and Barry Staw. Greenwich, CT: JAI Press.

Alchian, Armen. 1950. "Uncertainty, Evolution, and Economic Theory." *Journal of Political Economy* 58:211-21.

Alchian, Armen A. and Harold Demsetz. 1972. "Production, Information Costs, and Economic Organization." *American Economic Review* 62:777-95.

Aldrich, Howard E. 1999. *Organizations Evolving*. Thousand Oaks, CA: Sage.

Aldrich, Howard E. and C. Marlene Fiol. 1994. "Fools Rush In? The Institutional Context of Industry Creation." *Academy of Management Review* 19:645-70.

Alexander, Ernest R. 1995. *How Organizations Act Together: Interorganizational Coordination in Theory and Practice.* Luxembourg: Gordon and Breach.

Alexander, Jeffrey C. 1983. *Theoretical Logic in Sociology,* vols. 1-4. Berkeley: University of California Press.

Alexander, Victoria D. 1996. "Pictures at an Exhibition: Conflicting Pressures in Museums and the Display of Art." *American Journal of Sociology* 101:797-839.

Alford, Robert R. 1998. *The Craft of Inquiry: Theories, Methods, Evidence.* New York: Oxford University Press.

Anand, Narasimhan and Richard A. Peterson. 2000. "When Market Information Constitutes Fields: Sensemaking of Markets in the Commercial Music Industry." *Organization Science* 11:260-84.

Archer, Margaret S. 1988. *Culture and Agency: The Place of Culture in Social Theory.* Cambridge, UK: Cambridge University Press.

Armour, H. O. and David Teece. 1978. "Organizational Structure and Economic Performance." *Bell Journal of Economics* 9:106-22.

Aronowitz, Stanley. 1992. *The Politics of Identity: Class, Culture, and Social Movements.* New York: Routledge, Chapman and Hall.

Arthur, W. Brian. 1988. "Self-Reinforcing Mechanisms in Economics." Pp. 9-32 in *The Economy as an Evolving Complex System,* edited by P. W. Anderson and Kenneth J. Arrow. Menlo Park, CA: Addison-Wesley.

Ashforth, Blake E. and Barrie W. Gibbs. 1990. "The Double-Edge of Organizational Legitimation." *Organization Science* 1:177-94.

Axelrod, Robert. 1984. *The Evolution of Cooperation.* New York: Basic Books.

Barley, Stephen R. 1986. "Technology as an Occasion for Structuring: Evidence From Observations of CT Scanners and the Social Order of Radiology Departments." *Administrative Science Quarterly* 31:78-108.

Barley, Stephen R. and Pamela S. Tolbert. 1997. "Institutionalization and Structuration: Studying the Links between Action and Institution." *Organization Studies* 18:93-117.

Barnard, Chester I. 1938. *The Functions of the Executive.* Cambridge, MA: Harvard University Press.

Barnett, William P. and Glenn R. Carroll. 1993a. "How Institutional Constraints Affected the Organization of Early U.S. Telephony." *Journal of Law, Economics, and Organization* 9:98-126.

————.1993b. "Organizational Ecology Approaches to Institutions." Pp. 171-81 in *Interdisciplinary Perspectives on Organization Studies,* edited by Siegwart M. Lindenberg and Hein Schreuder. Oxford, UK: Pergamon.

Baron, James N., Frank R. Dobbin, and P. Deveraux Jennings. 1986. "War and Peace: The Evolution of Modern Personnel Administration in U.S. Industry." *American Journal of Sociology* 92:350-83.

Baron, James N., Michael T. Hannan, and M. Diane Burton. 1999. "Building the Iron Cage: Determinants of Managerial Intensity in the Early Years of Organizations." *American Sociological Review* 64:527-47.

Baron, James N., P. Deveraux Jennings, and Frank R. Dobbin. 1988. "Mission Control? The Development of Personnel Systems in U.S. Industry." *American Sociological Review* 53:497-514.

Baum, Joel A. C. 1996. "Organizational Ecology." Pp. 77-114 in *Handbook of Organization Studies*, edited by Stewart R. Clegg, Cynthia Hardy, and Walter R. Nord. London: Sage.

Baum, Joel A. C. and Jane E. Dutton, eds. 1996. *Advances in Strategic Management*, Vol. 13, *The Embeddedness of Strategy*, edited by Paul Shrivastava, Anne S. Huff, and Jane E. Dutton. Greenwich, CT: JAI Press.

Baum, Joel A. C. and Christine Oliver. 1992. "Institutional Imbeddedness and the Dynamics of Organizational Populations." *American Sociological Review* 57:540-59

Baum, Joel A. C. and Jintendra V. Singh, eds. 1994. *Evolutionary Dynamics of Organizations*. New York: Oxford University Press.

Baum, Joel A. C. and Walter W. Powell. 1995. "Cultivating an Institutional Ecology of Organizations: Comment on Hannan, Carroll, Dundon, and Torres." *American Sociological Review* 60:529-38.

Becker, Howard S. 1982. *Art Worlds*. Berkeley: University of California Press.

Becker, Howard S., Blanche Geer, Everett C. Hughes, and Anselm Strauss. 1961. *Boys in White: Student Culture in Medical School*. Chicago: University of Chicago Press.

Bellah, Robert N., Richard Madsen, William M. Sullivan, Ann Swidler, and Steven M. Tipton. 1985. *Habits of the Heart: Individualism and Commitment in American Life*. Berkeley: University of California Press.

Bendix, Reinhard. 1960. *Max Weber: An Intellectual Portrait*. Garden City, NY: Doubleday.

Berger, Peter L., Brigitte Berger, and Hansfried Kellner. 1973. *The Homeless Mind: Modernization and Consciousness*. New York: Random House.

Berger, Peter L. and Hansfried Kellner. 1981. *Sociology Interpreted: An Essay On Method and Vocation*. Garden City, NY: Doubleday Anchor.

Berger, Peter L. and Thomas Luckmann. 1967. *The Social Construction of Reality*. New York: Doubleday Anchor.

Berman, Harold J. 1983. *Law and Revolution: The Formation of the Western Legal Tradition*. Cambridge, MA: Harvard University Press.

Biggart, Nicole Woolsey and Mauro F. Guillén. 1999. "Developing Difference: Social Organization and the Rise of the Auto Industries of South Korea, Taiwan, Spain, and Argentina." *American Sociological Review* 64:722-47.

Biggart, Nicole Woolsey and Gary G. Hamilton. 1992. "On the Limits of a Firm-Based Theory to Explain Business Networks: The Western Bias of Neoclassical Economics." Pp. 471-90 in *Networks and Organizations: Structure, Form, and Action*, edited by Nitin Nohria and Robert G. Eccles. Boston: Harvard Business School Press.

Bijker, W. E., Thomas Hughes, and Trevor Pinch, eds. 1987. *The Social Construction of Technological Systems: New Directions in the Sociology and History of Technology*. Cambridge: MIT Press.

Bill, James A. and Robert L. Hardgrave, Jr. 1981. *Comparative Politics: The Quest for Theory*. Washington, DC: Bell & Howell, University Press of America.

Blau, Peter M. 1955. *The Dynamics of Bureaucracy*. Chicago: University of Chicago Press.

Blau, Peter M., Cecilia McHugh Falbe, William McKinley, and Phelps K. Tracy. 1976. "Technology and Organization in Manufacturing." *Administrative Science Quarterly* 21:20-40.

Blau, Peter M. and W. Richard Scott. 1962. *Formal Organizations: A Comparative Approach.* San Francisco: Chandler.

Boeker, Warren P. 1989. "The Development and Institutionalization of Subunit Power in Organizations." *Administrative Science Quarterly* 34:388-410.

Boli, John and George M. Thomas. 1997. "World Culture in the World Polity: A Century of International Non-Governmental Organization." *American Sociological Review* 62:171-90.

———, eds. 1999. *Constructing World Culture: International Nongovernmental Organizations Since 1875.* Stanford, CA: Stanford University Press.

Bourdieu, Pierre. 1977. *Outline of a Theory of Practice.* Cambridge, UK: Cambridge University Press.

———. 1988. *Homo Academicus.* Stanford, CA: Stanford University Press.

Bourdieu, Pierre and Loic J. D. Wacquant. 1992. *An Invitation to Reflexive Sociology.* Chicago: University of Chicago Press.

Brint, Steven and Jerome Karabel. 1991. "Institutional Origins and Transformations: The Case of American Community Colleges." Pp. 337-60 in *The New Institutionalism in Organizational Analysis,* edited by Walter W. Powell and Paul J. DiMaggio. Chicago: University of Chicago Press.

Brinton, Mary C. and Victor Nee, eds. 1998. *The New Institutionalism in Sociology.* New York: Russell Sage Foundation.

Brown, Lawrence A. 1981. *Innovation Diffusion: A New Perspective.* London: Methuen.

Brunsson, Nils. 1989. *The Organization of Hypocrisy: Talk, Decisions and Actions in Organizations.* New York: John Wiley.

———. 1998. "A World of Standards: Standardization as a Social Form." Working Paper, Stockholm Center for Organizational Research, Stockholm, Sweden.

Brunsson, Nils and Bengt Jacobsson, eds. 2000. *A World of Standards.* Oxford, UK: Oxford University Press.

Buchanan, James M. and Gordon Tullock. 1962. *The Calculus of Consent.* Ann Arbor: University of Michigan Press.

Buckley, Walter. 1967. *Sociology and Modern Systems Theory.* Englewood Cliffs, NJ: Prentice Hall.

Burawoy, Michael. 1979. *Manufacturing Consent: Changes in the Labor Process Under Monopoly Capitalism.* Chicago: University of Chicago Press.

Burgess, John William. 1902. *Political Science and Comparative Constitutional Law.* Boston: Ginn.

Burke, Peter J. and Donald C. Reitzes. 1981. "The Link Between Identity and Role Performance." *Social Psychology Quarterly* 44:83-92.

Burns, Lawton R. and Douglas R. Wholey. 1993. "Adoption and Abandonment of Matrix Management Programs: Effects of Organizational Characteristics and Interorganizational Networks." *Academy of Management Journal* 36:106-38.

Burrell, Gibson and Gareth Morgan. 1979. *Sociological Paradigms and Organisational Analysis.* London: Heinemann.

Burt, Ronald S. 1987. "Social Contagion and Innovation: Cohesion Versus Structural Equivalence." *American Journal of Sociology* 92:1287-1335.

Calhoun, Craig. 1991. "The Problem of Identity in Collective Action." Pp. 51-75 in *Macro-Micro Linkages in Sociology*, edited by Joan Huber. Beverly Hills, CA: Sage.

Camic, Charles. 1992. "Reputation and Predecessor Selection: Parsons and the Institutionalists." *American Sociological Review* 57:421-45.

Campbell, John L. 1997. "Mechanisms of Evolutionary Change in Economic Governance: Interaction, Interpretation, and Bricolage." Pp. 10-31 in *Evolutionary Economics and Path Dependence*, edited by Lars Magnusson and Jan Ottosson. Cheltenham, UK: Edward Elgar.

Campbell, John L., J. Rogers Hollingsworth, and Leon N. Lindberg, eds. 1991. *Governance of the American Economy*. New York: Cambridge University Press.

Campbell, John L. and Leon N. Lindberg. 1990. "Property Rights and the Organization of Economic Activity by the State." *American Sociological Review* 55:634-47.

———. 1991. "The Evolution of Governance Regimes." Pp. 319-55 in *Governance of the American Economy*, edited by John L. Campbell, J. Rogers Hollingsworth, and Leon N. Lindberg. New York: Cambridge University Press.

Campbell, John L. and Ove K. Pedersen, eds. 1996. *Legacies of Change: Transformations of Postcommunist European Economies*. New York: Aldine de Gruyter.

Carroll, Glenn R. 1984. "Organizational Ecology." *Annual Review of Sociology* 10:71-93.

———. 1987. *Publish and Perish: The Organizational Ecology of Newspaper Industries*. Greenwich, CT: JAI Press.

Carroll, Glenn R. and Jacques Delacroix. 1982. "Organizational Mortality in the Newspaper Industries of Argentina and Ireland: An Ecological Approach." *Administrative Science Quarterly* 27:169-98.

Carroll, Glenn R., Jacques Delacroix, and Jerry Goodstein. 1988. "The Political Environments of Organizations: An Ecological View." Pp. 359-92 in *Research in Organizational Behavior* (Vol. 10), edited by Barry M. Staw and L. L. Cummings. Greenwich, CT: JAI Press.

Carroll, Glenn R., Jerry Goodstein, and Antal Gyenes. 1988. "Organizations and the State: Effects of the Institutional Environment on Agricultural Cooperatives in Hungary." *Administrative Science Quarterly* 33:233-56.

Carroll, Glenn R. and Michael T. Hannan. 1989. "Density Dependence in the Evolution of Populations of Newspaper Organizations." *American Sociological Review* 54:524-48.

Carroll, Glenn R. and Yangchung Paul Huo. 1986. "Organizational Task and Institutional Environments in Ecological Perspective: Findings from the Local Newspaper Industry." *American Journal of Sociology* 91:838-73.

Cawson, Alan, ed. 1985. *Organized Interests and the State: Studies in Meso-Corporatism*. Beverly Hills, CA: Sage.

Certina, Karin Knorr. 1999. *Epistemic Cultures: How the Sciences Make Knowledge*. Cambridge, MA: Harvard University Press.

Chandler, Alfred D., Jr. 1962. *Strategy and Structure: Chapters in the History of the American Industrial Enterprise*. Cambridge: MIT Press.

———. 1977. *The Visible Hand: The Managerial Revolution in American Business*. Cambridge, MA: Belknap Press of Harvard University Press.

Christensen, Søren, Peter Karnøe, Jesper Strangaard Pedersen, and Frank Dobbin, eds. 1997. "Action in Institutions" [Special issue]. *American Behavioral Scientist* 40:389-538.

Cicourel, Aaron V. 1968. *The Social Organization of Juvenile Justice.* New York: John Wiley.

Clark, Burton R. 1960. *The Open Door College.* New York: McGraw-Hill.

———. 1970. *The Distinctive College: Antioch, Reed, and Swarthmore.* Chicago: Aldine de Gruyter.

Clemens, Elisabeth S. 1993. "Organizational Repertoires and Institutional Change: Women's Groups and the Transformation of U.S. Politics, 1890-1920." *American Journal of Sociology* 98:755-98.

Clemens, Elisabeth S. and James M. Cook. 1999. "Politics and Institutionalism: Explaining Durability and Change." *Annual Review of Sociology* 25:441-66.

Coase, Ronald H. 1937. "The Nature of the Firm."*Economica* N.S. 4:385-405.

———. 1972. "Industrial Organization: A Proposal for Research." Pp. 59-73 in *Policy Issues and Research Opportunities in Industrial Organization,* edited by Victor R. Fuchs. New York: National Bureau of Economic Research.

———. 1983. "The New Institutional Economics." *Journal of Institutional and Theoretical Economics* 140:229-31.

Cole, Robert E. 1989. *Strategies for Learning: Small-group Activities in American, Japanese, and Swedish Industry.* Berkeley: University of California Press.

———. 1999. *Managing Quality Fads: How American Business Learned to Play the Quality Game.* New York: Oxford University Press.

Cole, Robert E. and W. Richard Scott, eds. 2000. *The Quality Movement & Organization Theory.* Thousand Oaks, CA: Sage.

Coleman, James R. 1974. *Power and the Structure of Society.* New York: Norton.

———. 1990. *Foundations of Social Theory.* Cambridge, MA: Belknap Press of Harvard University Press.

———. 1994. "A Rational Choice Perspective on Economic Sociology." Pp. 166-80 in *The Handbook of Economic Sociology,* edited by Neil J. Smelser and Richard Swedberg. Princeton, NJ: Princeton University Press and Russell Sage Foundation.

Commons, John R. 1924. *The Legal Foundations of Capitalism.* New York: Macmillan.

———. [1950] 1970. *The Economics of Collective Action.* Madison: University of Wisconsin Press.

Cooley, Charles Horton. [1902] 1956. *Social Organization.* Glencoe, IL: Free Press.

Cooper, David J., Bob Hinings, Royston Greenwood, and John L. Brown. 1996. "Sedimentation and Transformation in Organizational Change: The Case of Canadian Law Firms." *Organization Studies* 17:632-47.

Covaleski, Mark A. and Mark W. Dirsmith. 1988. "An Institutional Perspective on the Rise, Social Transformation, and Fall of a University Budget Category." *Administrative Science Quarterly* 33:562-87.

Czarniawska, Barbara. 1997. *Narrating the Organization: Dramas of Institutional Identity.* Chicago: University of Chicago Press.

Dacin, M. Tina. 1997. "Isomorphism in Context: The Power and Prescription of Institutional Norms." *Academy of Management Journal* 40:46-81.

Dacin, M. Tina, Marc J. Ventresca, and Brent D. Beal. 1999. "The Embeddedness of Organizations: Dialogue and Directions." *Journal of Management* 25:317-56.

Daft, Richard and Karl E. Weick. 1984. "Toward a Model of Organizations as Interpretation Systems." *Academy of Management Review* 9:284-95.

D'Andrade, Roy G. 1984. "Cultural Meaning Systems." Pp. 88-119 in *Culture Theory: Essays on Mind, Self, and Emotion,* edited by Richard A. Shweder and Robert A. LeVine. Cambridge, UK: Cambridge University Press.

D'Aunno, Thomas, Robert I. Sutton, and Richard H. Price. 1991. "Isomorphism and External Support in Conflicting Institutional Environments: A Study of Drug Abuse Treatment Units." *Academy of Management Journal* 14:636-61.

David, Paul A. 1985. "Clio and the Economics of QWERTY." *American Economic Review* 75:332-37.

David, Paul A. 1992. "Why are Institutions the 'Carriers of History'? Notes on Path-Dependence and the Evolution of Conventions, Organizations, and Institutions." Presented to the Stanford Institute for Theoretical Economics, July, Stanford University.

Davis, Gerald F. 1994. "The Corporate Elite and Politics of Corporate Control." Pp. 245-68 in *Current Perspectives in Social Theory,* Sup. 1, edited by Christopher Prendergast and J. David Knottnerus. Greenwich, CT: JAI Press.

Davis, Gerald F., Kristina A. Diekmann, and Catherine H. Tinsley. 1994. "The Decline and Fall of the Conglomerate Firm in the 1980s: The Deinstitutionalization of an Organizational Form." *American Sociological Review* 59:547-70.

Davis, Gerald F. and Henrich R. Greve. 1997. "Corporate Elite Networks and Governance Changes in the 1980s." *American Journal of Sociology* 103:1-37.

Davis, Kingsley. 1949. *Human Society.* New York: Macmillan.

Deephouse, David L. 1996. "Does Isomorphism Legitimate?" *Academy of Management Journal* 39:1024-39.

Delacroix, Jacques and Hayagreeva Rao. 1994. "Externalities and Ecological Theory: Unbundling Density Dependence." Pp. 255-68 in *Evolutionary Dynamics of Organizations,* edited by Joel A. C. Baum and Jitendra V. Singh. New York: Oxford University Press.

Dezalay, Yves and Bryant G. Garth. 1996. *Dealing in Virtue: International Commercial Arbitration and the Construction of a Transnational Legal Order.* Chicago: University of Chicago Press.

DiMaggio, Paul J. 1983. "State Expansion and Organization Fields." Pp. 147-61 in *Organization Theory and Public Policy,* edited by Richard H. Hall and Robert E. Quinn. Beverly Hills, CA: Sage.

———. 1986. "Structural Analysis of Organizational Fields: A Blockmodel Approach." Pp. 355-70 in *Research in Organization Behavior,* vol. 8, edited by Barry M. Staw and L. L. Cummings. Greenwich, CT: JAI Press.

———. 1988. "Interest and Agency in Institutional Theory." Pp. 3-21 in *Institutional Patterns and Organizations: Culture and Environment,* edited by Lynne G. Zucker. Cambridge, MA: Ballinger.

———. 1990. "Cultural Aspects of Economic Organization and Behavior." Pp. 113-36 in *Beyond the Marketplace: Rethinking Economy and Society,* edited by Roger Friedland and A. F. Robertson. New York: Aldine de Gruyter.

————. 1991. "Constructing an Organizational Field as a Professional Project: U.S. Art Museums, 1920-1940." Pp. 267-92 in *The New Institutionalism in Organizational Analysis*, edited by Walter W. Powell and Paul J. DiMaggio. Chicago: University of Chicago Press.

————. 1997. "Culture and Cognition: An Interdisciplinary Review." *Annual Review of Sociology* 23:263-87.

DiMaggio, Paul J. and Walter W. Powell. 1983. "The Iron Cage Revisited: Institutional Isomorphism and Collective Rationality in Organizational Fields." *American Sociological Review* 48:147-60.

————. 1991. "Introduction." Pp. 1-38 in *The New Institutionalism in Organizational Analysis*, edited by Walter W. Powell and Paul J. DiMaggio. Chicago: University of Chicago Press.

Dobbin, Frank R. 1994a. "Cultural Models of Organization: The Social Construction of Rational Organizing Principles." Pp. 117-53 in *The Sociology of Culture: Emerging Theoretical Perspectives*, edited by Diana Crane. Oxford, UK: Blackwell.

————. 1994b. *Forging Industrial Policy: The United States, Britain, and France in the Railway Age*. Cambridge, UK: Cambridge University Press.

Dobbin, Frank R., Lauren Edelman, John W. Meyer, W. Richard Scott, and Ann Swidler. 1988. "The Expansion of Due Process in Organizations." Pp. 71-100 in *Institutional Patterns and Organizations: Culture and Environment*, edited by Lynne G. Zucker. Cambridge, MA: Ballinger.

Dobbin, Frank R. and John R. Sutton. 1998. "The Strength of a Weak State: The Rights Revolution and the Rise of Human Resources Management Divisions." *American Journal of Sociology* 104:441-76.

Dobbin, Frank R., John R. Sutton, John W. Meyer, and W. Richard Scott. 1993. "Equal Opportunity Law and the Construction of Internal Labor Markets." *American Journal of Sociology* 99:396-427.

Dornbusch, Sanford M. and W. Richard Scott, with the assistance of Bruce C. Busching and James D. Laing. 1975. *Evaluation and the Exercise of Authority*. San Francisco: Jossey-Bass.

Douglas, Mary. 1982. "The Effects of Modernization on Religious Change." *Daedalus* (Winter):1-19.

————. 1986. *How Institutions Think*. Syracuse, NY: Syracuse University Press.

Dowling, John and Jeffrey Pfeffer. 1975. "Organizational Legitimacy: Social Values and Organizational Behavior." *Pacific Sociological Review* 18:122-36.

Durkheim, Émile. [1893] 1949. *Division of Labor in Society*. Glencoe, IL: Free Press.

————. [1901] 1950. *The Rules of Sociological Method*. Glencoe, IL: Free Press.

————. [1912] 1961. *The Elementary Forms of Religious Life*. New York: Collier Books.

Easton, David. 1965. *A Framework for Political Analysis*. Englewood Cliffs, NJ: Prentice Hall.

Eckstein, Harry. 1963. "A Perspective on Comparative Politics, Past and Present." Pp. 3-32 in *Comparative Politics*, edited by Harry Eckstein and David E. Apter. New York: Free Press of Glencoe.

Edelman, Lauren B. 1992. "Legal Ambiguity and Symbolic Structures: Organizational Mediation of Civil Rights Law." *American Journal of Sociology* 97:1531-76.

Edelman, Lauren B. and Mark C. Suchman. 1997. "The Legal Environment of Organizations." *Annual Review of Sociology* 23:479-515.

Edelman, Lauren B., Christopher Uggen, and Howard S. Erlanger. 1999. "The Endogeneity of Legal Regulation: Grievance Procedures as Rational Myth." *American Journal of Sociology* 105:406-54.

Ellul, Jacques. [1954] 1964. *The Technological Society*. New York: Knopf.

Elsbach, Kimberly D. and Robert I. Sutton. 1992. "Acquiring Organizational Legitimacy Through Illegitimate Actions: A Marriage of Institutional and Impression Management Theories." *Academy of Management Journal* 35:699-738.

Elster, Jon. 1983. *Explaining Technical Change: A Case Study in the Philosophy of Science.* Cambridge, UK: Cambridge University Press.

Emirbayer, Mustafa. 1997. "Manifesto for a Relational Sociology." *American Journal of Sociology* 103:281-317.

Emirbayer, Mustafa and Ann Mische. 1998. "What is Agency?" *American Journal of Sociology* 103:962-1023.

Espeland, Wendy Nelson and Mitchell L. Stevens. 1998. "Commensuration as a Social Process." *Annual Review of Sociology* 24:313-43.

Fine, Gary Alan and Lori J. Ducharme. 1995. "The Ethnographic Present: Images of Institutional Control in Second-School Research." Pp. 108-35 in *A Second Chicago School? The Development of a Postwar American Sociology,* edited by Gary Allan Fine. Chicago: University of Chicago Press.

Fligstein, Neil. 1985. "The Spread of the Multidivisional Form among Large Firms, 1919-1979." *American Sociological Review* 50:377-91.

———. 1987. "The Intraorganizational Power Struggle: The Rise of Finance Presidents in Large Corporations, 1919-1979." *American Sociological Review* 52:44-58.

———. 1990. *The Transformation of Corporate Control.* Cambridge, MA: Harvard University Press.

———. 1991. "The Structural Transformation of American Industry: An Institutional Account of the Causes of Diversification in the Largest Firms, 1919-1979." Pp. 311-36 in *The New Institutionalism in Organizational Analysis,* edited by Walter W. Powell and Paul J. DiMaggio. Chicago: University of Chicago Press.

Flood, Ann Barry and W. Richard Scott. 1987. *Hospital Structure and Performance.* Baltimore, MD: Johns Hopkins University Press.

Frank, David John, Ann Hironaka, John W. Meyer, Evan Schofer, and Nancy Brandon Tuma. 1999. "The Rationalization and Organization of Nature in World Culture." Pp. 81-99 in *Constructing World Culture: International Nongovernmental Organizations Since 1875,* edited by John Boli and George M. Thomas. Stanford, CA: Stanford University Press.

Freidson, Eliot. 1970. *Profession of Medicine.* New York: Dodd, Mead.

———. 1986. *Professional Powers: A Study of the Institutionalization of Formal Knowledge.* Chicago: University of Chicago Press.

Friedland, Roger and Robert R. Alford. 1991. "Bringing Society Back In: Symbols, Practices, and Institutional Contradictions." Pp. 232-263 in *The New Institutionalism in Organizational Analysis,* edited by Walter W. Powell and Paul J. DiMaggio. Chicago: University of Chicago Press.

Fromm, Gary, ed. 1981. *Studies in Public Regulation.* Cambridge: MIT Press.

Galaskiewicz, Joseph and Wolfgang Bielefeld. 1998. *Nonprofit Organizations in an Age of Uncertainty: A Study of Organizational Change.* New York: Aldine de Gruyter.

Galaskiewicz, Joseph and Ronald S. Burt. 1991. "Interorganizational Contagion in Corporate Philanthropy." *Administrative Science Quarterly* 36:88-105.

Garfinkel, Harold. 1967. *Studies in Ethnomethodology.* Englewood Cliffs, NJ: Prentice Hall.

———. 1974. "The Origins of the Term 'Ethnomethodogy'." Pp. 15-18 in *Ethnomethodology: Selected Readings,* edited by Roy Turner. Harmondworth, UK: Penguin Books.

Garud, Raghu and Michael A. Rappa. 1994. "A Socio-Cognitive Model of Technology Evolution: The Case of Cochlear Implants." *Organization Science* 5:344-62.

Geertz, Clifford. 1971. *Islam Observed: Religious Development in Morocco and Indonesia.* Chicago: University of Chicago Press.

———. 1973. *The Interpretation of Cultures.* New York: Basic Books.

Georgopoulos, Basil S. 1972. "The Hospital as an Organization and Problem-Solving System." Pp. 9-48 in *Organization Research on Health Institutions,* edited by Basil S. Georgopoulos. Ann Arbor: Institute for Social Research, University of Michigan.

Gergen, Kenneth J. and Keith E. Davis, eds. 1985. *The Social Construction of the Person.* New York: Springer-Verlag.

Ghoshal, Sumantra and D. Eleanor Westney, eds. 1993. *Organization Theory and the Multinational Corporation.* New York: St. Martin's.

Giddens, Anthony. 1979. *Central Problems in Social Theory: Action, Structure, and Contradiction in Social Analysis.* Berkeley: University of California Press.

———. 1984. *The Constitution of Society.* Berkeley: University of California Press.

Glassman, Robert. 1973. "Persistence and Loose Coupling in Living Systems." *Behavioral Science* 18:83-98.

Goffman, Erving. 1961. *Asylums.* Garden City, NY: Doubleday, Anchor Books.

———. 1974. *Frame Analysis.* Cambridge, MA: Harvard University Press.

———. 1983. "The Interaction Order." *American Sociological Review* 48:1-17.

Goodrick, Elizabeth and Gerald R. Salancik. 1996. "Organizational Discretion in Responding to Institutional Practices: Hospitals and Cesarean Births." *Administrative Science Quarterly* 41:1-28.

Gouldner, Alvin W. 1954. *Patterns of Industrial Bureaucracy.* Glencoe, IL: Free Press.

Granovetter, Mark. 1985. "Economic Action and Social Structure: The Problem of Embeddedness." *American Journal of Sociology* 91:481-510.

Greening, Daniel W. and Barbara Gray. 1994. "Testing a Model of Organizational Response to Social and Political Issues." *Academy of Management Journal* 37:467-98.

Greenwood, Royston and C. R. Hinings. 1993. "Understanding Strategic Change: The Contribution of Archetypes." *Academy of Management Journal* 36:1052-81.

———. 1996. "Understanding Radical Organizational Change: Bringing Together the Old and the New Institutionalism." *Academy of Management Review* 21:1022-54.

Greve, Henrich R. 1995. "Jumping Ship: The Diffusion of Strategy Abandonment." *Administrative Science Quarterly* 40:444-73.

———. 1998. "Managerial Cognition and the Mimetic Adoption of Market Positions: What You See Is What You Do." *Strategic Management Journal* 19:967-88.

Griswold, Wendy. 1992. "Recent Developments in the Sociology of Culture: Four Good Arguments (and One Bad One)." *Acta Sociologica* 35:323-28.

Guillén, Mauro F. 1994. *Models of Management: Work, Authority, and Organization in a Comparative Perspective*. Chicago: University of Chicago Press.

Gulick, Luther and L. Urwick, eds. 1937. *Papers in the Science of Administration*. New York: Institute of Public Administration, Columbia University.

Gusfield, Joseph R. 1955. "Social Structure and Moral Reform: A Study of the Women's Christian Temperance Union." *American Journal of Sociology* 61:221-32.

Hall, Peter A. 1986. *Governing the Economy: The Politics of State Intervention in Britain and France*. Cambridge, UK: Polity Press.

Hall, Richard H. 1992. "Taking Things a Bit Too Far: Some Problems with Emergent Institutional Theory." Pp. 71-87 in *Issues, Theory, and Research in Industrial Organizational Psychology*, edited by Kathryn Kelley. Amsterdam: Elsevier.

Halliday, Terence C., Michael J. Powell, and Mark W. Granfors. 1993. "After Minimalism: Transformation of State Bar Associations From Market Dependence to State Reliance, 1918 to 1950." *American Sociological Review* 58:515-35.

Hamilton, Gary and Nicole W. Biggart. 1988. "Market, Culture, and Authority: A Comparative Analysis of Management and Organization in the Far East." *American Journal of Sociology* 94 (Supplement):S52-S94.

Hannan, Michael T. and Glenn Carroll, eds. 1995. *Organizations in Industry*. Oxford, UK: Oxford University Press.

Hannan, Michael T., Glenn R. Carroll, Elizabeth A. Dundon, and John Charles Torres. 1995. "Organizational Evolution in a Multinational Context: Entries of Automobile Manufacturers in Belgium, Britain, France, Germany, and Italy." *American Sociological Review* 60:509-28.

Hannan, Michael T. and John Freeman. 1977. "The Population Ecology of Organizations." *American Journal of Sociology* 82:929-64.

———. 1984. "Structural Inertia and Organizational Change." *American Sociological Review* 49:149-64.

———. 1989. *Organizational Ecology*. Cambridge, MA: Harvard University Press.

Hasenclever, A., P. Mayer, and V. Rittberger. 1997. *Theories of International Regimes*. Cambridge, UK: Cambridge University Press.

Haunschild, Pamela R. 1993. "Interorganizational Imitation: The Impact of Interlocks on Corporate Acquisition Activity." *Administrative Science Quarterly* 38:564-92.

Haunschild, Pamela R. and Christine M. Beckman. 1998. "When Do Interlocks Matter? Alternative Sources of Information and Interlock Influence." *Administrative Science Quarterly* 43:815-44.

Haunschild, Pamela R. and Anne S. Miner. 1997. "Modes of Interorganizational Imitation: The Effects of Outcome Salience and Uncertainty." *Administrative Science Quarterly* 42:472-500.

Haveman, Heather A. 1993. "Follow the Leader: Mimetic Isomorphism and Entry into New Markets." *Administrative Science Quarterly* 38:593-627.

Haveman, Heather A. and Hayagreeva Rao. 1997. "Structuring a Theory of Moral Sentiments: Institutional and Organizational Coevolution in the Early Thrift Industry." *American Journal of Sociology* 102:1606-51.

———. Forthcoming. "Hybrid Forms and Institution/Organization Co-Evolution in the Early California Thrift Industry." In *How Institutions Change*, edited by Walter W. Powell and Daniel L. Jones. Chicago: University of Chicago Press.

Hawley, Amos. 1950. *Human Ecology.* New York: Ronald Press.

———. 1968. *Human Ecology: A Theoretical Essay.* Chicago: University of Chicago Press.

Hay, Peter. 1993. "Royal Treatment." *Performing Arts*, March, p. 70.

Hayek, Friedrich A. 1948. *Individualism and Economic Order.* Chicago: University of Chicago Press.

Hechter, Michael. 1987. *Principles of Group Solidarity.* Berkeley: University of California Press.

Hechter, Michael, Karl-Dieter Opp, and Reinhard Wippler, eds. 1990. *Social Institutions: Their Emergence, Maintenance, and Effects.* New York: Aldine de Gruyter.

Hegel, G. W. F. [1807] 1967. *The Phenomenology of Mind.* New York: Harper & Row.

Heilbroner, Robert L. 1985. *The Nature and Logic of Capitalism.* New York: Norton.

Heimer, Carol A. 1999. "Competing Institutions: Law, Medicine, and Family in Neonatal Intensive Care." *Law and Society Review* 33:17-66.

Helper, Susan, John Paul MacDuffie, and Charles Sabel. 2000. "Pragmatic Collaborations: Advancing Knowledge While Controlling Opportunism." Unpublished manuscript, Wharton School, University of Pennsylvania.

Hirsch, Paul M. 1972. "Processing Fads and Fashions: An Organization-Set Analysis of Cultural Industry Systems." *American Sociological Review* 77:639-59.

———. 1985. "The Study of Industries." Pp. 271-309 in *Research in the Sociology of Organizations*, vol. 4, edited by Sam B. Bacharach and S. M. Mitchell. Greenwich, CT: JAI Press.

———. 1986. "From Ambushes to Golden Parachutes: Corporate Takeovers as an Instance of Cultural Framing and Institutional Integration." *American Journal of Sociology* 91:800-37.

———. 1997. "Review Essay: Sociology Without Social Structure: Neoinstitutional Theory Meets Brave New World." *American Journal of Sociology* 102:1702-23.

Hirsch, Paul M. and Michael D. Lounsbury. 1996. "Rediscovering Volition: The Institutional Economics of Douglass C. North." *Academy of Management Review* 21:872-84.

Hochshild, Arlie Russell. 1983. *The Managed Heart: Commercialization of Human Feeling.* Berkeley: University of California Press.

Hodgson, Geoffrey. 1991. "Institutional Economic Theory: The Old versus the New." Pp. 194-213 in *After Marx and Sraffa: Essays in Political Economy* by Geoffrey M. Hodgson. New York: St. Martin's.

———, ed. 1993. *The Economics of Institutions.* Aldershot, UK: Edward Elgar.

———. 1994. "The Return of Institutional Economics." Pp. 58-76 in *The Handbook of Economic Sociology*, edited by Neil J. Smelser and Richard Swedberg. Princeton, NJ: Princeton University Press and Russell Sage Foundation.

Hoffman, Andrew W. 1997. *From Heresy to Dogma: An Institutional History of Corporate Environmentalism.* San Francisco: New Lexington Press.

Hollingsworth, J. Rogers and Robert Boyer, eds. 1997. *Contemporary Capitalism: The Embeddedness of Institutions.* Cambridge, UK: Cambridge University Press.

Holm, Petter. 1995. "The Dynamics of Institutionalization: Transformation Processes in Norwegian Fisheries." *Administrative Science Quarterly* 40:398-422.

Hopwood, Anthony and Peter Miller. 1994. *Accounting as a Social and Institutional Practice.* Cambridge, UK: Cambridge University Press.

Hughes, Everett C. 1936. "The Ecological Aspect of Institutions." *American Sociological Review* 1:180-189.

———. 1939. "Institutions." Pp. 281-330 in Robert E. Park, ed., *An Outline of the Principles of Sociology.* New York: Barnes & Noble.

———. 1958. *Men and Their Work.* Glencoe, IL: Free Press. (Collected essays dating from 1928)

Hult, Karen M. and Charles Walcott. 1990. *Governing Public Organizations: Politics, Structures, and Institutional Design.* Pacific Grove, CA: Brooks/Cole.

Huntington, Samuel P. 1996. *The Clash of Civilizations and the Remaking of World Order.* New York: Simon & Schuster.

Hybels, Ralph C. and Allan R. Ryan. 1996. "The Legitimization of Commercial Biotechnology Through the Business Press, 1974-1989." Presented at the annual meeting of the Academy of Management, Cincinnati, Ohio.

Jaccoby, Sanford M. 1990. "The New Institutionalism: What Can It Learn from the Old?" *Industrial Relations* 29:316-59.

Jensen, Michael C. and William H. Meckling. 1976. "Theory of the Firm: Managerial Behavior, Agency Costs, and Ownership Structure." *Journal of Financial Economics* 3:305-60.

Jepperson, Ronald L. 1991. "Institutions, Institutional Effects, and Institutionalization." Pp. 143-63 in *The New Institutionalism in Organizational Analysis,* edited by Walter W. Powell and Paul J. DiMaggio. Chicago: University of Chicago Press.

Jepperson, Ronald L. and John W. Meyer. 1991. "The Public Order and the Construction of Formal Organizations." Pp. 204-31 in *The New Institutionalism in Organizational Analysis,* edited by Walter W. Powell and Paul J. DiMaggio. Chicago: University of Chicago Press.

Jepperson, Ronald L. and Ann Swidler. 1994. "What Properties of Culture Should We Measure?" *Poetics* 22:359-71.

Jones, Edward E. and Keith E. Davis. 1965. "From Acts to Dispositions: The Attribution Process in Person Perception." Pp. 220-66 in *Advances in Experimental Social Psychology,* vol. 2, edited by Leonard Berkowitz. New York: Academic Press.

Jowell, Jeffrey L. 1975. *Law and Bureaucracy: Administrative Discretion and the Limits of Legal Action.* Port Washington, NY: Dunellen.

Kahn, Robert L. and Mayer N. Zald, eds. 1990. *Organizations and Nation-States: New Perspectives on Conflict and Cooperation.* San Francisco: Jossey-Bass.

Kalleberg, Arne L., David Knoke, Peter V. Marsden, and Joe L. Spaeth. 1996. *Organizations in America: Analyzing Their Structures and Human Resource Practices.* Thousand Oaks, CA: Sage.

Kaplan, Marilyn R. and J. Richard Harrison. 1993. "Defusing the Director Liability Crisis: The Strategic Management of Legal Threats." *Organization Science* 4:412-32.

Katz, Daniel and Robert L. Kahn. 1966. *The Social Psychology of Organizations.* New York: John Wiley.

Katz, M. L. and C. Shapiro. 1985. "Network Externalities, Competition, and Compatibility." *American Economic Review* 75:424-40.

Keohane, Robert O., ed. 1989. *International Institutions and State Power: Essays in International Relations Theory.* Boulder, CO: Westview.

Kerr, Clark, John T. Dunlop, Frederick Harbison, and Charles A. Myers. 1964. *Industrialism and Industrial Man.* 2nd ed. New York: Oxford University Press.

Kilduff, Martin. 1993. "The Reproduction of Inertia in Multinational Corporations." Pp. 259-74 in *Organization Theory and the Multinational Corporation,* edited by Sumantra Ghoshal and D. Eleanor Westney. New York: St. Martin's.

Kimberly, John R. 1975. "Environmental Constraints and Organizational Structure: A Comparative Analysis of Rehabilitation Organizations." *Administrative Science Quarterly* 20:1-9.

Kiser, Edgar and Michael Hechter. 1991. "The Role of General Theory in Comparative-Historical Sociology." *American Journal of Sociology* 97:1-30.

Kitschelt, Herbert. 1991. "Industrial Governance Structures, Innovation Strategies, and the Case of Japan: Sectoral or Cross-national Comparative Analysis?" *International Organization* 45:453-93.

Knudsen, Christian. 1993. "Modelling Rationality, Institutions and Processes in Economic Theory." Pp. 265-99 in *Rationality, Institutions, and Economic Methodology,* edited by Uskali Mäki, Bo Gustafsson, and Christian Knudsen. London: Routledge.

———. 1995. "Theories of the Firm, Strategic Management, and Leadership." Pp. 179-217 in *Resource-Based and Evolutionary Theories of the Firm: Toward a Synthesis,* edited by Cynthia A. Montgomery. Boston: Kluwer.

Kraatz, Matthew S. 1998. "Learning by Association? Interorganizational Networks and Adaptation to Environmental Change." *Academy of Management Journal* 41:621-43.

Krasner, Stephen D., ed. 1983. *International Regimes.* Ithaca, NY: Cornell University Press.

———. 1988. "Sovereignty: An Institutional Perspective." *Comparative Political Studies* 21:66-94.

Kuhn, Thomas. 1970. *The Structure of Scientific Revolutions.* 2nd ed. Chicago: University of Chicago Press.

Kunda, Gideon. 1992. *Engineering Culture: Control and Commitment in a High-Tech Corporation.* Philadelphia: Temple University Press.

Landy, M., M. Roberts, and S. Thomas. 1990. *The Environmental Protection Agency: Asking the Wrong Questions.* New York: Oxford University Press.

Langlois, Richard N. 1986a. "The New Institutional Economics: An Introductory Essay." Pp. 1-25 in *Economics as a Process: Essays in the New Institutional Economics,* edited by Richard M. Langlois. New York: Cambridge University Press.

———. 1986b. "Rationality, Institutions, and Explanations." Pp. 225-55 in *Economics as a Process: Essays in the New Institutional Economics,* edited by Richard M. Langlois. New York: Cambridge University Press.

Lant, Theresa K. and Joel A. C. Baum. 1995. "Cognitive Sources of Socially Constructed Competitive Groups: Examples from the Manhattan Hotel Industry." Pp. 15-38 in *The Institutional Construction of Organizations: International and Longitudinal Studies,* edited by W. Richard Scott and Schøn Christensen. Thousand Oaks, CA: Sage.

Lasswell, Harold. 1936. *Politics: Who Gets What, When, How?* New York: Whittlesey House.

Lave, Charles A. and James G. March. 1975. *An Introduction to Models in the Social Sciences.* New York: Harper & Row.

Laumann, Edward O. and David Knoke. 1987. *The Organizational State: Social Choice in National Policy Domains.* Madison: University of Wisconsin Press.

Leblebici, Husayin and Gerald R. Salancik. 1982. "Stability in Interorganizational Exchanges: Rulemaking Processes of the Chicago Board of Trade." *Administrative Science Quarterly* 27:227-42.

Leblebici, Husayin, Gerald R. Salancik, Anne Copay, and Tom King. 1991. "Institutional Change and the Transformation of Interorganizational Fields: An Organizational History of the U.S. Radio Broadcasting Industry." *Administrative Science Quarterly* 36:333-63.

Levitt, Barbara and James G. March. 1988. "Organization Learning." *Annual Review of Sociology* 14:319-40.

Lewin, Kurt. 1951. *Field Theory in Social Psychology.* New York: Harper.

Lindblom, Charles E. 1977. *Politics and Markets: The World's Political-Economic Systems.* New York: Basic Books.

Lipset, Seymour Martin, Martin A. Trow, and James S. Coleman. 1956. *Union Democracy.* Glencoe, IL: Free Press.

Lipsky, Martin. 1980. *Street-Level Bureaucracy.* New York: Russell Sage Foundation.

Loya, Thomas A. and John Boli. 1999. "Standardization in the World Polity: Technical Rationality over Power." Pp. 169-97 in *Constructing World Culture: International Nongovernmental Organizations Since 1875,* edited by John Boli and George M. Thomas. Stanford, CA: Stanford University Press.

Macaulay, Stewart. 1963. "Non-contractual Relations in Business." *American Sociological Review* 28:55-70.

McAdam, Doug. 1982. *Political Process and the Development of Black Insurgency, 1930-1970.* Chicago: University of Chicago Press.

McAdam, Doug, John D. McCarthy, and Mayer N. Zald. 1996. "Introduction: Opportunities, Mobilizing Structures, and Framing Processes—Toward a Synthetic, Comparative Perspective on Social Movements." Pp. 1-22 in *Comparative Perspectives on Social Movements: Political Opportunities, Mobilizing Structures, and Cultural Framings,* edited by Doug McAdam, John D. McCarthy, and Mayer N. Zald. Cambridge, UK: Cambridge University Press.

McCarthy, John D. and Mayer N. Zald. 1977. "Resource Mobilization and Social Movements: A Partial Theory." *American Journal of Sociology* 82:1212-41.

McKelvey, Bill. 1982. *Organizational Systematics.* Berkeley: University of California Press.

McLaughlin, Milbrey W. 1975. *Evaluation and Reform: The Elementary and Secondary Education Act of 1965.* Cambridge, MA: Ballinger.

McPherson, J. Miller. 1983. "An Ecology of Affiliation." *American Sociological Review* 61:179-202.

Mäki, Uskali, Bo Gustafsson, and Christian Knudsen, eds. 1993. *Rationality, Institutions, and Economic Methodology.* London: Routledge.

March, James G., ed. 1965. *Handbook of Organizations.* Chicago: Rand McNally.

————. 1981. "Decisions in Organizations and Theories of Choice." Pp. 205-44 in *Perspectives on Organization Design and Behavior*, edited by Andrew H. Van de Ven and William F. Joyce. New York: John Wiley, Wiley-Interscience.

————. 1994. *A Primer on Decision Making: How Decisions Happen.* New York: Free Press.

March, James G. and Johan P. Olsen 1984. "The New Institutionalism: Organizational Factors in Political Life." *American Political Science Review* 78:734-49.

————. 1989. *Rediscovering Institutions: The Organizational Basis of Politics.* New York: Free Press.

March, James G. and Herbert A. Simon 1958. *Organizations.* New York: John Wiley.

Mares, David R. and Walter W. Powell. 1990. "Cooperative Security Regimes: Preventing International Conflicts." Pp. 55-94 in *Organizations and Nation-States: New Perspectives on Conflict and Cooperation*, edited by Robert L. Kahn and Mayer N. Zald. San Francisco: Jossey-Bass.

Markus, Hazel and R. B. Zajonc. 1985. "The Cognitive Perspective in Social Psychology." Pp. 137-230 in *Handbook of Social Psychology*, vol. 1, edited by Gardner Lindzey and Elliot Aronson. 3rd ed. New York: Random House.

Martin, Joanne. 1992. *Cultures in Organizations: Three Perspectives.* New York: Oxford University Press.

————. 1994. "The Organization of Exclusion: The Institutionalization of Sex Inequality, Gendered Faculty Jobs, and Gendered Knowledge in Organizational Theory and Research." *Organizations* 1:401-31.

Marx, Karl. [1844] 1972. "Economic and Philosophic Manuscripts of 1944: Selections." Pp. 52-106 in *The Marx-Engels Reader*, edited by Robert C. Tucker. New York: Norton.

Marx, Karl. [1845-1846] 1972. "The German Ideology: Part I." Pp. 110-64 in *The Marx-Engels Reader*, edited by Robert C. Tucker. New York: Norton.

Masten, Scott E. 1986. "The Economic Institutions of Capitalism: A Review Article." *Journal of Institutional and Theoretical Economics* 142:445-51.

Mead, George Herbert. 1934. *Mind, Self, and Society.* Chicago: University of Chicago Press.

Melnick, R. Shep. 1983. *Regulation and the Courts: The Case of the Clean Air Act.* Washington, DC: Brookings Institution.

Menger, Carl. [1883] 1981. *Problems of Economics and Sociology.* Translated by F. J. Nock. Urbana: University of Illinois Press.

Merton, Robert K. 1936. "The Unanticipated Consequences of Purposive Social Action." *American Sociological Review* 1:894-904.

————. [1940] 1957. "Bureaucratic Structure and Personality." Pp. 195-206 in *Social Theory and Social Structure*, by Robert K. Merton. 2nd ed. Glencoe, IL: Free Press.

Merton, Robert K., Ailsa P. Gray, Barbara Hockey, and Hanan C. Selvin, eds. 1952. *Reader in Bureaucracy.* Glencoe, IL: Free Press.

Meyer, John W. 1977. "The Effects of Education as an Institution." *American Journal of Sociology* 83:55-77.

————. 1983. "Conclusion: Institutionalization and the Rationality of Formal Organizational Structure." Pp. 261-82 in *Organizational Environments: Ritual and Rationality*, edited by John W. Meyer and W. Richard Scott. Beverly Hills, CA: Sage.

———. 1994. "Rationalized Environments." Pp. 28-54 in *Institutional Environments and Organizations: Structural Complexity and Individualism*, edited by W. Richard Scott and John W. Meyer. Thousand Oaks, CA: Sage.

Meyer, John W., John Boli, and George M. Thomas. 1987. "Ontology and Rationalization in the Western Cultural Account." Pp. 12-37 in *Institutional Structure: Constituting State, Society, and the Individual*, edited by George M. Thomas, John W. Meyer, Francisco O. Ramirez, and John Boli. Newbury Park, CA: Sage.

Meyer, John W., John Boli, George M. Thomas, and Francisco O. Ramirez. 1997. "World Society and the Nation State." *American Journal of Sociology* 103:144-81.

Meyer, John W. and Michael T. Hannan. 1979. *National Development and the World System*. Chicago: University of Chicago Press.

Meyer, John W., David Kamens, Aaron Benavot, Y. K. Cha, and S. Y. Wong. 1992. *School Knowledge for the Masses: World Models and National Primary Curriculum Categories in the Twentieth Century*. London: Falmer.

Meyer, John W. and Brian Rowan. 1977. "Institutionalized Organizations: Formal Structure as Myth and Ceremony." *American Journal of Sociology* 83:340-63.

Meyer, John W. and W. Richard Scott. 1983a. "Centralization and the Legitimacy Problems of Local Government." Pp. 199-215 in *Organizational Environments: Ritual and Rationality*, edited by John W. Meyer and W. Richard Scott. Beverly Hills, CA: Sage.

Meyer, John W. and W. Richard Scott, with the assistance of Brian Rowan and Terrence E. Deal. [1983b] 1992. *Organizational Environments: Ritual and Rationality*. Beverly Hills, CA: Sage.

Meyer, John W., W. Richard Scott, and Terrence E. Deal. 1981. "Institutional and Technical Sources of Organizational Structure: Explaining the Structure of Educational Organizations." Pp. 151-78 in *Organization and the Human Services*, edited by Herman D. Stein. Philadelphia: Temple University Press.

Meyer, John W., W. Richard Scott, and David Strang. 1987. "Centralization, Fragmentation, and School District Complexity." *Administrative Science Quarterly* 32:186-201.

Meyer, John W., W. Richard Scott, David Strang, and Andrew L. Creighton. 1988. "Bureaucratization Without Centralization: Changes in the Organizational System of U.S. Public Education, 1940-80." Pp. 139-68 in *Institutional Patterns and Organizations: Culture and Environment*, edited by Lynne G. Zucker. Cambridge, MA: Ballinger.

Mezias, Stephen J. 1990. "An Institutional Model of Organizational Practice: Financial Reporting at the Fortune 200." *Administrative Science Quarterly* 35:431-57.

Miles, Robert H. 1982. *Coffin Nails and Corporate Strategy*. Englewood Cliffs, NJ: Prentice Hall.

Milgrom, Paul and John Roberts. 1992. *Economics, Organization, and Management*. Englewood Cliffs, NJ: Prentice Hall.

Miller, Jon. 1994. *The Social Control of Religious Zeal: A Study of Organizational Contradictions*. New Brunswick, NJ: Rutgers University Press.

Miner, Anne S. 1991. "The Social Ecology of Jobs." *American Sociological Review* 56:772-85.

Mizruchi, Mark S. and Lisa C. Fein. 1999. "The Social Construction of Organizational Knowledge: A Study of the Uses of Coercive, Mimetic, and Normative Isomorphism." *Administrative Science Quarterly* 44:653-83.

Moe, Terry M. 1984. "The New Economics of Organization." *American Journal of Political Science* 28:739-77.

———. 1989. "The Politics of Bureaucratic Structure." Pp. 267-329 in *Can the Government Govern?* edited by John Chubb and Paul Peterson. Washington, DC: Brookings Institution.

———. 1990a. "Political Institutions: The Neglected Side of the Story." *Journal of Law, Economics, and Organizations* 6:213-53.

———. 1990b. "The Politics of Structural Choice: Toward a Theory of Public Bureaucracy." Pp. 116-53 in *Organization Theory: From Chester Barnard to the Present and Beyond*, edited by Oliver E. Williamson. New York: Oxford University Press.

Mohr, John W. 1994. "Soldiers, Mothers, Tramps, and Others: Discourse Roles in the 1907 New York City Charity Directory." *Poetics* 22:327-57.

Mohr, John W. and Francesca Guerra-Pearson. Forthcoming. "The Differentiation of Institutional Space: Organizational Forms in the New York Social Welfare Sector, 1888-1917." In *How Institutions Change*, edited by Walter W. Powell and Daniel L. Jones. Chicago: University of Chicago Press.

Mohr, Lawrence B. 1982. *Explaining Organizational Behavior.* San Francisco: Jossey-Bass.

Montgomery, Kathleen. 1990. "A Prospective Look at the Specialty of Medical Management." *Work and Occupations* 17:178-97.

Morrill, Calvin. Forthcoming. "Institutional Change Through Interstitial Emergence: The Growth of Alternative Dispute Resolution in American Law, 1965-1995." In *How Institutions Change*, edited by Walter W. Powell and Daniel L. Jones. Chicago: University of Chicago Press.

Mouritsen, Jan and Peter Skærbæk. 1995. "Civilization, Art, and Accounting: The Royal Danish Theater—An Enterprise Straddling Two Institutions." Pp. 91-112 in *The Institutional Construction of Organizations*, edited by W. Richard Scott and Søren Christensen. Thousand Oaks, CA: Sage.

National Commission on Excellence in Education. 1983. *A Nation at Risk: The Imperative for Educational Reform.* Washington, DC: Government Printing Office.

Nee, Victor. 1998. "Sources of the New Institutionalism." Pp. 1-16 in *The New Institutionalism in Sociology*, edited by Mary C. Brinton and Victor Nee. New York: Russell Sage Foundation.

Neisser, U. 1976. *Cognition and Reality: Principles and Implications of Cognitive Psychology.* San Francisco: Freeman.

Nelson, Richard R. and Sidney G. Winter. 1982. *An Evolutionary Theory of Economic Change.* Cambridge, MA: Belknap Press of Harvard University Press.

Nisbett, Richard and Lee Ross. 1980. *Human Inference: Strategies and Shortcomings of Social Judgment.* Englewood Cliffs, NJ: Prentice Hall.

Nohria, Nitin and Robert G. Eccles, eds. 1992. *Networks and Organizations: Structure, Form, and Action.* Boston: Harvard Business School Press.

Noll, Roger T., ed. 1985. *Regulatory Policy and the Social Sciences.* Berkeley: University of California Press.

North, Douglass C. 1989. "Institutional Change and Economic History." *Journal of Institutional and Theoretical Economics* 145:238-45.

———. 1990. *Institutions, Institutional Change, and Economic Performance*. Cambridge, UK: Cambridge University Press.

North, Douglass C. and Robert Paul Thomas. 1973. *The Rise of the Western World: A New Economic History*. Cambridge, UK: Cambridge University Press.

Oliver, Christine. 1991. "Strategic Responses to Institutional Processes." *Academy of Management Review* 16:145-79.

———. 1992. "The Antecedents of Deinstitutionalization." *Organization Studies* 13:563-88.

Orlikowski, Wanda J. 1992. "The Duality of Technology: Rethinking the Concept of Technology in Organizations." *Organization Science* 3:398-427.

Orren, Karen and Stephen Skowronek. 1994. "Beyond the Iconography of Order: Notes for 'New' Institutionalism." Pp. 311-32 in *The Dynamics of American Politics*, edited by L. D. Dodd and C. Jillson. Boulder, CO: Westview.

Orrù, Marco, Nicole Woolsey Biggart, and Gary G. Hamilton. 1997. *The Economic Organization of East Asian Capitalism*. Thousand Oaks, CA: Sage.

Orton, J. Douglas and Karl E. Weick. 1990. "Loosely Coupled Systems: A Reconceptualization." *Academy of Management Review* 15:203-23.

Padgett, John F. and Christopher K. Ansell. 1993. "Robust Action and the Rise of the Medici, 1400-1434." *American Journal of Sociology* 98:1259-1318.

Palmer, Donald A., P. Devereaux Jennings, and Xueguang Zhou. 1993. "Late Adoption of the Multidivisional Form by Large U.S. Corporations: Institutional, Political, and Economic Accounts." *Administrative Science Quarterly* 38:100-31.

Parsons, Talcott. 1937. *The Structure of Social Action*. New York: McGraw-Hill.

———. 1951. *The Social System*. New York: Free Press.

———. 1953. "A Revised Analytical Approach to the Theory of Social Stratification." Pp. 92-129 in *Class, Status, and Power: A Reader in Social Stratification*, edited by Reinhard Bendix and Seymour M. Lipset. Glencoe, IL: Free Press.

———. [1956] 1960a. "A Sociological Approach to the Theory of Organizations." Pp. 16-58 in *Structure and Process in Modern Societies*, edited by Talcott Parsons. Glencoe, IL: Free Press.

———. [1956] 1960b. "Some Ingredients of a General Theory of Formal Organization." Pp. 59-96 in *Structure and Process in Modern Societies*, edited by Talcott Parsons. Glencoe, IL: Free Press.

———. [1934] 1990. "Prolegomena to a Theory of Social Institutions." *American Sociological Review* 55:319-39.

Parsons, Talcott, Robert F. Bales, and Edward A. Shils. 1953. *Working Papers in the Theory of Action*. Glencoe, IL: Free Press.

Pedersen, Jesper Standgaard and Frank Dobbin. 1997. "The Social Invention of Collective Actors: On the Rise of the Organization." *American Behavioral Scientist* 40:431-43.

Perrow, Charles. 1961. "The Analysis of Goals in Complex Organizations." *American Sociological Review* 26:854-66.

———. 1985. "Review Essay: Overboard with Myth and Symbols." *American Journal of Sociology* 91:151-55.

————. 1986. *Complex Organizations: A Critical Essay.* 3rd ed. New York: Random House.

Peters, B. Guy. 1988. "The Machinery of Government." Pp. 19-53 in *Organizing Governance; Governing Organizations,* edited by Colin Campbell and B. Guy Peters. Pittsburgh, PA: University of Pittsburgh Press.

————. 1999. *Institutional Theory in Political Science: The "New Institutionalism."* London: Pinter.

Peterson, Paul E., Barry G. Rabe, and Kenneth K. Wong. 1986. *When Federalism Works.* Washington, DC: Brookings Institution.

Pfeffer, Jeffrey and Yinon Cohen. 1984. "Determinants of Internal Labor Markets in Organizations." *Administrative Science Quarterly* 29:550-72.

Pfeffer, Jeffrey and Gerald Salancik. 1978. *The External Control of Organizations.* New York: Harper & Row.

Porac, Joseph F. and H. Thomas. 1990. "Taxonomic Mental Models in Competitor Definition." *Academy of Management Review* 15:224-40.

Porac, Joseph F., H. Thomas, and C. Badden-Fuller. 1989. "Competitive Groups as Cognitive Communities: The Case of the Scottish Knitwear Manufacturers." *Journal of Management Studies* 26:397-415.

Porac, Joseph F., James B. Wade, and Timothy G. Pollock. 1999. "Industry Categories and the Politics of the Comparable Firm in CEO Compensation." *Administrative Science Quarterly* 44:112-44.

Powell, Walter W. 1988. "Institutional Effects on Organizational Structure and Performance." Pp. 115-36 in *Institutional Patterns and Organizations: Culture and Environment,* edited by Lynne G. Zucker. Cambridge, MA: Ballinger.

————. 1991. "Expanding the Scope of Institutional Analysis." Pp. 183-203 in *The New Institutionalism in Organizational Analysis,* edited by Walter W. Powell and Paul J. DiMaggio. Chicago: University of Chicago Press.

————. 1999. "The Social Construction of an Organizational Field: The Case of Biotechnology." *International Journal of Biotechnology* 1:42-66.

Powell, Walter W. and Paul J. DiMaggio, eds. 1991. *The New Institutionalism in Organizational Analysis.* Chicago: University of Chicago Press.

Powell, Walter W. and Daniel L. Jones, eds. Forthcoming. *How Institutions Change.* Chicago: University of Chicago Press.

Pratt, John W. and Richard J. Zeckhauser, eds. 1985. *Principals and Agents: The Structure of Business.* Boston, MA: Harvard Business School Press.

President's Research Committee on Social Trends. 1934. *Recent Social Trends in the United States.* New York: McGraw-Hill.

Ranger-Moore, James, Jane Banaszak-Holl, and Michael T. Hannan. 1991. "Density-Dependent Dynamics in Regulated Industries: Founding Rates of Banks and Life Insurance Companies." *Administrative Science Quarterly* 36:36-65.

Rao, Hayagreeva. 1994. "The Social Construction of Reputation: Certification Contests, Legitimation, and the Survival of Organizations in the American Automobile Industry, 1895-1912." *Strategic Management Journal* 15(S2):29-44.

————. 1998. "Caveat Emptor: The Construction of Nonprofit Consumer Watchdog Organizations." *American Journal of Sociology* 103:912-61.

Reed, Michael. 1985. *Redirections in Organizational Analysis.* London: Tavistock.

Regier, D. A., I. D. Goldberg, and C. A. Taub. 1978. "The de facto U.S. Mental Health Services System." *Archives of General Psychiatry* 35:685-93.

Rittberger, V. 1993. *Regime Theory and International Relations.* Oxford, UK: Clarendon.

Roethlisberger, Fritz J. and William J. Dickson. 1939. *Management and the Worker.* Cambridge, MA: Harvard University Press.

Rogers, Everett. 1995. *Diffusion of Innovation.* 4th ed. New York: Free Press.

Rorty, Richard. 1989. *Contingency, Irony, and Solidarity.* New York: Cambridge University Press.

Rosenberg, Morris. 1979. *Conceiving the Self.* New York: Basic Books.

Rosenberg, Nathan and L. E. Birdzell, Jr. 1986. *How the West Grew Rich: The Economic Transformation of the Industrial World.* New York: Basic Books.

Rowan, Brian. 1982. "Organizational Structure and the Institutional Environment: The Case of Public Schools." *Administrative Science Quarterly* 27:259-79.

Roy, Donald. 1952. "Quota Restriction and Goldbricking in a Machine Shop." *American Journal of Sociology* 57:427-42.

Roy, William G. 1997. *Socializing Capital: The Rise of the Large Industrial Corporation in America.* Princeton, NJ: Princeton University Press.

Ruef, Martin and W. Richard Scott. 1998. "A Multidimensional Model of Organizational Legitimacy: Hospital Survival in Changing Institutional Environments." *Administrative Science Quarterly* 43:877-904.

Rumelt, Richard. 1974. *Strategy, Structure, and Economic Performance.* Boston, MA: Harvard Business School Press.

Salaman, Graeme. 1978. "Toward a Sociology of Organizational Structure." *The Sociological Review* 26:519-54.

Saxenian, Annalee. 1994. *Regional Advantage: Culture and Competition in Silicon Valley and Route 128.* Cambridge, MA: Harvard University Press.

Schank, R. C. and R. P. Abelson. 1977. *Scripts, Plans, Goals, and Understanding.* Hillsdale, NJ: Lawrence Erlbaum.

Scharpf, Fritz W. 1997. *Games Real Actors Play.* Boulder, CO: Westview.

Schmitter, Philippe. 1990. "Sectors in Modern Capitalism: Models of Governance and Variations in Performance." Pp. 3-39 in *Labour Relations and Economic Performance,* edited by Renato Brunetta and Carlo Dell'Aringa. Houndmills, UK: Macmillan.

Schmoller, Gustav von. 1900-1904. *Grundriss der Allgemeinen Volkswirtschaftslehre.* Leipzig: Duncker & Humbolt.

Schotter, Andrew. 1986. "The Evolution of Rules." Pp. 117-34 in *Economics as a Process: Essays in the New Institutional Economics,* edited by Richard N. Langlois. New York: Cambridge University Press.

Schrödinger, Erwin. 1945. *What Is Life?* New York: Cambridge University Press.

Schumpeter, Joseph A. [1926] 1961. *The Theory of Economic Development.* New York: Oxford University Press.

Schutz, Alfred. [1932] 1967. *The Phenomenology of the Social World.* Translated by George Walsh and Frederick Lehnert. Evanston, IL: Northwestern University Press.

Scott, W. Richard. 1965. "Reactions to Supervision in a Heteronomous Professional Organization." *Administrative Science Quarterly* 10:65-81.

————. 1977. "The Effectiveness of Organizational Effectiveness Studies." Pp. 63-95 in *New Perspectives on Organizational Effectiveness,* edited by Paul S. Goodman and Johannes M. Pennings. San Francisco: Jossey-Bass.

————. 1982. "Health Care Organizations in the 1980s: The Convergence of Public and Professional Control Systems." Pp. 177-95 in *Contemporary Health Services: Social Science Perspectives,* edited by Allen W. Johnson, Oscar Grusky, and Bertram H. Raven. Boston: Auburn House.

————. 1985. "Conflicting Levels of Rationality: Regulators, Managers, and Professionals in the Medical Care Sector." *Journal of Health Administration Education* 3(part 2):113-31.

————. 1987. "The Adolescence of Institutional Theory." *Administrative Science Quarterly* 32:493-511.

————. 1994a. "Conceptualizing Organizational Fields: Linking Organizations and Societal Systems." Pp. 203-21 in *Systemrationalitat und Partialinteresse [Systems Rationality and Partial Interests],* edited by Hans-Ulrich Derlien, Uta Gerhardt, and Fritz W. Scharpf. Baden-Baden, Germany: Nomos Verlagsgesellschaft.

————. 1994b. "Institutional Analysis: Variance and Process Theory Approaches." Pp. 81-99 in *Institutional Environments and Organizations: Structural Complexity and Individualism,* edited by W. Richard Scott and John W. Meyer. Thousand Oaks, CA: Sage.

————. 1994c. "Institutions and Organizations: Toward a Theoretical Synthesis." Pp. 55-80 in *Institutional Environments and Organizations: Structural Complexity and Individualism,* edited by W. Richard Scott and John W. Meyer. Thousand Oaks, CA: Sage.

————. 1994d. "Law and Organizations." Pp. 3-18 in *The Legalistic Organization,* edited by Sim B. Sitkin and Robert J. Bies. Thousand Oaks, CA: Sage.

————. 1998. *Organizations: Rational, Natural, and Open Systems.* 4th ed. Englewood Cliffs, NJ: Prentice Hall.

————. Forthcoming. "Organizations, general." In *International Encyclopedia of the Social and Behavioral Sciences,* Vol. 5, *Organizational and Management Studies,* edited by Neil J. Smelser and Paul B. Baltes. Amsterdam: Pergamon, Elsevier Science.

Scott, W. Richard and Elaine V. Backman. 1990. "Instititutional Theory and the Medical Care Sector." Pp. 20-52 in *Innovations in Health Care Delivery: Insights for Organization Theory,* edited by Stephen S. Mick. San Francisco: Jossey-Bass.

Scott, W. Richard and Bruce L. Black, eds. 1986. *The Organization of Mental Health Services: Societal and Community Systems.* Beverly Hills, CA: Sage.

Scott, W. Richard and Søren Christensen. 1995a. "Crafting a Wider Lens." Pp. 302-13 in *The Institutional Construction of Organizations: International and Longitudinal Studies.* Thousand Oaks, CA: Sage.

Scott, W. Richard, and Søren Christensen, eds. 1995b. *The Institutional Construction of Organizations: International and Longitudinal Studies.* Thousand Oaks, CA: Sage.

Scott, W. Richard, Peter J. Mendel, and Seth Pollack. Forthcoming. "Environments and Fields: Studying the Evolution of a Field of Medical Care Organizations." In *How Institutions Change,* edited by Walter W. Powell and Daniel L. Jones. Chicago: University of Chicago Press.

Scott, W. Richard and John W. Meyer. 1983. "The Organization of Societal Sectors." Pp. 129-53 in *Organizational Environments: Ritual and Rationality,* edited by John W. Meyer and W. Richard Scott. (Revised version, pp. 108-140 in *The New Institutionalism in Organizational Analysis,* edited by Walter W. Powell and Paul J. DiMaggio. Chicago: University of Chicago Press, 1991.)

———. 1988. "Environmental Linkages and Organizational Complexity: Public and Private Schools." Pp. 128-60 in *Comparing Public and Private Schools,* Vol. 1, *Institutions and Organizations,* edited by Tom James and Henry M. Levin. Philadelphia, PA: Falmer.

———, eds. 1994. *Institutional Environments and Organizations: Structural Complexity and Individualism.* Thousand Oaks, CA: Sage.

Scott, W. Richard, Martin Ruef, Peter J. Mendel, and Carol A. Caronna. 2000. *Institutional Change and Healthcare Organizations: From Professional Dominance to Managed Care.* Chicago: University of Chicago Press.

Searle, John R. 1995. *The Construction of Social Reality.* New York: Free Press.

Seavoy, Ronald E. 1982. *The Origins of the American Business Corporation, 1784-1855: Broadening the Concept of Public Service during Industrialization.* Westport, CT: Greenwood Press.

Selznick, Philip. 1948. "Foundations of the Theory of Organization." *American Sociological Review* 13:25-35.

———. 1949. *TVA and the Grass Roots.* Berkeley: University of California Press.

———. 1957. *Leadership in Administration.* New York: Harper & Row.

———. 1969. *Law, Society, and Industrial Justice.* New York: Russell Sage Foundation.

———. 1996. "Institutionalism 'Old' and 'New.' " *Administrative Science Quarterly* 41:270-77.

Sewell, William H., Jr. 1992. "A Theory of Structure: Duality, Agency, and Transformation." *American Journal of Sociology* 98:1-29.

Shenhav, Yehouda. 1995. "From Chaos to Systems: The Engineering Foundations of Organizational Theory, 1879-1932." *Administrative Science Quarterly* 40:557-86.

———. 1999. *Manufacturing Rationality: The Engineering Foundations of the Managerial Revolution.* Oxford: Oxford University Press.

Shepsle, Kenneth A. 1989. "Studying Institutions: Lessons from the Rational Choice Approach." *Journal of Theoretical Politics* 1:131-47.

Shepsle, Kenneth A. and Barry Weingast. 1987. "The Institutional Foundations of Committee Power." *American Political Science Review* 81:85-104.

Sherif, Muzafer. 1935. "A Study of Some Social Factors in Perception." *Archives of Psychology,* No. 187.

Shonfield, Alfred. 1965. *Modern Capitalism.* London: Oxford University Press.

Silverman, David. 1971. *The Theory of Organizations: A Sociological Framework.* New York: Basic Books.

———. 1972. "Some Neglected Questions about Social Reality." Pp. 165-82 in *New Directions in Sociological Theory,* edited by Paul Filmer, Michael Phillipson, David Silverman, and David Walsh. Cambridge: MIT Press.

Silverman, David and J. Jones. 1976. *Organizational Work: The Language of Grading and the Grading of Language.* London: Macmillan.

Simon, Herbert A. [1945] 1997. *Administrative Behavior: A Study of Decision-Making Processes in Administrative Organization*. 4th ed. New York: Free Press.

——. 1991. *Models of My Life*. New York: Basic Books.

Singh, Jitendra V. 1993. "Review Essay: Density Dependence Theory—Current Issues, Future Promise." *American Journal of Sociology* 99:464-73.

Singh, Jitendra V. and Charles J. Lumsden. 1990. "Theory and Research in Organizational Ecology." *Annual Review of Sociology* 16:161-95.

Singh, Jitendra V., David J. Tucker, and Robert J. House. 1986. "Organizational Legitimacy and the Liability of Newness." *Administrative Science Quarterly* 31:171-93.

Sitkin, Sim B. and Robert J. Bies, eds. 1994. *The Legalistic Organization*. Thousand Oaks, CA: Sage.

Sjöstrand, Sven-Erik. 1995. "Toward a Theory of Institutional Change." Pp. 19-44 in *On Economic Institutions: Theory and Applications,*" edited by John Groenewegen, Christos Pitelis, and Sven-Erik Sjöstrand. Aldershot, UK: Edward Elgar.

Skocpol, Theda. 1979. *States and Social Revolutions*. Cambridge, UK: Cambridge University Press.

——. 1984. "Emerging Agendas and Recurrent Strategies in Historical Sociology." Pp. 356-91 in *Vision and Method in Historical Sociology,* edited by Theda Skocpol. Cambridge, UK: Cambridge University Press.

——. 1985. "Bringing the State Back In: Strategies of Analysis in Current Research." Pp. 3-37 in *Bringing the State Back In,* edited by Peter B. Evans, Dietrich Rueschemeyer, and Theda Skocpol. Cambridge, UK: Cambridge University Press.

Skowronek, Stephen. 1982. *Building a New American State: The Expansion of National Administrative Capacities, 1877-1920*. Cambridge, UK: Cambridge University Press.

Smelser, Neil J. and Richard Swedberg, eds. 1994. *The Handbook of Economic Sociology*. New York: Princeton University Press and Russell Sage Foundation.

Snow, David A., E. Burke Rochford, Jr., Steven K. Worden, and Robert D. Benford. 1986. "Frame Alignment Processes, Micromobilization, and Movement Participation." *American Sociological Review* 51:464-81.

Somers, Ann R. 1969. *Hospital Regulation: The Dilemma of Public Policy*. Princeton, NJ: Princeton University.

Somers, Margaret R. and Gloria Gibson. 1994. "Reclaiming the Epistemological 'Other': Narrative and the Social Constitution of Identity." Pp. 37-99 in *Social Theory and the Politics of Identity,* edited by Craig Calhoun. Oxford, UK: Basil Blackwell.

Spencer, Herbert. 1876-1896, 1910. *The Principles of Sociology,* 3 vols. New York: Appleton-Century-Crofts.

Stark, David. 1996. "Recombinant Property in East European Capitalism." *American Journal of Sociology* 101:993-1027.

Starr, Paul. 1982. *The Social Transformation of American Medicine*. New York: Basic Books.

Stern, Robert N. 1979. "The Development of an Interorganizational Control Network: The Case of Intercollegiate Athletics." *Administrative Science Quarterly* 24:242-66.

Stigler, George J. 1968. *The Organization of Industry*. Homewood, IL: Richard D. Irwin.

Stinchcombe, Arthur L. 1965. "Social Structure and Organizations." Pp. 142-93 in *Handbook of Organizations,* edited by James G. March. Chicago: Rand McNally.

———. 1968. *Constructing Social Theories.* Chicago: University of Chicago Press.

———. 1997. "On the Virtues of the Old Institutionalism." *Annual Review of Sociology* 23:1-18.

Strang, David and John W. Meyer. 1993. "Institutional Conditions for Diffusion." *Theory and Society* 22:487-511.

Strang, David and Sarah A. Soule. 1998. "Diffusion in Organizations and Social Movements: From Hybrid Corn to Poison Pills." *Annual Review of Sociology* 24:265-90.

Streeck, Wolfgang and Philippe C. Schmitter. 1985. "Community, Market, State—and Associations? The Prospective Contribution of Interest Governance to Social Order." Pp. 1-29 in *Private Interest Government: Beyond Market and State,* edited by Wolfgang Streeck and Philippe C. Schmitter. Beverly Hills, CA: Sage.

Stryker, Robin. 1994. "Rules, Resources, and Legitimacy Processes: Some Implications for Social Conflict, Order, and Change." *American Journal of Sociology* 99:847-910.

———. 2000. "Legitimacy Processes as Institutional Politics: Implications for Theory and Research in the Sociology of Organizations." Pp. 179-223 in *Research in the Sociology of Organizations,* vol. 17, edited by Samuel B. Bacharach. Greenwich, CT: JAI Press.

Stryker, Sheldon. 1980. *Symbolic Interactionism: A Social Structural Version.* Menlo Park, CA: Cummings.

Stubbart, C. I. and A. Ramaprasad. 1988. "Probing Two Chief Executives' Schematic Knowledge of the U.S. Steel Industry Using Cognitive Maps." Pp. 139-64 in *Advances in Strategic Management,* vol. 5, edited by R. Lamb and P. Shrivastava. Greenwich, CT: JAI Press.

Suchman, Mark C. 1994. "On Advice of Counsel: Legal and Financial Firms as Information Intermediaries in the Structuration of Silicon Valley." Unpublished doctoral dissertation, Department of Sociology, Stanford University.

———. 1995a. "Localism and Globalism in Institutional Analysis: The Emergence of Contractual Norms in Venture Finance." Pp. 39-63 in *The Institutional Construction of Organizations: International and Longitudinal Studies,* edited by W. Richard Scott and Søren Christensen. Thousand Oaks, CA: Sage.

———. 1995b. "Managing Legitimacy: Strategic and Institutional Approaches." *Academy of Management Review* 20:571-610.

———. Forthcoming. "Constructed Ecologies: Reproduction and Structuration in Emerging Organizational Communities." In *How Institutions Change,* edited by Walter W. Powell and Daniel L. Jones. Chicago: University of Chicago Press.

Suchman, Mark C. and Lauren B. Edelman. 1997. "Legal Rational Myths: The New Institutionalism and the Law and Society Tradition." *Law and Social Inquiry* 21:903-41.

Sugden, Robert. 1986. *The Economics of Rights, Cooperation, and Welfare.* Oxford, UK: Basic Blackwell.

Sumner, William Graham. 1906. *Folkways.* Boston: Ginn & Co.

Sutton, John R., Frank R. Dobbin, John W. Meyer, and W. Richard Scott. 1994. "The Legalization of the Workplace." *American Journal of Sociology* 99:944-71.

Swedberg, Richard. 1991. "Major Traditions of Economic Sociology." *Annual Review of Sociology* 17:251-76.

———. 1998. *Max Weber and the Idea of Economic Sociology.* Princeton, NJ: Princeton University Press.

Swidler, Ann. 1986. "Culture in Action: Symbols and Strategies." *American Sociological Review* 51:273-86.

Taylor, Serge. 1984. *Making Bureaucracies Think: The Environment Impact Statement Strategy of Administrative Reform.* Stanford, CA: Stanford University Press.

Teece, David J. 1981. "Internal Organization and Economic Performance: An Empirical Study of the Profitability of Principal Firms." *Journal of Industrial Economics* 30(December):173-200.

Thelen, Kathleen. 1999. "Historical Institutionalism in Comparative Politics." *Annual Review of Political Science* 2:369-404.

Thelen, Kathleen and Sven Steinmo. 1992. "Historical Institutionalism in Comparative Politics." In *Structuring Politics: Historical Institutionalism in Comparative Analysis,* edited by Sven Steinmo, Kathleen Thelen, and Frank Longstreth. Cambridge, UK: Cambridge University Press.

Thomas, George M. and John W. Meyer. 1984. "The Expansion of the State." *Annual Review of Sociology* 10:461-82.

Thomas, George M., John W. Meyer, Francisco O. Ramirez, and John Boli, eds. 1987. *Institutional Structure: Constituting State, Society, and the Individual.* Newbury Park, CA: Sage.

Thompson, James D. 1967. *Organizations in Action.* New York: McGraw-Hill.

Thornton, Patricia H. 1995. "Accounting for Acquisition Waves: Evidence from the U.S. College Publishing Industry." Pp. 199-225 in *The Institutional Construction of Organizations: International and Longitudinal Studies,* edited by W. Richard Scott and Søren Christensen. Thousand Oaks, CA: Sage.

Tolbert, Pamela S. 1988. "Institutional Sources of Organizational Culture in Major Law Firms." Pp. 101-13 in *Institutional Patterns and Organizations: Culture and Environment,* edited by Lynne G. Zucker. Cambridge, MA: Ballinger.

Tolbert, Pamela S. and Wesley Sine. 1999. "Determinants of Organizational Compliance with Institutional Pressures: The Employment of Non-Tenure-Track Faculty in Four-Year Universities." Unpublished manuscript, School of Industrial Relations, Cornell University.

Tolbert, Pamela S. and Lynne G. Zucker. 1983. "Institutional Sources of Change in the Formal Structure of Organizations: The Diffusion of Civil Service Reform, 1880-1935." *Administrative Science Quarterly* 30:22-39.

———. 1996. "The Institutionalization of Institutional Theory." Pp. 175-90 in *Handbook of Organization Studies,* edited by Stewart R. Clegg, Cynthia Hardy, and Walter R. Nord. London: Sage.

Trice, Harrison M. and Janice M. Beyer. 1993. *The Cultures of Work Organizations.* Englewood Cliffs, NJ: Prentice Hall.

Tucker, Robert C. 1972. "Introduction: The Writings of Marx and Engels." Pp. xv-xxxiv in *The Marx-Engels Reader,* edited by Robert C. Tucker. New York: Norton.

Tullock, Gordon. 1976. *The Vote Motive.* London: Institute for Economic Affairs.

Tuma, Nancy B. and Michael T. Hannan. 1984. *Social Dynamics: Models and Methods.* New York: Academic Press.

Tuma, Nancy B., Michael T. Hannan, and Lyle P. Groeneveld. 1979. "Dynamic Analysis of Event Histories." *American Journal of Sociology* 76:187-206.

Turner, Roy, ed. 1974. *Ethnomethodology: Selected Readings.* Harmondsworth, UK: Penguin.

Tushman, Michael L. and Philip Anderson. 1986. "Technological Discontinuities and Organizational Environments." *Administrative Science Quarterly* 31:439-65.

Tversky, Amos and Donald Kahneman. 1974. "Judgment Under Uncertainty." *Science* 185:1124-31.

Uzzi, Brian D. 1996. "The Sources and Consequences of Embeddedness for the Economic Performance of Organizations: The Network Effect." *American Sociological Review* 61:674-98.

Vanberg, Viktor. 1989. "Carl Menger's Evolutionary and John R. Commons's Collective Action Approach to Institutions: A Comparison." *Review of Political Economy* 1:334-60.

Van Maanen, John and Gideon Kunda. 1989. " 'Real Feelings': Emotional Expression and Organizational Culture." Pp. 43-103 in *Research in Organizational Behavior,* vol. 11, edited by L. L. Cummings and Bary M. Staw. Greenwich, CT: JAI Press.

Van de Ven, Andrew H. 1993. "The Institutional Theory of John R. Commons: A Review and Commentary." *Academy of Management Review* 18:129-52.

Van de Ven, Andrew H. and Raghu Garud. 1989. "A Framework for Understanding the Emergence of New Industries." Pp. 195-225 in *Research on Technological Innovation, Management, and Policy,* edited by Richard S. Rosenbloom. Greenwich, CT: JAI Press.

—————. 1994. "The Coevolution of Technical and Institutional Events in the Development of an Innovation." Pp. 425-43 in *Evolutionary Dynamics of Organizations,* edited by Joel A. C. Baum and Jitendra Singh. New York: Oxford University Press.

Van de Ven, Andrew H. and George P. Huber, eds. 1990. "Longitudinal Field Research Methods for Studying Processes of Organizational Change." Special issues. *Organization Science* 1(3):213-335; and (4):375-439.

Vaughn, Diane. 1996. *The Challenger Launch Decision: Risky Technology, Culture, and Deviance at NASA.* Chicago: University of Chicago Press.

—————. 1999. "The Dark Side of Organizations: Mistakes, Misconduct, and Disaster." *Annual Review of Sociology* 25:271-305.

Veblen, Thorstein B. 1898. "Why Is Economics Not an Evolutionary Science?" *Quarterly Journal of Economics* 12:373-97.

—————. 1909. "The Limitations of Marginal Utility." *Journal of Political Economy* 17:235-45.

—————. 1919. *The Place of Science in Modern Civilization and Other Essays.* New York: Huebsch.

Walker, Gordon and David Weber. 1984. "A Transaction Cost Approach to Make-or-Buy Decisions." *Administrative Science Quarterly* 29:373-91.

Wallerstein, Immanuel. 1979. "From Feudalism to Capitalism: Transition or Transitions?" Pp. 138-51 in *The Capitalist World-Economy: Essays by Immanuel Wallerstein.* Cambridge, UK: Cambridge University Press.

Weber, Max. [1906-1924] 1946. *From Max Weber: Essays in Sociology.* Translated and edited by Hans H. Gerth and C. Wright Mills. New York: Oxford University Press.

———. [1924] 1947. *The Theory of Social and Economic Organization.* Translated and edited by A. M. Henderson and Talcott Parsons. New York: Oxford University Press.

———. [1904-1918] 1949. *The Methodology of the Social Sciences.* Translated and edited by Edward A. Shils and Henry A. Finch. Glencoe, IL: Free Press.

———. [1924] 1968. *Economy and Society: An Interpretive Sociology,* 3 vols., edited by Guenther Roth and Claus Wittich. New York: Bedminister Press.

Weick, Karl E. 1976. "Educational Organizations as Loosely Coupled Systems." *Administrative Science Quarterly* 21:1-19.

———. 1979. *The Social Psychology of Organizing.* 2nd ed. Reading, MA: Addison-Wesley.

———. 1995. *Sensemaking in Organizations.* Thousand Oaks, CA: Sage.

———. 2000. "Quality Improvement: A Sensemaking Perspective." Pp. 155-72 in *The Quality Movement & Organization Theory,* edited by Robert E. Cole and W. Richard Scott. Thousand Oaks, CA: Sage.

Weingast, Barry R. 1989. "The Political Institutions of Representative Government." Working Paper in Political Science P-89-14, Hoover Institution, Stanford University.

Westney, D. Eleanor. 1987. *Imitation and Innovation: The Transfer of Western Organizational Patterns to Meiji Japan.* Cambridge, MA: Harvard University Press.

———. 1993. "Institutional Theory and the Multinational Corporation." Pp. 53-76 in *Organization Theory and the Multinational Corporation,* edited by Sumantra Ghoshal and D. Eleanor Westney. New York: St. Martin's.

Westphal, James D., Ranjay Gulati, and Stephen M. Shortell. 1997. "Customization or Conformity? An Institutional and Network Perspective on the Content and Consequences of TQM Adoption." *Administrative Science Quarterly* 42:366-94.

Westphal, James D. and Edward J. Zajac. 1994. "Substance and Symbolism in CEOs' Long-term Incentives Plans." *Administrative Science Quarterly* 39:367-90.

———. 1998. "The Symbolic Management of Stockholders: Corporate Governance Reforms and Shareholder Reactions." *Administrative Science Quarterly* 43:127-53.

Whetten, David A. and Paul C. Godfrey, eds. 1999. *Identity in Organizations: Building Theory Through Conversations.* Thousand Oaks, CA: Sage.

White, William D. 1982. "The American Hospital Industry since 1900: A Short History." Pp. 143-70 in *Advances in Health Economics and Health Services Research,* vol. 3, edited by Richard M. Scheffler. Greenwich, CT: JAI Press.

Whitley, Richard. 1992a. *Business Systems in East Asia: Firms, Markets, and Societies.* London: Sage.

———. 1992b. "The Social Construction of Organizations and Markets: The Comparative Analysis of Business Recipes." Pp. 120-43 in *Rethinking Organizations: New Directions in Organization Theory and Analysis,* edited by Michael Reed and Michael Hughes. Newbury Park, CA: Sage.

———. 1992c. "Societies, Firms, and Markets: The Social Structuring of Business Systems." Pp. 5-44 in *European Business Systems: Firms and Markets in Their National Contexts,* edited by Richard Whitley. London: Sage.

Wholey, Douglas R. and Susan M. Sanchez. 1991. "The Effects of Regulatory Tools on Organizational Populations." *Academy of Management Review,* 16:743-67.

Wiley, Mary Glenn and Mayer N. Zald. 1968. "The Growth and Transformation of Educational Accrediting Agencies: An Exploratory Study in Social Control of Institutions." *Sociology of Education* 41:36-56.

Wilks, Stephen and Maurice Wright, eds. 1987. *Comparative Government-Industry Relations*. Oxford, UK: Clarendon Press.

Williamson, Oliver E. 1975. *Markets and Hierarchies: Analysis and Antitrust Implications*. New York: Free Press.

———. 1985. *The Economic Institutions of Capitalism*. New York: Free Press.

———. 1991. "Comparative Economic Organization: The Analysis of Discrete Structural Alternatives." *Administrative Science Quarterly* 36:269-96.

———. 1994. "Transaction Cost Economics and Organization Theory." Pp. 77-107 in *The Handbook of Economic Sociology*, edited by Neil J. Smelser and Richard Swedberg. Princeton, NJ: Princeton University Press and Russell Sage Foundation.

Willoughby, Westel Woodbury. 1896. *An Examination of the Nature of the State*. New York: Macmillan.

———. 1904. *The American Constitutional System*. New York: Century.

Wilson, James Q., ed. 1980. *The Politics of Regulation*. New York: Basic Books.

———. 1989. *Bureaucracy: What Government Agencies Do and Why They Do It*. New York: Basic Books.

Wilson, Woodrow. 1889. *The State and Federal Governments of the United States*. Boston: D.C. Heath.

Winter, Sidney F. 1964. "Economic 'Natural Selection' and the Theory of the Firm." *Yale Economic Essays* 4:225-72.

———. 1990. "Survival, Selection, and Inheritance in Evolutionary Theories of Organization." Pp. 269-97 in *Organizational Evolution: New Directions*, edited by Jitendra V. Singh. Newbury Park, CA: Sage.

Woodward, Joan. 1958. *Management and Technology*. London: Her Majesty's Stationery Office.

Wuthnow, Robert. 1987. *Meaning and Moral Order: Explorations in Cultural Analysis*. Berkeley: University of California Press.

Wuthnow, Robert, James Dividson Hunter, Albert J. Bergesen, and Edith Kurzwell. 1984. *Cultural Analysis: The Work of Peter L. Berger, Mary Douglas, Michel Foucault, and Jurgen Habermas*. Boston: Routledge & Kegan Paul.

Zald, Mayer N. 1990. "History, Sociology, and Theories of Organization." Pp. 81-108 in *Institutions in American Society: Essays in Market, Political, and Social Organizations*, edited by John E. Jackson. Ann Arbor: University of Michigan Press.

Zald, Mayer N. and Patricia Denton. 1963. "From Evangelism to General Service: The Transformation of the YMCA." *Administrative Science Quarterly* 8:214-34.

Zald, Mayer N. and Roberta Ash Garner. 1966. "Social Movement Organizations: Growth, Decay, and Change," *Social Forces* 44:327-40.

Zimmerman, Donald H. 1969. "Record-keeping and the Intake Process in a Public Welfare Agency." Pp. 319-54 in *On Record: Files and Dossiers in American Life*, edited by Stanton Wheeler. New York: Russell Sage Foundation.

Znaniecki, Florian. 1945. "Social Organization and Institutions." Pp. 172-217 in *Twentieth Century Society*, edited by Gerges Gurvitch and Wilbert E. Moore. New York: The Philosophical Library.

Zucker, Lynne G. 1977. "The Role of Institutionalization in Cultural Persistence." *American Sociological Review* 42:726-43.

———. 1987. "Institutional Theories of Organization." *Annual Review of Sociology* 13:443-64.

———, ed. 1988a. *Institutional Patterns and Organizations: Culture and Environment.* Cambridge, MA: Ballinger.

———. 1988b. "Where Do Institutional Patterns Come From? Organizations as Actors in Social Systems." Pp. 23-49 in *Institutional Patterns and Organizations: Culture and Environment,* edited by Lynne G. Zucker. Cambridge, MA: Ballinger.

———. 1989. "Combining Institutional Theory and Population Ecology: No Legitimacy, No History (Comment on Carroll-Hannan, 1989)." *American Sociological Review* 54:542-45.

———. 1991. "Postscript: Microfoundations of Institutional Thought." Pp. 103-106 in *The New Institutionalism in Organizational Analysis,* edited by Walter W. Powell and Paul J. DiMaggio. Chicago: University of Chicago Press.

Zuckerman, Ezra W. 1999. "The Categorical Imperative: Securities Analysts and the Illegitimacy Discount," *American Journal of Sociology* 104: 1398-1438.

Zysman, John. 1983. *Governments, Markets, and Growth: Finance and the Politics of Industrial Change.* Ithaca, NY: Cornell University.

Index

About the Author

W. Richard (Dick) Scott (Ph.D., University of Chicago) is Professor Emeritus in the Department of Sociology with courtesy appointments in the Graduate School of Business, School of Education, and School of Medicine, Stanford University. He has spent his entire professional career at Stanford and served as the founding director of the Stanford Center for Organizations Research. He is the author of many articles and more than a dozen scholarly books, including two widely used texts in the area of organizations: an early book, *Formal Organizations* (1962), coauthored with Peter M. Blau, and the more recent volume, *Organizations: Rational, Natural, and Open Systems* (1981/1987/ 1992/1998), now in its 4th edition. Scott is a past fellow of the Center for Advanced Study in the Behavioral Sciences and was the recipient in 1988 of the Distinguished Scholar Award from the Management and Organization Theory Division of the Academy of Management. In 1996, he received the Richard D. Irwin Award for Scholarly Contributions to Management from the Academy of Management.